THE TRULY GREAT

THE 200 BEST

PRO FOOTBALL PLAYERS

OF ALL TIME

Rick Korch

FOREWORD BY

GALE SAYERS

TAYLOR PUBLISHING COMPANY

DALLAS, TEXAS

ALSO BY

RICK KORCH

_____

The Official Pro Football Hall of Fame Playbook
The Sports Encyclopedia: Pro Football (co-author)
The Fantasy Football Abstract

Published by Taylor Publishing Company
          1550 West Mockingbird Lane
          Dallas, Texas 75235
Designed by David Timmons

Library of Congress Cataloging-in-Publication Data

Korch, Rick
    The truly great : the 200 best football players of all time / by Rick Korch
        p.   cm.
    ISBN 0-87833-831-4
    1. Football players—United States—Biography. I. Title
GV939.A1K67   1993
796.332'092'2—dc20
[B]   93-14797
                                                                              CIP

Printed in the United States of America
10   9   8   7   6   5   4   3   2   1

Contents

Foreword

It's been over seventy years since pro football really got going with the formation of the National Football League. Thousands and thousands of men in the NFL and the several other leagues since then. A lot of them were excellent athletes. I played with and against some of the best: Jim Brown . . . Johnny Unitas . . . Bob Lilly . . . Dick Butkus . . . Raymond Berry . . . Larry Wilson . . . Jim Parker . . . Ray Nitschke . . . Paul Warfield. . . .

Anyone would be proud to be in that kind of company, and I'm honored to be in there with them.

Rick Korch has set himself a tough task, but he's done his homework. He talked to past and present players and coaches and combined their opinions with statistics, records, and other factors, some of them not as easy to put a finger on.

Was the player a leader, a winner? Did his teammates play better because of him? Have his records stood the test of time? Did he revolutionize his position? How is he still remembered? These factors and others have been taken into consideration. I think the author has done a great job, and he's come up with some interesting picks. It's not easy, picking the greatest players ever, position by position. You try it.

I haven't played football for over twenty years, so it makes me feel good to be remembered. Just about every year people talk about running backs, my position. I played only sixty-eight ballgames. I didn't play ten years, and I didn't gain that many yards when I was playing. But I must have done something good. People remember me as a player who gave them some excitement. I think they remember Gale Sayers as someone who, when he touched the football, was going to do something exciting.

This book is exciting, too. Rick Korch scores a touchdown with *The Truly Great.* Read on—you won't be disappointed.

GALE SAYERS

Acknowledgments

There are two ways this book could have been written. I could have done it myself with just my opinions, but then it would have been a purely subjective book. Or I could have interviewed several hundred experts—players, former players, coaches, assistant coaches, historians, and sportswriters.

I chose the latter. While still being very subjective because of its nature, I wanted this to be as close to a consensus as to who is the best player at a particular position as has ever been written.

I don't even agree with all of the rankings. But nobody does, so perhaps it is fair and impartial.

More than 300 interviews were conducted, many of them in 1990 when I wrote a nine-part series for *Pro Football Weekly* called "The Best Ever" that was judged the best feature story that year by the Pro Football Writers of America.

This book couldn't have been written without the special help of several pro football historians who gave me their insights and opinions from having seen and studied the game for many decades. They include Jim Campbell, who, in my opinion, is the most knowledgeable person on pro football alive today; Joe Horrigan, the historian at the Pro Football Hall of Fame; Bob Carroll, the foremost authority on pro football's first few decades; David Neft, a co-author of *The Football Encyclopedia* who is responsible for an enormous amount of research; and Beau Riffenburgh, the author of *The Official NFL Encyclopedia*.

Also from the Hall of Fame, research assistant Pete Fierle provided a large volume of background information, and public relations director Don Smith was always available for assistance.

And thanks to all the members of the NFL Alumni, who, during the five years I served as public relations director of that organization, told me countless stories about their own teammates, opponents, and boyhood idols. Several NFL Alumni staffers also helped, including Dick Szymanski, Tim Williams, Doug Lang, and Hans Humphrey.

Many sportswriters provided their insights, particularly Bob Oates of the *Los Angeles Times*, John Steadman of the *Baltimore Morning News*, Cooper Rollow of the *Chicago Tribune*, Jerry Magee of the *San Diego Union*, Sid Hartman of the

Minneapolis Star-Tribune, Art Rosenbaum of the *San Francisco Chronicle*, Chuck Heaton of the *Cleveland Plain Dealer*, Bill Wallace of *The New York Times*, and Art Daley of the *Green Bay Press-Gazette*.

The list of former players is too long to list here; you'll see their quotes throughout the book.

Several current and former head coaches provided much input, but perhaps the people I enjoyed talking to the most were the many current and former assistant coaches.

And a real special thanks to Gale Sayers, one of the true legends of the game, for writing the foreword.

Also to my brother, Jody, for proofreading the manuscript.

To Jim Donovan, my editor at Taylor Publishing, who came up with the idea for this book two years ago.

And to Angela Miller, my literary agent, for telling Jim that I was the one who should write this book.

A special thanks to my two mentors, Bob Hardin and Dick Kirkpatrick, two outstanding writers who like to stay out of the limelight but who know the English language like no two people I know.

Loving thanks to, as I write this, my fiancé Jacquie, who, when this book comes out, will be my wife. And Erik and Jennifer, her children. Yes, there are some Packers in this book.

To my dad, the first talent scout in professional football, who, although he died when I was two, somehow gave me an incredible thirst for knowledge of the history of professional football. And to my mom, for letting me read his library of football books when I was young so I could learn about many of the players I wrote about—and interviewed—for this book.

The many interviews I conducted were meant to find out who the best players were. But they were also a lot of fun. There was a back-and-forth exchange—through me—between two former Colts, Jim Parker and Dick Szymanski. Sizzy told me to razz Parker about forgetting the snap count so many times decades ago. Parker roared when I told him, and said, "Nooooo. That was Sizzy. I never forgot the snap count."

And Howard Mudd, a pretty good guard himself, after a long interview one day during football season when he was the Chiefs' offensive line coach, said to me, "Hey, it was a lot of fun reminiscing like this. Thanks for calling."

Well, everybody, thanks for talking to me. You made this book what it is.

I think continually of those who were truly great . . .
Who wore at their hearts the fire's center

STEPHEN SPENDER

INTRODUCTION

A FEW GOOD MEN

Who's the greatest pro football player of all time?

Then again, is it even fair to single out one player as the best ever?

It's a difficult subject, because the eras change and the players change, the rules change and the stadiums change. And players' talents are so different, even the great ones.

But everyone has an opinion, and everyone always asks the same questions.

Who's better: Joe Montana or Johnny Unitas? Or was Walter Payton better than Jim Brown?

If you ask football players and coaches, even they have their own opinions. At very few positions is there one clear favorite.

Too often, a player picks a person from the era in which he played. Sportswriters are partial to the players on the teams they covered. Everybody—especially the fan—favors the players they watched.

And injuries play a factor. Kenny Easley would have been one of the greatest safeties ever if he hadn't been injured in his seventh season. Gale Sayers played in only sixty-eight games but has to be included because he was a true legend.

But there has to be a way to determine the best pro football player of all time. So current and former players, NFL coaches, sportswriters, and pro football historians were sought to determine the best ever. More than 300 interviews were conducted, and certain conclusions were easily drawn.

Although everyone has his own opinion—and a few held their own and simply described players' abilities—it didn't take long before a consensus could be formed, no matter the position or the players.

But it wasn't easy. Take quarterbacks, for example. That's the one position where three players clearly drew nominations for the best ever—Johnny Unitas, Joe Montana, and Otto Graham. All three of them won championships and all three were the best during their respective time.

Some players clearly revolutionized their position. Don Hutson pioneered the passing game, while Jerry Rice is the most prolific scorer in the game today. But both of them scored 100 or so touchdowns in about the same number of games. So the nod goes to Hutson, who did it in a time when few teams threw the ball.

It's hard to compare players from the first three decades of pro football because it was such a different game then. It was strictly a running game then, with shoulder blocking, cross-body tackling, and little of the technical skills that are inherent in the game today. And there was certainly little of the specialization of today's game. In football's first three decades, players played both offense and defense, usually sixty minutes a game.

Certainly, everybody is entitled to his opinion, but something needs to be said about fans' opinions: Far too many people overrate players from the teams in their city.

Take running backs, for example. In Chicago, where I live, fans say Walter Payton was the best ever. Around the rest of the country, it's clearly Jim Brown. It's always difficult for fans from a particular city to be objective.

Also, as time passes and the heroes of yesterday loom bigger in our memories, there is a tendency to believe they were better than they really were, or to believe their kind will never be seen again. New players will come, records will be broken. and the game will go on. Someday Jerry Rice will seem as old to the football public as Don Hutson seems today. And somebody else will be the greatest receiver of all time.

Many people are entranced with the past. I hope I am not one of them. But I think the rankings in this book are fair and impartial—and split fairly between the oldtimers and today's players.

The lists in this book do not stop at ten, or some other round number, for every position. Each position includes the players who are truly the best at that position, after which there is a drop off to the next tier of top players. For example, there are sixteen running backs analyzed but only four nose tackles. There are ten middle linebackers, but only three inside linebackers.

Not all of the players in this book are in the Pro Football Hall of Fame, and not all of the Hall of Famers are in this book.

But these are the truly great.

QUARTERBACKS

*You can plan and plan and work and work, and it all comes down to
the man who pulls the trigger.*
WEEB EWBANK

The position of quarterback is like no other in sports. The quarterback is the one true leader on the field, and, to win a championship in the NFL, you have to have a truly great quarterback.

Look at the Super Bowls. The first ten were won by quarterbacks who are in the Pro Football Hall of Fame. Most of the rest were won by quarterbacks who are either now in the Hall or destined for it.

In fact, nearly every NFL championship since the invention of the T-formation has been won by a team with a great quarterback. There are flukes, such as the victory by Washington and Doug Williams in Super Bowl XXII, but at least Williams did have a Hall of Fame-caliber performance that day.

Teams just won't win championships without a great quarterback, and that's why a quarterback who can win championships is the most precious commodity in pro football.

Imagine what the Chicago Bears might have done in the latter half of the 1980s with Dan Marino or Boomer Esiason at quarterback. Or imagine how many championships the Green Bay Packers would *not* have won in the 1960s with Zeke Bratkowski playing instead of Bart Starr.

Ex-Colts and Jets coach Weeb Ewbank put it this way: "You can plan and plan and work and work, and it all comes down to the man who pulls the trigger."

Quarterbacks are like fingerprints—no two are alike. It is certainly the most demanding position in pro football. As Paul Brown once said, "Playing quarterback in the NFL is so tough it is almost impossible. The basic reason [is] the degree required is so high it is virtually unimaginable to outsiders."

Intelligence and perception are the intangibles coaches talk about, the undefined parts of a quarterback that place him a cut above other athletes. But a great quarterback also needs size, speed, mobility, a quick release, touch, creativity, and leadership. And then there're the team aspects—the supporting cast and the system they play in.

As former 49ers coach Bill Walsh put it, "You usually find that every good quarterback is a good athlete in almost everything he tries."

And there's one more: In the final moments of a close game, the great quarterbacks take total control of their own team and control of winning the game. They always want one last chance at getting the ball because they feel they can win any game in the last moment.

Noted sportswriter Mickey Herskowitz of the *Houston Post* once said, "Winning is a quarterback's excuse for living."

"Quarterbacks judge other quarterbacks on just one thing—winning," said Len Dawson, the Hall of Fame quarterback for the Chiefs.

Bobby Layne said, "There's something about being a winner that's the greatest thing in the world. You can spot a winner by the way he walks down the street. When you're a winner, you don't have to park your car by yourself; somebody parks it for you."

So forget what Alex Karras once said—"I never met a quarterback I liked. They're all candy-asses"—because, as Don Meredith put it, "Quarterback is where it's at, pardner."

So who's the best ever?

Statistically, it's Joe Montana. The numbers are there, pure and simple.

For winning, you have to go with Otto Graham. He quarterbacked the Browns to ten straight championship games from 1946 to '55. Nobody has ever come close to that streak.

For the all-around package, Johnny Unitas is the one. He had the numbers and he won.

And you couldn't go wrong with any one of the three at quarterback.

"I'd like to have any one of them," says Sid Gillman, the Hall of Fame coach for the Rams and Chargers who is considered football's top passing expert. "I couldn't pick one of them over the other. I don't see how anybody can."

More than any other position, it's almost impossible to name the best quarterback. At other positions, the best-ever players can, arguably, be picked. But it's very difficult at quarterback.

But all three of these quarterbacks—Montana, Graham, and Unitas—were also winners. It could be a three-way tie for the best quarterback in NFL history, because nobody has won more than Unitas, Graham and Montana. But somebody has to be the best, so . . .

1. JOHNNY UNITAS—When you think of Johnny Unitas, you think of crew cuts, high-topped shoes, and composure. He was signed off the Pittsburgh semipro lots in 1956 and was voted the quarterback on the NFL's all-time team thirteen years later. He played on four NFL championship teams and holds perhaps the one unbreakable record in the NFL—forty-seven consecutive games throwing a touchdown pass.

JOHNNY UNITAS

Unitas didn't always win and he didn't have the greatest statistics ever, but he is most often considered the best quarterback ever.

"He was the first of the daring quarterbacks," says Ted Marchibroda, the former NFL quarterback and current Colts head coach. "That's what made Johnny great—the willingness to gamble and take chances."

Unitas did just that in the 1958 NFL championship, still called "the greatest game ever played." Baltimore was driving in overtime and needed just a field goal to win. Instead of setting up in the middle of the field with runs, Unitas surprised everyone by passing to Jim Mutscheller down to the one-yard line. A play later, Alan Ameche dove over for the winning touchdown.

"That was the best single drive in NFL history," claims Beau Riffenburgh, the author of *The Official NFL Encyclopedia.*

Unitas simply said, "When you know what you're doing, you don't get intercepted."

"He was beyond intimidation," remembered John Steadman, the longtime Baltimore sportswriter. "He was immune to pressure, totally immune. He never second-guessed himself after a game, win or lose."

"He had tremendous courage to stay in the pocket," says Bears Hall of Famer Sid Luckman. "He just said, 'I'm going back; come and get me.' When you talk about how to set up, it's Johnny Unitas. The way he faced the sideline when he went back, how he held the ball up, how he threw."

"One way you judge is how far ahead of his competition he was," says historian Bob Carroll. "First, there was Benny Friedman, then Sammy Baugh, then Unitas. He was on a plane ahead of the others."

But he was cut from the Steelers. Pittsburgh coach Walt Kiesling once explained why he cut Unitas in 1955: "Too dumb. The kid was just too dumb to be a pro quarterback."

Hardly. A three-time NFL Most Valuable Player (1959, '64, and '67) and five-time All-Pro, Unitas lent new definition to the terms poise and cool. When he retired after the 1973 season, he held virtually every meaningful pro passing record—2,830 completions in 5,186 attempts for 40,239 yards, 290 touchdowns, and 26 games of over 300 yards passing. He played in ten Pro Bowls and was inducted into the Hall of Fame in 1979.

As a kid, former Chargers quarterback Dan Fouts idolized Unitas. "When I was growing up, it was Johnny U. He was just head and shoulders above everybody else in his era," Fouts said. "There was no doubt when he was playing who the best quarterback was."

"The thing that makes John Unitas the greatest quarterback of all time," said Merlin Olsen, "isn't his arm or even his football sense. It's his courage."

Unitas summed up his talents thusly: "You try to take what they give you. They always give you something and you try to take it."

Perhaps John Mackey, the Colts' Hall of Fame tight end, summed up Unitas best: "It's like being in the huddle with God."

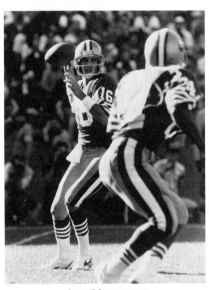

JOE MONTANA

2. JOE MONTANA—If the best quarterback is chosen either on the basis of winning or on his statistics, Joe Montana can make a very strong case as the best ever. Picked in the third round of the 1979 draft, he surprised every personnel expert in the NFL. He is the top-rated passer of all time.

"If Joe's not the best of all time, you would have a heck of an argument against anyone who wanted to go in any other direction," says John Madden, the former Raiders coach and current CBS broadcaster.

The only three-time Super Bowl MVP, Montana always played best in the big games. Says Miami quarterback Dan Marino, "Every opportunity he's had to win, Joe's done what he had to win. He's been in four Super Bowls, and he could have won two and lost two, but he's won all four. He's a big-time player and he plays great in big ballgames. The one thing I admire most about Joe is he doesn't make big mistakes. He doesn't throw a lot of interceptions."

Montana's status as a great quarterback is sometimes knocked because of the 49ers' system, which features a short passing game that revolves around getting the ball to great receivers who turn 10-yard passes into 80-yard touchdowns. It gives Montana an advantage, but the system isn't an easy one to master. "It took me a while to realize it takes a special person to run any successful system," says ex-Steeler Terry Bradshaw. "I don't think I ever could have mastered the 49ers' system, because I don't think I would have had the patience."

"I detect a feeling going around of people not wanting to give credit for what he is," says Cooper Rollow, the veteran *Chicago Tribune* sportswriter. "Unitas is my personal favorite, but Montana puts all aspects of the game together better than anyone in the history of the game."

"Quarterbacks today think long," says Otto Graham. "They should think short, and if long presents itself you take it. Montana never throws long, hardly ever. But that's not a knock. He can throw long, but he takes what you give him."

Pro football historian Jim Campbell says, "He realizes his full potential as much as any athlete in sports. He comes as close as anyone to changing my thinking about Unitas being the best quarterback ever, and the fourth Super Bowl (victory) did it."

And like all great quarterbacks, Montana excels when the game is on the line. Bill Walsh, who coached Montana and the 49ers to three Super Bowls, says, "When the game is on the line, you need someone to go in there and win it right now. I would rather have Joe Montana as my quarterback than anybody else who has ever played the game. I don't know if he is the best in any one category, but if you put it all together, he's the best all-around quarterback that ever was."

In his thirteen seasons, Montana has completed 63.7 percent of his 4,600 passes for 35,124 yards and 244 touchdowns and only 123 interceptions.

Dan Fouts compares Montana with Unitas this way: "Montana's got the numbers and the rings and everything, but when you're a kid, you're so much more influenced by the players that you watched that I think I'm a little biased toward Johnny U. But if there could be co-greatest of all time, I think Montana is fantastic, too."

3. OTTO GRAHAM—Otto Graham played for some of the greatest teams in pro football history, making it to ten championship games in ten years. Nine members of the Browns are already in the Hall of Fame. But Graham was the key to the team.

He has stood the test of time, too. Not only were his statistics the best back then, but, until the 1980s, Graham was still the top-rated pro passer of all time. He completed 55.8 percent of his passes for 23,584 yards and 174 touchdowns.

"Otto Graham was the best quarterback in my time," says Saints general manager Jim Finks. "If there was one game on the line that you had to win, I would pick Otto Graham."

Graham's teams won league championships in seven of his ten seasons.

OTTO GRAHAM

"When you ask what a quarterback is supposed to do, coaches say the bottom line is to win, and no one did it better than Graham," says Beau Riffenburgh.

Graham could do it all. "He had the best touch, long or short," said his coach, Paul Brown. "And he could run with the ball."

Brown considered Graham the greatest quarterback ever. "The test of a quarterback is where his teams finish, so Otto Graham, by that standard, is the best of all time. . . . To put it simply, find me another quarterback who took his team to as many championships."

Graham also was tough. The only negative thing about him was that he didn't call his own plays; Brown did. But Graham was capable of doing it himself. Graham threw somewhat sidearm, but he was accurate, one of the best long-ball passers ever.

Like most people, Graham says one person can't pick the greatest quarterback ever. The game has changed so much, and today's athletes are bigger, faster, and stronger than those of yesteryear. "Guys today are better than I was," he admits. "There's no doubt about that."

Graham switched from single-wing tailback in college to one of the finest T-formation quarterbacks in the pros. He led the All-American Football Conference in passing four times and the NFL twice, and was the MVP twice in each league. But he saved many of his best performances for the big games. In the 1954 NFL championship game, he passed for three touchdowns and ran for three. In his final game, for the 1955 title, he passed for two scores and ran for two more. The first player signed by Brown, his teams had a record of 114-20-4. A nine-time All-League selection, he was inducted into the Hall of Fame in 1965.

Graham had fine peripheral vision, total composure on the field, the ability to find his receivers, and the arm to get the ball to them. Brown said Graham's hand–eye coordination was most unusual.

But the knock against him was that he was a stoic automaton who never would have dreamed about interfering with his coach's play-calling.

4. ROGER STAUBACH—Most people rank Roger Staubach as the greatest come-from-behind quarterback ever. Time and time again, Staubach pulled out victories in the final two minutes of a game, usually big games. Staubach didn't invent the name of the "Hail Mary" pass—he threw it.

"Roger can make a positive play out of one that starts out like a loser," said ex-Miami quarterback Bob Griese.

Between the time of Johnny Unitas and Joe Montana, Staubach was the NFL's best quarterback. He was a great improviser and was very mobile. "He had an air about him," says Hall of Famer Sid Luckman. "You knew someone special was on the field."

"He was a great competitor," says Ted Marchibroda. "Staubach could do it more ways than most quarterbacks."

Tom Landry, who was Staubach's coach, agrees. "Roger Staubach might be the best combination of a passer, an athlete, and a leader ever to play in the NFL." And that is incredible praise from someone who played or coached against the greatest passers of the last five decades.

ROGER STAUBACH

"I coached the College All-Star game for ten years, and of all the quarterbacks, Roger was the best I ever had," said Otto Graham. "He was a great leader—that's the most important thing for a quarterback."

Staubach was simply unwilling to take no for an answer. He led the NFL in passing in 1971, '73, '78, and '79 and is the highest-rated passer of all retired players. Surprisingly, he was never voted to an All-Pro team. He was also an outstanding scrambler and runner, adding 2,264 yards and a 5.5-yard average. During his eleven-year career, he led the Cowboys to an unbelievable 23 come-from-behind victories (fourteen in the final two minutes or overtime), and he almost pulled out Super Bowls X and XIII.

But the odds were against him at the outset. He was drafted as a future in the tenth round of the 1964 draft when he still owed a year at Navy and a four-year commitment. Said Landry, "I never thought we would see this Heisman Trophy winner in a Cowboys' uniform." Staubach joined the Cowboys in 1969 but didn't gain a starting job until midway through the '71 season. He led Dallas to ten consecutive victories, including the team's first Super Bowl victory.

Staubach passed for 22,700 yards and 153 touchdowns in basically eight years as a starter (and he averaged only 351 passes a season). He also ran for 20 scores.

In his final press conference, on how he wanted to be remembered, Staubach replied, understating to the very end, "As a pretty darn consistent quarterback."

SAMMY BAUGH

5. SAMMY BAUGH—Sammy Baugh was the first and best of the T-formation quarterbacks. "Slingin' Sammy," as he was known, was the greatest passer of the NFL's first three decades. He was one of the greatest athletes who ever lived, according to Sid Luckman, his chief rival. Baugh also was a great defensive back and punter.

"He was before my time, but they tell me he was the greatest passer of them all," says Ted Marchibroda.

Some people think Baugh just might have been the greatest player to ever have played pro football.

Baugh changed the sport forever. He was the leading passer during pro football's evolution from a ground to an air game. When he came on the scene, passing was merely a desperation tactic for most teams; by the time he left, it was the most important weapon in a team's arsenals.

"It was Baugh," wrote Arthur Daley of *The New York Times*, "who revolutionized football and altered all previous strategic concepts."

Baugh had a great arm. In fact, in 1945 he completed 70.33 percent of his passes, while other quarterbacks of the time hit on only 40 percent of theirs. That record lasted until 1989. Baugh also played sixteen seasons (1937–52), which was unheard of in those days.

Baugh started his career as a single-wing tailback, not making the switch to quarterback until midway through his career in 1944. That's why he made the All-NFL team three times as a halfback and only once as a quarterback. He also led the league in passing a record six times, three at each position.

The 6-foot-2, 178-pound Baugh was marvelously gifted in every facet of the game. He holds the records for career and single-season punting average, and his four interceptions in one game are still tied for the record (he also threw four TD passes in the same game). Baugh completed 1,693 of 2,995 passes (56.5 percent) for 21,886 yards and 186 touchdowns, all records when he retired. Twice he threw six TD passes in a game.

He was the No. 1 choice of the Redskins in 1937, the second draft. That was the year the team moved from Boston to Washington. Baugh responded by taking them to an NFL championship as a rookie. Washington won four other divisional titles and one more championship during his career.

"In his worst game," said the late football historian Roger Treat, "he was as good as the rest of the quarterbacks on their best days."

"I played quarterback for sixteen years, and I loved it," recalled Baugh. "I wished I could have played all my life or until I was sixty, like in most jobs. Being quarterback in the big league is the best job on earth."

6. DAN MARINO—The two best quarterbacks in the NFL over the last decade have been Joe Montana and Dan Marino. "They are head and shoulders over anyone else in the league," says Johnny Unitas. "If I had his personnel, I'd go with Montana. But, if I didn't have that overall personnel, in a key game I'd probably go with Marino."

Marino burst on the NFL scene in 1984, his second season, quickly becoming the NFL's most prolific single-season passer ever. He passed for 48 touchdowns and 5,084 yards that season.

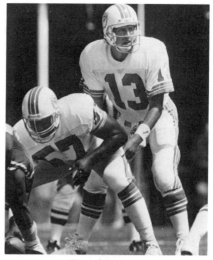

DAN MARINO

"There is no doubt in my mind that Marino is the greatest pure passer to ever play the game," says Edwin Pope, sports editor of *The Miami Herald*. "I've seen them all, back to Sammy Baugh, Graham, Waterfield, Van Brocklin, Unitas, Starr, Jurgensen, Namath, Staubach, Bradshaw, Montana. No question. None of them had that God-given skill to just throw, to flick the ball like he does."

Marino has both a beautiful, feathery touch and a rocket for an arm. "I love his arm," says Sid Luckman. "He has the quickest release ever."

Marino's release has made him the least-sacked quarterback ever. He isn't very mobile, but opponents fear Marino's willingness to throw long at any time.

"I love watching him," says Dan Fouts, to whom Marino is often compared. "I think if I had a choice of going to a game and I could pick any quarterback to go see right now, I'd pick Marino. I just think it's his style and his flair for the game that excites me."

"I remember a couple of occasions that he threw unbelievable balls," recalled Len Dawson. "The margin for error was so minimal; he had the ball right there at the right time."

Don Shula coached both Unitas and Marino. "John Unitas had a pretty good gun. Marino has that gun. He also has quickness and he sees downfield well," Shula says. "He has a toughness about him, a real desire to win. He did some things early in his career that no other player had ever done."

The sixth quarterback taken in 1983's legendary first-round quarterback bonanza, Marino has taken passing to new heights. He holds every meaningful Miami passing record and is pro football's second-rated passer of all time. In ten seasons, he has thrown for 39,502 yards and 290 touchdowns.

Marino relies on the aggressiveness of his receivers more than other quarterbacks. He fires an extremely fast pass.

"Only Sonny Jurgensen and Joe Namath have been able to get rid of the ball as quickly as Marino," says Shula, who has had to compare Marino with the greats for years. "There simply are times when you have to put it up in a certain spot before that defensive lineman grinds you into the ground. Marino can do that. He can find the open receiver, or the receiver who'll shortly be getting open, and deliver the ball almost instantaneously."

Shula then compares Marino with Fouts. "Fouts was a much more controlled passer and as efficient as anyone at the short passing game. Fouts could see the entire field and then throw to the most open receiver. On the other hand, Marino likes the deep game more than Fouts and he takes more chances with it. He doesn't always go to the wide-open receiver but sometimes to the one with the most potential to be the most dangerous."

Before his career is over, Marino will probably hold every career passing record. And, if he can lead the Dolphins to a couple of Super Bowl victories, he might also go down as the greatest quarterback ever. He has the numbers—he just needs the wins.

DAN FOUTS

7. DAN FOUTS—In 1981, Dan Fouts threw for 4,802 yards—a figure unheard of before that time.

If Dan Marino has been more daring, it was Fouts who mastered the short passing game. Fouts was a very intelligent passer who could read defenses. He was tough, and when he was at his peak, the Chargers had the greatest passing attack in football history.

"God, he could throw a football," raves Sid Luckman, the Bears Hall of Famer. "I went into raptures of joy watching him throw the football."

Ted Marchibroda says Fouts threw from the three-step pattern more than Johnny Unitas, Sammy Baugh, Sonny Jurgensen, or most of the other great quarterbacks did. "He hit the quick patterns; now that's the trend," Marchibroda says.

Fouts had perhaps the greatest vision of any quarterback ever, especially going to his second and third receivers. "He would look at all four receivers, then all four again, then decide who to throw to," observes Beau Riffenburgh.

But it wasn't always easy for Fouts. He was a third-round draft choice from Oregon in 1973—the sixth quarterback chosen that year—who didn't do much until Don Coryell became the Chargers' head coach in 1978.

"In my career, it didn't turn around for me until my sixth year when Coryell took over. Up 'til then, I was a fair-to-mediocre quarterback."

And after that time, he was the greatest passer in the game.

The next year, in 1979, Fouts directed the Chargers to their first divisional title in fourteen years. He led the AFC in passing and broke Joe Namath's record for season passing yards. And he was named AFC Player of the Year.

He trails only Fran Tarkenton on the all-time lists for passing attempts, completions, and yards. His 254 touchdown passes tied for fourth all-time, and he went to the Pro Bowl six times.

Few quarterbacks made the kind of impact Fouts did over his career. But he doesn't look at the personal accolades.

"I don't like to talk about myself. Football's a team game," he says. "The satisfaction comes in winning and that's not an individual thing. [The highlight of my career was] the way we helped change the game. Playing for Coryell. Leading the league in total offense and passing a lot. If you look back in the record books, we were number one for quite a good while there. I think nobody has come close to the string we had. We led the league six years in a row in passing, and I think that's pretty phenomenal. We had a lot of fun."

It was also a lot of fun for his receivers. As Charlie Joiner once said, "When you have a pure passer such as Dan, from a receiver's standpoint, it's like dying and going to heaven."

A final word from Bill Walsh: "Dan is enormously strong once he sets to throw, and he has no fear about being hit. Dan Fouts is the best leader I've seen."

8. BOBBY LAYNE—Bobby Layne was renowned for partying, but it didn't seem to affect his play on the field. In fact, football historians call Layne the greatest leader ever. So do his peers.

"I played with Bobby Layne in Pittsburgh," Len Dawson remembers. "You hear all the stories off the field, but he was a very intelligent player out there."

Layne was the heart and soul of Detroit teams that won championships in 1952, '53, and '57. But most of the teams he played on were quite average. All of them, however, played better than they would have played with anyone else at quarterback.

When he retired in 1962 after fifteen seasons, he had completed 1,814 passes in 3,700 attempts for 26,768 yards and 196 touchdowns. All were NFL records at the time. He also ran for 25 scores. Still, numbers never were Layne's strong suit; leadership and winning were. He was even known to draw game-winning plays in the dirt on the field.

Red Hickey, who coached the 49ers, once said, "Layne, as bad as he looked throwing the ball, was a winner. You'd work him out and you wouldn't want him, but you'd want him in your huddle. Players feel that way about a quarterback. When a leader's in there, they'll perform. They'll go."

Layne agreed. "As a quarterback," he said, "you have to make the boys believe in you. Just the way you bark out the signals tells them you have confidence in the play you called. And they have to want to make it work. They have to be willing to want to put out an extra ten percent."

"He was a rough, tough kid," said Sid Luckman, who was a teammate of Layne's when Layne was a rookie in Chicago. "Coach [George] Halas told me that trading Layne was the biggest mistake he ever made." Layne went from the Bears to the Lions and then to the Steelers.

"His leadership was maybe unparalleled among quarterbacks," says Ted Marchibroda. "It was win-at-all-costs with Bobby."

But there was the other side to Layne, the side that formed the legend. He was hell-raising and free-wheeling. Teammate Yale Lary once commented, "When Bobby said 'drink,' we drank. When Bobby said 'play,' we played."

"He could have three hours of sleep and a splitting hangover, but he'd come to play," said Cooper Rollow.

"Bobby Layne never lost a game," said former Lion teammate and close friend Doak Walker. "Time just ran out. Nobody hated to lose more than Bobby."

9. SONNY JURGENSEN—Sonny Jurgensen is pro football's best pure passer ever, and his ability to lead receivers and get them the ball on the run is legendary. He had a great touch—he could lay the ball over linebackers and in front of defensive backs—and he could throw as he backpedaled.

Jurgensen, who threw almost with a side-arm delivery, passed to two Hall of Famers, Bobby Mitchell and Charley Taylor. He established some great records with some poor teams. If he had the kind of offensive line, running backs, and defense Johnny Unitas had, Jurgensen might have been the greatest quarterback of all time.

In fact, Unitas once said, "If I threw as much as Jurgensen, my arm would fall off, and if I could throw as well, my head would swell up too big to get into a helmet."

And Vince Lombardi said: "Jurgensen is a great quarterback. He may be the best the league has ever seen. He is the best I've seen."

Jurgensen played seven years for Philadelphia and eleven with Washington (1957–74). He completed 2,433 of 4,262 passes for 32,224 yards and 255 touchdowns, third all-time. He won league passing titles in 1967 and '69.

A classic drop-back passer, Jurgensen could deliver the ball at the last second under the pressure of a heavy rush. "All I ask of my blockers is four seconds," he said. "I try to stay on my feet and try not be forced out. Any time they make me do something I'm second-best at, they're defeating me. I beat people by throwing, not running. And I won't let them intimidate me."

Don Meredith, Dallas' quarterback in the sixties, said, "We go into Washington every year with the best defense in the NFL, and Sonny still scares me to death. He's the one person who can pass a defense to death no matter who is rushing him and no matter who is in the secondary. He is an uncanny passer, simply the best the game has had."

"I see guys today diving for the ball, jumping for it. . . . Sonny put the ball on the numbers," said Len Dawson.

Jurgensen's induction into the Hall of Fame in 1983 provided proof that a star can get there on the strength of his own merits rather than those of the teams for which he played. "This is the ultimate," he said of his enshrinement. "It takes the place of all those frustrations and disappointments. This makes it all worthwhile."

10. NORM VAN BROCKLIN—Norm Van Brocklin was another of pro football's great leaders. His 1960 Eagles weren't the best in the league, but Van Brocklin carried that team on his shoulders and it won the NFL title.

It was said of Van Brocklin many times that he couldn't run and he was too frail—all he could do was pass. "I'm not paid to do anything but throw and call plays," he said. "I think I've been doing pretty well with the invention."

A colorful, competitive, stormy individual, Van Brocklin was one of the first pocket passers, because he couldn't run at all. He was smart and a fine passer. In 1951, he passed for 554 yards in a single game, which is still the record. Once he led the Rams to 41 points in a single quarter.

Van Brocklin would challenge opponents, and even his teammates. His temper was legendary. "If he had one fault, it was that he would make up his mind in the huddle who he was going to throw to," said Cooper Rollow.

"The Dutchman" won passing titles in three of his first five seasons (as well as twice in punting). He passed for 23,611 yards and 173 touchdowns.

But Van Brocklin's greatness is often overlooked because he split time in Los Angeles from 1949 to '52 with Bob Waterfield, another Hall of Famer. In fact, in 1950, the two quarterbacks alternated quarters of games. Van Brocklin took over in '53, but was then stymied because he wanted to be a "coach on the field." He threatened retirement several times and finally demanded a trade, going to Philadelphia. There, Eagles coach Buck Shaw gave him almost free rein with the offense.

When the Eagles beat the Packers for the 1960 championship, it marked the only time a Vince Lombardi-coached team ever lost a championship game. "The job he did that year was the best ever done by any quarterback," recalls Marion Campbell, then an Eagle and later the team's head coach. "We did not have the physical talent, but we had the mental talent, and he was a great leader."

Van Brocklin retired a month after the game and became the head coach of the expansion Vikings.

11. TERRY BRADSHAW—Terry Bradshaw's four Super Bowl championships say it all. He was a terrific winner and one of the best of the big-play quarterbacks. But he always had his detractors.

Bob Carroll calls him "the most exciting quarterback I ever saw—but sometimes that would result in a disastrous mistake. He could throw an eighty-yard pass or a five-yard interception."

There was a supposition that Bradshaw wasn't smart enough to be a big-time quarterback. As the Cowboys' Hollywood Henderson once said, "Bradshaw couldn't spell cat if you spotted him the C and the T."

But Bradshaw got satisfaction proving people wrong. Halfway through Bradshaw's career, Len Dawson remembers telling a writer, "A lot of us would like to be so dumb to quarterback two Super Bowl [winning] teams." And that was before he won two more.

The Steelers were primarily a running team early in Bradshaw's career, and he started slowly as a passer. In his rookie season, he completed only 38.1 percent of his passes and had 24 interceptions. But later he carried them with his passing, throwing for 100 touchdowns in a four-year span from 1978–81. He had one of the strongest arms ever, with a great long touch, and he had superior receivers in Lynn Swann and John Stallworth. Bradshaw was tough, and he was a great big-play quarterback in big games.

The first player drafted in 1970, the 6-foot-3, 210-pound Bradshaw passed for 27,989 yards and 212 touchdowns (12th all-time). He also ran for 32 TDs. But he was named All-Pro only once and was selected to just two Pro Bowls.

In four Super Bowls, he threw for 932 yards and nine touchdowns. He was the Most Valuable Player of Super Bowls XIII and XIV. He also holds the postseason records of 3,833 yards and 30 TDs.

He was inducted into the Hall of Fame in 1989, his first year of eligibility.

12. LEN DAWSON—Len Dawson was the best of the quarterbacks who failed in their first opportunities in the NFL only to succeed in the new AFL. Cleveland had wanted him with the fourth pick of the first round of the 1957 draft but lost a coin flip and had to settle for Jim Brown. Dawson threw only 45 passes in five years with the Steelers and Browns (to whom he was traded in '60) before he signed with the AFL and turned into a star quickly. He quarterbacked the Chiefs to two of the first four Super Bowls.

Dawson and the Chiefs mastered the moving pocket, and he was equally adept at play-action. His coach, Hank Stram, once called him "the most accurate passer in football." Dawson never completed less than 53.4 percent of his passes in a season, and he wound up with a 57.6 career percentage.

In fourteen seasons with the Chiefs, the 6-foot, 190-pound signal caller led the AFL in passing in 1962, '64, '66, and '68. For many years he was ranked as the No. 1 passer in history. In nineteen seasons, Dawson completed 2,136 of

3,741 passes for 28,711 yards and 239 touchdowns. He was elected to the Hall of Fame in 1987.

"Lenny the Cool" is remembered as the losing quarterback in the first Super Bowl, but he prefers to remember Super Bowl IV, when he was named the Most Valuable Player as Kansas City upset Minnesota. In that game, he completed 12 of 17 passes for 142 yards, including a game-breaking 46-yard touchdown to Otis Taylor.

"Dawson had all the qualities you look for in a quarterback—leadership and a very intangible confidence that you don't see in a lot of people," says Stram.

RUNNING BACKS

If you have the football and eleven guys are after you,
if you're smart, you'll run.
RED GRANGE

Jim Thorpe was the first great runner in professional football, but his best years were spent playing for the Canton Bulldogs before the start of what we now know as the NFL. Red Grange was the star of the twenties, then it was Bronko Nagurski in the thirties and Steve Van Buren and Marion Motley in the forties. Jim Brown was next, and he was pretty much considered the best until O.J. Simpson and Walter Payton came along in the seventies.

Along the way, football fans have been thrilled by Hugh McElhenny, Gale Sayers, Tony Dorsett, Earl Campbell, Eric Dickerson, and a lot of other stars.

Brown is considered the best running back ever by most experts, but it is certainly not a unanimous declaration. In nine seasons with the Browns, from 1957 to '65, he rushed for 12,312 yards, a total that shattered Van Buren's previous record. Brown is probably the greatest pure runner ever. He was big at 6-foot-2, 228 pounds, and he had speed and power to match. His NFL average of 5.2 yards per carry is untouched by any other runner.

Payton broke Brown's rushing record in 1984 and went on to rush for 16,726 yards in thirteen seasons with the Bears. He was the back who could do it all—run, catch, and block. Few people know that, when Payton retired, he had also caught more passes than any other running back ever (492).

Simpson was the best back between Brown and Payton. He rushed for 11,236 yards for Buffalo and San Francisco between 1969 and '79 and set a then-single-season record of 2,003 yards in a 14-game season in 1973. He had size, world-class speed, and great moves.

With 2,210 yards in his second season in 1984, Dickerson broke Simpson's single-season record, although it took sixteen games. With 13,168 yards in ten seasons with the Rams, Colts, and Raiders, he was within reach of Payton's all-time record until he slipped drastically the last three years.

Marion Motley was Brown's predecessor in Cleveland, a punishing runner who gained 4,720 yards (he didn't play his first pro game until he was twenty-six), mostly in the All-American Football Conference that played from 1946 to '49 before being absorbed by the NFL. His two-league average of 5.7 yards per carry shatters even Brown's mark, but the competition in the AAFC wasn't usually up to NFL standards.

Those are the five backs most often considered the best ever, and everyone has his own reason for favoring one of them.

So who's the best running back ever?

Paul Brown coached both Motley and Brown. "As a pure runner, Jim Brown was the best ever," he said before his death in 1991. "He had a combination of power, intense speed, and a shuffling foot action that made it difficult to stop him. Jim rarely fumbled, and his durability was unusual." Brown missed only one game in his career.

Joe Horrigan, the historian for the Pro Football Hall of Fame, calls Payton the best ever. "He had great all-around abilities. He did everything, including blocking. Payton dominated an era of great running backs, whereas, when Brown played, Jim Taylor was his only competition."

John Steadman, the longtime Baltimore sportswriter who is a member of the Hall of Fame selection committee and was a publicist for the Colts in the fifties, votes for Motley. "He was the best power back. Motley was awesome, 240 pounds, and a masterful blocker. Jim Brown didn't shine Motley's shoes as a football player."

Paul Zimmerman, the esteemed writer for *Sports Illustrated*, also favors Motley, calling him "the greatest player ever . . . a steamroller, a gathering force."

Bob Oates of the *Los Angeles Times* has covered pro football for fifty-five years. He's seen all of the great running backs, and picks Simpson as the best ever. "O.J. had size, speed, and moves. Brown had just size and speed; he didn't have the moves of Simpson. Payton had quickness, but no speed. His durability stands out. Motley was like Brown, with more power but not the speed of Simpson and Dickerson. Dickerson is right there, close to O.J., but his personality hurts him so much."

Another football historian, Bob Carroll, who has authored eleven books, including *100 Greatest Running Backs,* chooses Brown. "He was the ultimate package of speed and power, and no one has ever combined them better. Teams set up their defenses strictly to stop him, but it seldom worked."

Jim Campbell also is one of the foremost pro football historians. He was Horrigan's predecessor at the Hall of Fame and also worked for NFL Properties and the NFL Alumni association. "No contest," says Campbell, "Brown was the best. A running back runs with the football; forget the other stuff. No one ever ran better than Brown."

In the early years of the NFL, there wasn't even the term "running back." It was just three or four players set up behind the line of scrimmage. They carried the ball, they got dirty. The tailback received most of the snaps from center, ran, passed, and frequently kicked. The right halfback or wingback in the Single Wing lined up outside the right end and was primarily a blocker. The fullback was a burly, up-the-middle runner. And, unlike today's quarterback, the old Single Wing quarterback was simply a blocking back who considered one carry a game to be heavy-duty work.

It wasn't until the T-formation in the forties that the modern running back started to evolve. Through the fifties and most of the sixties, the NFL officially divided the split backs behind the quarterback into the different positions of halfback and fullback. Fullbacks generally were the bruising power runners such as Motley and Cookie Gilchrist. Halfbacks were supposed to have the speed to get outside, as most did, and a few had deceptive moves like Hugh McElhenny and Gale Sayers without the fullback's size. That distinction slowly died as Vince Lombardi's Packers won championship after championship with two fullback-sized halfbacks in Jim Taylor and Paul Hornung.

But, for some reason, most of the great running backs were halfbacks, although there is some disagreement over which is the more important role.

As the legendary Red Grange once said, "This comment may surprise most people coming from me, but, to be honest, it's the guys who power up the middle, the guys who will lay down that all-important block for you, the guys who would take the ball, stick their heads into a linebacker and make that fourth-and-short a first-and-ten who win football games." Grange, obviously, liked fullbacks.

Larry Csonka, a Hall of Fame fullback for Miami, said, "I wouldn't ever have wanted to be a halfback. I like running up the gut. You see, a power runner can intimidate the defense and, if not, at least you can nail them down once in a while. Linebackers spend their entire careers beating up on ballcarriers who are twenty or thirty pounds lighter than they are, so I like to run in the middle and even the score a little for the offense."

Enough of the history lesson: Who is the best running back ever?

Historians and writers like to pick their favorites. Coaches and players don't. The coaches don't like to compare the great players, and the great players don't like to single somebody out.

"It's like apples and oranges," says Lou Saban, Simpson's coach in Buffalo. "It's totally unfair to judge one against the other. Each had some special talent that made them different from each other."

Jim Brown agrees. "No coach can 'make' a great runner. Great runners are works of God. Great running is an art so intensely personal, no two men do it quite alike."

Current Lions star Barry Sanders says, "It's sort of a vain discussion. When you start getting into who's the best, there's really no way of ever finding that out. I don't think we've seen anybody who was so good you could just say he was the best. If a guy comes and rushes for 5,000 yards a season, you might be able to say he's the best, but I don't think we've seen anybody like that."

Brown considers himself the greatest running back ever, but he groups Payton, Simpson, Gale Sayers, and Earl Campbell right with him. "The bottom line is: Did he dominate?" asks Brown. "When I think of domination, I think of Gale and Walter and Earl and O.J., in no particular order. Give me Gale's cuts, Earl's power, O.J.'s speed, and Walter's heart. That would be the perfect back."

"Remember, we're talking about players who are all very close," remarked Oates.

But one was just a little better than all the rest.

JIM BROWN

1. JIM BROWN—"He's number one in my book," says Gale Sayers, "and he'll always be. Coming out of high school and college, I looked to be as good as him. He played in tough times, on the frozen fields of Cleveland and Green Bay and the quagmire of Kezar Stadium [in San Francisco]. He could've had 2,000 yards on AstroTurf. Walter Payton was the most durable back I've ever seen. Gale Sayers was probably the most exciting. But I really feel Jim Brown is the best."

"Brown was a franchise player," said Lou Saban. "He just said, 'Give me the ball; I'll get it there.'"

"He was a great runner," remembers Rams coach Chuck Knox. " 'Run to daylight' was designed for Jim Brown by Blanton Collier. He would take those flips outside. They would pull a guard or a tackle, then crack back with the flanker. Then he'd split the crease. And he prepared for games more than he is given credit for."

"He just had it," said Hall of Famer Hugh McElhenny. However, although McElhenny said it's hard to criticize Brown's record, blocking wasn't exactly his strong suit.

"He never blocked anyone," said John Steadman.

"He wasn't called upon to block," said Joe Horrigan. "And he didn't catch the ball. But, as a ballcarrier, he was the best."

"He was never very interested in being a blocker," answered his coach, Paul Brown. "But he caught the ball beautifully." Brown caught 262 passes in his career.

The ultimate running back possessed both speed and power. Even after his career records have been broken, Brown's feats really haven't been equaled. He led the league in rushing eight times in nine years. When he retired in 1965, he held twenty NFL records. Perhaps his most impressive stat was that, despite repeatedly setting the record for carries in a season, he stills hold the NFL career record for a 5.22-yard average per carry.

Hall of Fame linebacker Chuck Bednarik said, "Good? He's superhuman. He had finesse, ability, sheer power and desire. Above all, desire. You knew he was going to carry the ball about thirty times. You could have five guys keying on him and you knew he was going to get the ball if it was third-and-one or third-and-two, and most of the time he'd get the first down no matter how hard you tried to stop him. You can forget your [Bronko] Nagurskis and Jim Thorpes— I'll take Jimmy Brown."

Sam Huff was another Hall of Fame linebacker who played against Brown. "In my opinion, he is the greatest football player to ever put on a uniform. It was difficult to play against Jim because, as a linebacker, you've got to play angry. He'd lull you to sleep, and the next time he'd come through, man he'd be heading like a freight train full speed ahead. When you hit him, it would be like running into an oak tree."

Alex Karras once described how the Lions should have tackled Brown: "Give each guy in the line an ax."

When he retired in 1966, Brown said, "It was the right time to retire. You have to go out on the top."

A quarter of a century later, he still is on top.

2. WALTER PAYTON—"When you played the Bears, the number-one defensive objective was to try to contain Walter Payton, slow him down," remembers Knox, whose teams had to try to do it a number of times in Los Angeles, Buffalo, and Seattle. "He had that stutter step once he got through the line. He finished off his runs better than anybody—he exploded into tacklers. And his enthusiasm infected everybody on the team."

"He was a hundred-percenter all the time," said Lou Saban. "He very seldom had a bad day. Totally consistent."

"Walter had the skills, the ultimate heart, a mix that can take a man anywhere," said Jim Brown, to whom Payton is most often compared. "He had a dynamic first step. He had striking power—Walter went about 195, struck like 220. The only quality Walter lacked, in my opinion, was what runners call a 'fourth gear.' It's the ability to get one step on a defender, be gone, for seventy, eighty yards. Within the fraternity of runners, that extra dimension is something we take special pride in. The Juice had it. Sayers, myself, but not Walter. Walter is as gutsy a runner as I've ever seen. But he didn't have that fourth gear."

WALTER PAYTON

"He was a totally unique little guy," observed Hugh McElhenny. "He had lateral movements like a bee."

"As a runner, there's no question he was great," says Gale Sayers, who preceded Payton as one of the Bears' great backs. "People talk about his durability, [but] he was in no better shape than me or O.J. We got hurt; he didn't. It's the luck of the draw. Luck was on his side."

Payton, who missed only one game in thirteen seasons, is considered the best blocking back ever and was probably the best receiver out of the backfield. When he retired, his 492 receptions was the record for a running back. He even played quarterback one game in 1984 when the Bears' passers were all injured—and he didn't do badly at all.

However, while Jim Brown averaged 5.22 yards every time he carried the ball, Payton's average was only 4.357 per carry.

Payton played early in his career behind a weak line. As former Chargers tight end Kellen Winslow points out, "For most of his career, he took on the NFL with no offensive line."

In 1977, his third season, on a damp, gray day, Payton ran the football 40 times for 275 yards in a 10–7 victory over the Vikings, which is farther than anyone has ever rushed in a single game. He had a bout of flu that day that almost sidelined him. That season, Payton was voted the NFL's Most Valuable Player at the age of twenty-three, the youngest player ever so honored.

When Payton finally retired after the 1987 season, he had rushed 3,838 times for 16,726 yards. He had scored 125 touchdowns. He rushed for at least 1,000 yards in ten of thirteen seasons (six of them consecutive), leading the league four times. He played in nine Pro Bowls and was a six-time All-Pro.

On December 20, 1987, the day of his last game, a banner hung in Soldier Field that read: "Santa: Please Send More Walter Paytons. First One Was Perfect."

O.J. SIMPSON

3. O.J. SIMPSON—O.J. Simpson was as close to a pure runner as anybody but Jim Brown. He brought a new dimension to football—the sharp-cutting, slicing ability that eludes most big backs.

Simpson was elusive; he got into and out of holes quickly. And he used "peripheral vision to avoid real hits," said Lou Saban, his former coach.

"Only Red Grange or Gale Sayers were more likely to break a long run," said Bob Carroll. Jim Campbell agreed: "He had a lot of three- and four-yard runs, but once a game he was going to get loose."

"I put Simpson between Brown and Motley," said Paul Brown. "He didn't have the power of Brown; he was like Sayers, only shaped."

"The Juice was fantastic," says Jim Brown. "[He had] a precise sense of when to accelerate. He also had a few nice moves. [But] Gale Sayers was pretty; the Juice was not. O.J. had this strange little humpback style of running."

Simpson's career got off to a slow start because he wasn't used much and Buffalo had a very weak offensive line, and he rushed for only 1,927 yards in his first three seasons. He was turned loose in 1972 when Lou Saban took over as Buffalo's head coach. Simpson responded by gaining 7,699 in his next five years and leading the AFC in rushing four times.

"It wasn't until my first 200-yard game against New England in that 1973 season opener that I was able to say to myself, 'I'm as good as anybody in this game,' " Simpson said. "For me, that was the first time all comparisons to Jim Brown, or at least the reports that put me in his class, seemed valid. Gaining 250 yards against the Patriots was the first time I was totally satisfied with my performance."

That season, Simpson became the first runner to crack the 2,000-yard barrier. "I knew the last game of the season going against the Jets that there was no way they were going to keep me from breaking Brown's single-season record," he said. "We knew we were going to win the game, and we knew we were going to get the sixty-one yards I needed to pass Brown. But I never would have imagined in my wildest expectations going over 2,000 yards for the season."

Two years later, he had what he calls an even better season, with 1,817 yards, 428 yards on 28 receptions, and 23 touchdowns. In a 1976 Thanksgiving contest, he rushed for the then-record of 273 yards in a single game. Simpson turned in five 1,000-yard seasons in a row and retired as the No. 2 rusher in NFL history with 11,236 yards.

Of his running style, Simpson once said, "I run like a coward. I bounce around the line. I hop around, looking for a place to run. They used to call it my stutter-step. If the hole's closed, I feel like I can still get four yards, but I'm always thinking fifty. So I try to find another place to run."

4. ERIC DICKERSON—If Eric Dickerson had kept his head in the game long enough, he might have been the greatest runner ever with his speed, quickness, and power. But, after seven outstanding seasons from 1983 to '89 when he gained 11,226 yards, he slipped quickly, and he rushed for only 1,942 yards from 1990 to '92.

ERIC DICKERSON

Dickerson's downfall has been caused by eroding skills, injuries, suspensions, and a relatively weak line his last years in Indianapolis. His yards-per-carry average dropped every year from 1987–91. But, when he was on, he was a true superstar.

"He combined strength and speed. I thought he'd be a three- or four-year ballplayer," says Joe Horrigan, "but he's made a believer out of me."

"For a big back, he has great explosiveness through the hole to the secondary and the speed to run away," said Chuck Knox. "And to break a big run in the NFL today gets more difficult every year."

Jim Brown takes pride in comparing running backs. During the height of Dickerson's career, Brown said, "Eric's talent for running the football is superb. He can cut, he's got that pretty track man's stride, microwave acceleration [and] fine natural instincts. He's the most skilled runner in football. [But] I'm still unsure of his heart."

With the Rams, Dickerson ran in a system that showcased his talents. In Indianapolis, he *was* the offense. Now with the Raiders, he still occasionally shows flashes of his old self, but they are few and far between. Like many backs, he seems to have aged quickly, which is why he won't break Payton's rushing record.

In 1991, Bears running back Neal Anderson said, "I don't know if his body will be able to last all those years, and that's how Walter did it. Eric's been, to me, as good as any running back that's ever played the game. But whether he can take it on for four or five more years at that level remains to be seen. Walter was able to do it for all those years at pretty much a consistent level."

A real thoroughbred, Dickerson broke into the NFL in 1983 like no rookie ever. He set the rookie season records for carries (390, an all-time high for any runner), yards (1,808), and touchdowns rushing (18). He reached the 10,000-yard plateau faster than any player ever.

Dickerson is now the second all-time leading rusher with 13,168 yards. A six-time Pro Bowler, he led the league in rushing four times (1983, '84, '86, and '88), second to Brown's eight.

Former Rams coach John Robinson recently reflected on how Dickerson forced the 1987 trade that sent him from Los Angeles to Indianapolis. "I have great sadness that our divorce had to happen like that," Robinson said. "If he had stayed, I think he would have become the greatest back of all time. Now . . ."

MARION MOTLEY

5. MARION MOTLEY—

Marion Motley defined the position of fullback, bringing it into the modern era from a line-plunger to a back who could block and run. He might have been the first big back with elusiveness.

Paul Zimmerman calls Motley the best fullback ever. "I watched Motley until his last hopeless days when he tried to come back with the Pittsburgh Steelers in 1955, and if there's a better football player who ever snapped on a helmet, I would like to know his name," Zimmerman said. "He ran, of course, he caught flare passes and turned them into big gains, and backed up the line in an era in which the rest of the world was switching to two platoons, and he pass-blocked like no other back who ever played the game."

Otto Graham, who was Motley's quarterback, agreed, calling him "the best fullback I ever saw. He was a better all-around player than Jimmy Brown. Of course, there's never been a better runner than Jimmy, and maybe he didn't have to block, but Marion was a great blocker, especially for a passer. I don't remember anybody ever knocking him off his feet. When they came at him, he just stopped them on a dime."

Motley's career average of 5.7 yards per carry (including four years in the All-American Football Conference) is half a yard higher than Jim Brown's. But some historians differ on those accomplishments. Joe Horrigan said although most people downplay his statistics in the AAFC, not all of the teams in that league were weak. Jim Campbell saw it differently: "He led the NFL in rushing in 1950, but he didn't do much else outside the AAFC." Motley gained only 878 yards in his final three seasons in Cleveland.

Motley was a 238-pound bull, and people underestimated his speed. The Browns invented the trap play for him. Motley once said, "We had only four plays for me, and that was all—an end run, a buck up the middle, a trap and a screen pass."

"He was like [Jim] Brown," said Bob Oates, a sportswriter for the *Los Angeles Times*. "He didn't have the speed and quickness of Sayers, Simpson, or Dickerson. He had more power."

6. GALE SAYERS— "Writers often ask me if Walter [Payton] was the greatest back of all time, or if I was the greatest back of all time," says Jim Brown. "Man, I don't even know if Walter was the greatest Chicago Bear of all time. They used to have a man named Gale Sayers."

What else can you say? Sayers had world-class speed, but he also had moves that have rarely been seen in football. He could stop on a dime and cut without losing acceleration. No matter how many great backs have played the game, Sayers remains the standard of style because so many of his 4,956 yards and 991 carries were so memorable.

GALE SAYERS

"It's a cliche now, but, every time Sayers touched the ball, he had the potential of scoring—that's true," said Joe Horrigan.

"One way to rate backs is how they do on an off field, and Sayers, McElhenny and Dickerson performed extraordinarily on muddy fields," says Bob Oates.

Sayers led the NFL in rushing in 1966—the first halfback to do so since Steve Van Buren in 1949—and '69 and finished among the top five three other times. He gained only 4,956 yards from scrimmage, not enough to show up in the record books except for one revealing statistic of average per carry. At 5.0 yards per crack, Sayers ranks third all-time behind Jim Brown's 5.22 and Mercury Morris' 5.14. He finished his career as the all-time leading kickoff returner with a 30.56-yard average. And, although he didn't have enough returns to qualify, he averaged almost two yards per punt return more than the career record (he had a 14.5-yard average).

Sayers' statistics are even more remarkable because he spent his career with quarterbacks who didn't generate much of a passing game and because of nagging injuries that affected his final seasons.

After his six-touchdown game in 1965, Bears coach George Halas was telling locker room reporters something about "Red Grange, George McAfee and Gale Sayers, and not necessarily in that order, gentlemen. . . . This is the greatest football exhibition I have ever seen by one man in a game." Later, Sayers said, "That's when I really knew I belonged."

Sayers hasn't played football for over twenty years, but he is still revered like few players ever. "It makes me feel good," he says. "Just about every year, people talk about running backs. I only played sixty-eight ballgames. I didn't play ten years. But my name is always there. . . . I didn't gain that many yards when I was playing, but I must have done something good. I think they remember Gale Sayers as someone who, when he touched the football, was going to do something exciting."

At thirty-four, Sayers was the youngest player ever inducted into the Hall of Fame. At that time, Halas said, "The first time I saw Gale Sayers . . . I could not believe what I had seen. . . . If you want to see perfection as a running back, you had best get a hold of a film of Gale Sayers. He was poetry in motion. His like will never be seen again."

EARL CAMPBELL

7. EARL CAMPBELL—Earl Campbell was a pure power runner when he was with the Oilers, like a bull without fear. He finished his short eight-year NFL career with 9,407 yards and 74 touchdowns. Campbell is best remembered for his thighs—they were immense. "It was tough for one guy to get him down," says Chuck Knox. "He would run into piles and come out; he wouldn't go down."

"It was strictly power and elusiveness," said Paul Brown. "He had a low center of gravity, and he ran over people."

"What a punishing runner," remembers John Steadman. "He'd separate you from your senses just tackling him."

"Earl was frightening," says Jim Brown. "He'd come surging through about two inches off the ground with those gargantuan thighs and that Mt. Rushmore head. A lot of folks thought Earl was strictly a bruiser, but Earl also could cut. [He just] usually opted to pulverize."

Few backs ever exploded upon the NFL scene like Earl Campbell did in 1978. He rushed for 1,450 yards and the first of three consecutive league rushing titles, and was named Rookie of the Year as well as Most Valuable Player. Two years later, Campbell, who was 5-foot-11 and 234 pounds, gained 1,934 yards, the third-highest total ever (he had four 200-yard rushing games that season).

"Earl Campbell is the kind of player you can build an offense and an entire team around," said his coach, Bum Phillips. "He is such a dominating runner that he makes linemen better than they are, a quarterback look better than he is and, because he allows the offense to control the tempo of a game, the defense look better than it is."

Some people think the Oilers used Campbell too much his first few seasons. Campbell once admitted that running backs can get "shellshocked" by all the heavy-duty ball-carrying. "I didn't ever get that way," he said, "but I wasn't far from it."

After six years, Campbell had already moved into the No. 9 spot on the career rushing chart, and he had the best per-season average in history (1,382.7 yards). He was traded to New Orleans midway through the 1984 season and retired a year later. He was inducted into the Hall of Fame in 1991.

8. TONY DORSETT—Tony Dorsett retired as the second all-time leading rusher with 12,739 yards. Although he is remembered as a slashing runner for Dallas, Dorsett could take the punishment. He was a deceiving runner, with more speed than he showed, and he was stronger than he appeared.

"Dorsett had great ability to pick a hole," said Chuck Knox. "Then he would just explode."

Dorsett was nicknamed "The Hawk" because his eyes used to get very big just before he made a cut. He could cut quicker on two feet than practically any other back ever.

A number of football people thought Dorsett, at 5-foot-10 and 190 pounds, was too small to play in the NFL. When he was drafted in 1977 he changed that thinking in a hurry. He not only ran for more than 1,000 yards as a rookie, he did it in each of his first five seasons. That extended his 1,000-yard streak to eleven, including two in high school and four at the University of Pittsburgh.

"Tony Dorsett is our catalyst," Dallas coach Tom Landry said. "He's the one who makes us go on offense."

Jim Brown once said, "There is no small back in football who can touch him. He's the fastest runner in the league without a doubt, and he has great moves to go along with the speed."

Dorsett retired following the 1988 season, after one year in Denver. He was vastly underrated throughout his career, playing in only four Pro Bowls and being named All-Pro just once. But he was second in combined yards (16,326), third in rushing attempts (2,936), fourth in receptions by a running back (398), and fourth in rushing touchdowns (77). He rushed for 1,000 yards in eight of his twelve NFL seasons, and had five runs of 75 yards or longer, including a 99-yarder, and a 91-yard catch-and-run.

Ricky Watters, a running back with the 49ers, idolized Dorsett as a kid. "He made everything look easy," Watters said. "He wasn't the biggest guy out there, but somehow he made himself look the biggest by what he did on the field."

Dorsett is a sure bet to be elected to the Hall of Fame in 1994, his first year of eligibility.

9. BRONKO NAGURSKI—Bronko Nagurski was football's first power runner. He played for the Bears from 1930 to '37 and again in '43. His rushing totals look meager today (about 4,000 yards), but game accounts from that time show that he dominated games, and nobody disputes the fact he pounded out yardage at a thundering pace. He was a charter member of the Hall of Fame in 1963.

Nagurski was a bulldozer who flew into rages, and, at 6-foot-2 and 235 pounds, he was as big as the linemen he played with (which would translate to a 6-5, 290-pound back today). That's why he has been called "a lineman playing fullback." Nagurski was the best back of his day, the benchmark by which fullbacks were measured until Marion Motley's time. But he also had surprising speed.

Nagurski was an awesome, forward-moving machine, the best of a herd of fullbacks who thundered through the NFL in the thirties and forties. The thinking in those days was "I'm coming through the middle; why don't you see if you can stop me."

The Bears won the first official NFL championship game in 1933 over the Giants as Nagurski ran for a game-high 65 yards and threw two TD passes. Nagurski led the team in rushing that year with 533 yards.

One tackler was no match for Nagurski, and even two might not get it done. John Dell Isola, a bruising two-way guard for the Giants in the late 1930s, once remembered the first time he tackled Nagurski. It was a first down, when Nagurski charged the line and Dell Isola met him head on. "It was one of the hardest tackles I ever made. I figured he made a yard, maybe two, and I was congratulating myself until I heard the referee say, 'Second down and two.' "

Giants coach Steve Owen once said, "There's only one defense that can stop Bronko Nagurski—shoot him before he leaves the dressing room. He's the only back I ever saw who runs his own interference."

Mel Hein, the Hall of Fame center for the Giants, said, "If you went at him low, he would stomp you to death, and if you went at him high he just knocked you down and ran over you."

One legendary story about Nagurski concerned the 1933 title game. On one play Nagurski gathered speed and bowled over several defenders, and never slowed down as he crossed the goal line and straight out of the end zone and ran into the concrete wall of the baseball dugout in Wrigley Field. "Gee, that last guy hit me awfully hard," Nagurski reportedly said.

10. HUGH McELHENNY—Hugh McElhenny was poetry in motion, one of the prettiest runners ever. He was a slashing, sideline-to-sideline runner often compared with Gale Sayers and occasionally called the first of the modern runners.

Over thirteen seasons, McElhenny rushed for 5,281 yards, gained 11,369 all-purpose yards, and scored 60 touchdowns for teams that rarely were in contention. He was selected to six Pro Bowls and was inducted into the Hall of Fame in 1970.

He was one of those players whom you never forgot if you saw him play. Former NFL commissioner Pete Rozelle claims McElhenny was the reason the 49ers and Rams drew incredible crowds of over 100,000 back in the fifties. "Most exciting player I ever saw," Rozelle says.

NFL old-timers still swear that McElhenny was the most exciting runner of all time. He made his long, criss-crossing runs, sometimes running forty yards to gain five. And defenders were certain he had eyes in the back of his head because he could instinctively cut away from tacklers coming up behind him. He had a twisting, turning style of running. Once, on a 71-yard screen pass, he was touched by nine of the eleven defenders on the field.

"Mac was the best broken-field runner pro football has ever seen," said ex-49ers quarterback Y.A. Tittle.

Before McElhenny was drafted by the 49ers, he was scouted by Frankie Albert, the team's quarterback, in the Hula Bowl. Albert called owner Tony Morabito from Honolulu at two in the morning. "I've just seen the greatest running back I've ever seen. We've got to get him."

In his rookie season, in a game against Chicago, McElhenny started out on his own six-yard line and ran all the way for a touchdown. Afterward, Bears coach George Halas said, "That was the damnedest, greatest run I've ever seen in football." After the game, Albert said, "He's the King. McElhenny is the king of runners." The nickname stuck.

Hall of Fame tackle Bob St. Clair said, "We knew that if we did our job right on any of his plays, he could go for the big six."

Another Hall of Famer, Sam Huff, said, "I've always felt that Eastern fans were cheated because they had so few opportunities to see 'The King' in his prime. I saw too much of him. He gave me a heart attack every time he took the ball. I cannot ever remember tackling him solidly or throwing him for a loss."

11. FRANCO HARRIS—Franco Harris almost broke Jim Brown's rushing record before Walter Payton got to it, but the Steelers' fullback fell 192 yards short. For a big back, he had tremendous balance and a great ability to define a hole.

Ernie Stautner, a Hall of Fame defensive tackle in the fifties, said, "He can be running toward the hole he's supposed to go, and if the hole is closed, he'll stop, change directions very quickly, find another and get through it."

"He's 230 pounds, but he can stop and accelerate better than anyone I know outside of Tony Dorsett," said former Dallas linebacker D.D. Lewis. "He can run east and west, stop on a dime and then cut north and south."

Harris didn't have great moves, but he was hard to tackle. And he carried the Steelers offense for several years until the passing game matured in the mid-seventies. Harris was the big gun on the ground for the Steelers in each of their four Super Bowl victories.

"Franco was a key man on our ballclub. We were coming on every year, getting closer and closer to the right combination," said Joe Greene. "All we needed was that catalyst, and Franco was it. He could have come here four years earlier and not made any difference at all. But that year (1972, when he became only the sixth rookie to rush for 1,000 yards) he was just what we needed."

Linebacker Jack Ham said, "The constant factor became our running game—in bad weather, in good weather, in wind, whatever, you could always count on Harris and our running game."

The 6-foot-2, 225-pound Harris rushed 2,949 times for 12,120 yards and 91 touchdowns from 1972–84. He rushed for at least 1,000 yards eight times and was the sixth player to score 100 touchdowns. In his rookie season, he ran for 100 yards in six straight games. He was selected to nine straight Pro Bowls from 1972–80.

Harris usually downplayed his achievements. "Running is like anything else," he said. "You try to find a good groove. When you find that groove, well, you don't want anything to mess it up. When I'm going good, I want the ball as often as possible."

12. STEVE VAN BUREN—Steve Van Buren was the NFL's best back in the 1940s. He had the speed of a halfback and the size of a fullback, rushing for 5,860 yards and 58 touchdowns while leading the Eagles to championships in 1948 and '49. Van Buren wasn't flashy; he quietly went about his job, which is why he is underrated. And he gained 1,000 yards when it meant something.

"He was the kind of guy you could count on," said Hugh McElhenny. "He was tough, didn't have great speed, but he always gave 100 percent."

"Van Buren was unselfish; there's a big difference now," said Lou Saban, who played for the Browns during Van Buren's day.

"He was a punishing runner," said Joe Horrigan. "I try to avoid cliches, but here it's appropriate."

Van Buren was a terrific ballcarrier running off-tackle. He'd loop back and almost surrender a couple of yards—then he'd pivot and break upfield. He was a devastating blocker, a deadly tackler, and a good receiver. But running was his thing. He was one of the first halfbacks to combine speed, agility, and power.

Van Buren led the NFL in punt returns as a rookie in 1944. The next year he led the league in rushing, the first of four times, and also in scoring and kickoff returns. Twice he set the NFL single-season rushing record—in 1947 with 1,008 yards and two years later with 1,146. In the Eagles' 14–0 victory in the 1949 title game, he set records with 31 carries and 196 yards. When he retired after the 1954 season, he held records for rushing attempts, rushing yards, rushing touchdowns, most TDs in a season, most TDs rushing in a season, most yards gained rushing in a season, most years leading the league in rushing, and most yards gained rushing in a championship game. He was enshrined in the Hall of Fame in 1965.

Former Giants coach Allie Sherman said, "He was the Jimmy Brown of his time. People don't appreciate what Steve Van Buren did."

13. JIM TAYLOR—Jim Taylor was a throwback to the Bronko Nagurski era, and he typified the rugged power of the Packers' championship teams of the 1960s. He may have been the hardest player to tackle ever, and he often taunted opposing tacklers by saying, "Is that the hardest you can hit?"

Never was the fierceness of Taylor more evident than in the 1962 NFL championship game. On a bitter cold day against the Giants, Taylor carried 31 times for 85 yards and scored Green Bay's only touchdown in a 16–7 victory. He took seven stitches in his elbow at halftime and had a cut tongue.

"Taylor isn't human," said the Giants' Sam Huff. "No human could have withstood the punishment he got today. Every time he was tackled, it was like crashing down on a cement sidewalk. But he kept bouncing up, snarling at us and asking for more."

Taylor was the only player ever to beat Jim Brown out of a rushing title. In 1962, the bruising fullback for the Packers gained 1,474 yards to Brown's 996. Taylor finished second to Brown in 1960, '61, '63, and '64.

Says Jim Campbell, "I never saw a harder runner in my life. He just would not go down."

The first Packers player from the sixties to be inducted into the Hall of Fame (1976), Taylor was very important to the Green Bay offense, especially its keynote play, the power sweep.

"I think all purists loved Jimmy Taylor," said Jim Brown. "He didn't have special size, speed or moves, yet football in his hand, Jimmy Taylor was defiance."

Taylor and Brown were constantly compared with each other. Huff said, "Brown is strong. But he doesn't sting you like Taylor does." And Vince Lombardi commented, "Jim Brown will give you that leg and then take it away from you. Jim Taylor will give it to you and ram it through your chest."

Taylor gained 1,000 yards in five consecutive seasons (1960–64), something Brown never did. During his ten-year career—he spent nine with the Packers and a final 1967 campaign with the expansion Saints in his home state— Taylor rushed for 8,597 yards, caught 225 passes, compiled 10,538 combined yards, and scored 93 touchdowns.

14. JOHN RIGGINS—For sure power up the middle, few running backs could ever compare with John Riggins. Nicknamed the "Big Diesel," he was putting together 1,000-yard seasons well into his thirties, and he seemed to get better as he grew older.

Riggins is one of only three backs to rush for more than 1,000 yards with two different teams. He also is the oldest player to rush for 1,000 yards in a season—1,239 yards in 1984 when he was thirty-five.

Riggins had a good career with the Jets from 1971 to '75 before signing with Washington as a free agent. Then, after back-to-back 1,000-yard seasons in 1978 and '79, Riggins walked out of the Redskins' training camp and announced his retirement. He spent the next year on his farm in Kansas. The following spring, Joe Gibbs, the new Redskins coach, went to Kansas to talk to Riggins. Riggins was out hunting, so Gibbs told Riggins' wife he would be welcomed back. Shortly afterward, Riggins reappeared in Washington, announcing, "I'm bored, I'm broke, I'm back." Surely the NFL has rarely seen a character like Riggo.

And then his career took off again. In his last five seasons, Riggins ran for 4,530 yards and 62 touchdowns, added six 100-yard games in the playoffs, and led Washington to two Super Bowls. When his fourteen-year career ended, he had rushed for 11,352 yards (sixth best in NFL history) and scored 116 touchowns (third best). In 1983 he ran for an NFL-record 24 touchdowns.

The 1982 postseason was the pinnacle of Riggins' career. He rushed for over 100 yards in each game—119, 185, 140, and 166 in the Super Bowl. He was voted the Most Valuable Player in Super Bowl XVII, when his 43-yard touchdown run on fourth down broke Miami's back.

"He was incredible during that stretch," said Joe Theismann, his quarterback. "He was a man on a mission. John was about 6-foot-2, 235 pounds, ran faster than most smaller backs, delivered great power, had a very low center of gravity, and was very difficult to tackle. And he had a great work ethic. I've always believed that's what distinguishes the average player from the great player. John made no pretense about the fact that he felt he was just a guard who happened to carry the football."

Because of his eccentricity, Riggins never achieved the proper acclaim—he had five 1,000-yard seasons but was named All-Pro only once and played in just one Pro Bowl—until he was enshrined into the Hall of Fame in 1992.

15. LARRY CSONKA—Most running backs take punishment. Larry Csonka administered it. Csonka played fullback like a horse plowing a field.

"I like that style," said the 1987 Hall of Famer. "I preferred to run inside. It was kind of fun to me, head on. If I had not had the speed and a little bit of balance, I probably would have been a middle linebacker like Dick Butkus."

A first-round draft pick in 1968, Csonka started leaving his impact on pro football in 1970 when Don Shula arrived in Miami. He had speed and quickness uncommon for a fullback, and not since Bronko Nagurski had the NFL seen a player with such tackle-breaking power. The bigger the game, the better the 6-foot-3, 235-pound Csonka played.

Two of the league's best defensive tackles in the seventies were Pittsburgh's Joe Greene and Cincinnati's Mike Reid. "It was like trying to catch a runaway trunk on an incline. You try to grab it and there's no way," Greene commented. And Reid added, "Even if I got an even shot at him, I always got the sense I got the worst of the deal."

In eleven seasons, Csonka rushed for 8,081 yards and scored 68 touchdowns. He rushed for more than 1,000 yards in each of the Dolphins' Super Bowl seasons in 1971, '72, and '73. From 1970–74, he was selected to the Pro Bowl. He was the Most Valuable Player in Super Bowl VIII, when he rushed for 145 yards against Minnesota.

"My job is no big deal," he once said. "I am a fullback, a power back whose assignment is to establish an inside running game. That's my work."

And few fullbacks ever did it any better than Csonka.

16. BARRY SANDERS—Barry Sanders is the best running back in the NFL today, and if he can keep up his present pace, he'll move up the list quickly. In four seasons, he has already rushed for 5,674 yards, more than any other player in history after four seasons except Eric Dickerson.

"He's the best running back in the league—hands down, no questions asked," says Patriots coach Bill Parcells. "He's a rare talent that comes along seldom, and he's probably going to go down as one of the all-time greats before he's through."

Former Rams quarterback Pat Haden says simply, "He could make a linebacker miss in a telephone booth."

Sanders is often compared with Gale Sayers, although their skills differ. Detroit offensive tackle Lomas Brown said, "[Sayers] had moves but he would take a step to get those moves. Barry is more of a bounding runner, jumping into his moves, which make them that much quicker."

And Richie Petitbon, the Redskins head coach who was a Bears safety when Sayers played, says, "I always thought Gale Sayers was the best running back I've ever seen, but this guy [Sanders] is better."

Ask Sayers about Sanders, and he'll say, "I would go to see Barry Sanders play. He turns me on."

Once Sanders gets around the corner, he can turn it on. He has an extra burst of speed that makes him nearly impossible to catch from behind, but he also can back out of a hole faster than most backs can get through one. He can break tackles and he has a nose for the end zone.

"The first guy doesn't get Barry Sanders," says John Madden. "Neither does the second. It's usually the third, fourth, or fifth guy."

Sanders compares running with the football to "like when you were playing tag when you were a kid. When somebody tries to tag you, you can shape your body into all types of configurations and try to avoid the tag," he says. "A lot of times when I'm running, I just do whatever I can to stop from being tackled, you know?"

17. JIM THORPE—Damon Runyon once said, "More lies have been told about Jim Thorpe than about any other athlete."

That may be true, but the legendary Thorpe was also one of the greatest ballcarriers in pro football history. Considered the best all-around athlete in modern history, he was actually the first great running back in pro football and one of the few true legends of pro football.

Thorpe is one of only a half-dozen men who ever played both major-league baseball and professional football, but football was the game he loved best.

Rough by nature, Thorpe loved to hit and be hit. He was a fearsome running back who could fake past tacklers or run right over them and didn't mind handing out a little extra physical punishment.

Thorpe's best athletic days were behind him when he joined the Canton Bulldogs at the age of twenty-seven in 1915. He played with six different teams but rarely was effective after the NFL was organized in 1920 (he also was the first president of the NFL). He played until 1928, when he was forty-one.

Said a teammate, Pete Calac, "Jim had a way of running I had never seen. Not everyone wore helmets in those days, and Jim would shift his hip toward the guy who was about to tackle him and swing it away. And then when the player moved toward him, he would swing his hip back hard against the tackler's head and leave a line there."

THREE

WIDE RECEIVERS

*Going for the ball and catching it is pure fantasy. There is nothing
like it. It more than makes up for the beating I get.*
LANCE ALWORTH

Pick the two best wide receivers of all time and, if you come up with Don Hutson and Jerry Rice, you have a pretty good consensus. Hutson was the greatest receiver of pro football's first fifty years, setting records that only now are being broken. Rice is a shoo-in for the Pro Football Hall of Fame someday, at which time he will probably own every receiving record ever invented.

Through the years, NFL fans have seen a lot of great receivers. They all get the same results—they catch the ball and end up in the end zone. But their styles varied; each was an individual.

"You can't pick the best," says wide receiver Bobby Mitchell, a member of the Hall of Fame. "Take anybody you want, and I'll pick from the rest, and I can win with any of them."

As Tex Maule, the esteemed writer for *Sports Illustrated*, once wrote, "The great players come and create legends in their time and move on and inevitably youngsters replace them and break their records. Don Hutson and Tom Fears and Elroy 'Crazylegs' Hirsch and Mac Speedie and Dante Lavelli and Raymond Berry were wonderful ends with breaktaking moves and hands like butterfly nets. But, when they left, along came Lynn Swann and John Stallworth and Steve

Largent and the rest of the young men who play the position with almost balletic grace."

Lance Alworth put it best one time when he was reminiscing about his playing days. "Running to get free is beautiful," he said. "It feels good. And then going for the ball and catching it is pure fantasy. There is nothing else like it. It more than makes up for the beating I get, and for me that's a lot to say."

In the history of professional football, there have been speedsters like Hirsch and Paul Warfield, catch-and-run threats such as Rice and Mitchell, possession receivers like Berry and Steve Largent, big targets such as Charley Taylor and Art Monk, players with shifty moves like Alworth and Don Maynard, and those who just compiled the numbers, like Charlie Joiner and Wes Chandler. And the best, the one who combined all of those attributes, was Hutson.

DON HUTSON

1. DON HUTSON—Maybe more than any other player ever at any position, Don Hutson has stood the test of time. The former Packer caught 99 touchdown passes, a record that stood until 1989. He caught a pass in every game from 1937 through '45—at a time when few teams were even throwing the ball much. He revolutionized pro football with his graceful speed and leaping ability, and it wouldn't be wrong to say he invented the position of wide receiver. He definitely altered the philosophy of the sport.

"He was way ahead of everybody else," recalls Raymond Berry, the former Colts Hall of Famer who has seen film of Hutson. Paul Warfield, a Hall of Famer with the Browns and Dolphins, has also spent time watching footage of Hutson. "At the beginning of this interview, I was reluctant to label anyone," he says. "But, if you're talking about the greatest ever, you might almost say that about Hutson. He was the forerunner of the modern receiver."

"Hutson is still the receiver all others are measured against," says Joe Horrigan, the historian at the Hall of Fame. "He was the first to require double and triple coverage. He caught seventeen touchdown passes in 1942—more than all but one team that year."

In fact, when Hutson retired with 488 catches, the No. 2 man on the list trailed by 298 receptions.

One Hall of Famer who did see Hutson play was Elroy Hirsch. "He had a method of running where he seemed to be running top speed, and then he just turned it on," Hirsch said.

When *Sports Illustrated* picked its all-time "Dream Team" in 1992, Paul Zimmerman chose Hutson as one of his receivers. "In the forties I saw Hutson through a child's eyes," Zimmerman wrote. "I wasn't sure about him until I did a film study a few years ago. Yes, he would be terrific today."

Hutson's Green Bay coach, Curly Lambeau, once said he hadn't seen anyone cut like Hutson "since George Gipp, not even [Red] Grange."

Hutson could outmaneuver and outrace any defensive back in the game when he played, and he had tremendous, large hands. But he was also an excellent defensive player who intercepted 23 passes in his final four seasons, and a placekicker who scored almost 200 points by kicking.

Nicknamed "The Alabama Antelope," he was a charter member of the Hall of Fame, one of the first sixteen enshrinees. He was named All-Pro nine of his eleven seasons. In a 1945 game, he scored 29 points in a single quarter.

"He was so difficult to defend against because half the time he didn't know himself where he was going," said Luke Johnsos, for years a player and coach with the Bears.

Beattie Feathers, who was the first back to rush for 1,000 yards in a season, used to cover Hutson for the Bears. "I used to concede Don two touchdowns and hope we could get more," Feathers said. "If not more, at least as many plus a field goal."

"Hutson was so far ahead of his time—more than any other player at any position anytime—even Jim Brown and Sammy Baugh," says sports historian Bob Carroll.

2. JERRY RICE—If it took fifty years for someone to break Don Hutson's records, it might take another fifty years for somebody to break the records Jerry Rice is now setting.

JERRY RICE

Rice is the best receiver of the last half century, a player capable of catching a pass over the middle and taking it all the way or flying past a defender to catch a bomb on the run. He is the highest-paid non-quarterback in pro football history, a marked man who keeps on producing.

"He's got the whole package," says Raymond Berry. "The rate at which he's producing is phenomenal. He has the ideal environment that a receiver can be in, and he has the physical abilities, too."

Detroit assistant coach Dave Levy puts it another way: "Rice is in a world of his own, a freak of the game."

The biggest gamebreaker playing today, Rice has caught 103 touchdown passes in eight seasons (he caught 22 in 1987 alone). It took Hutson eleven years to catch 99 and Largent fourteen to score 100 times. In fact, in one out of every nine games during his career, Rice has outscored the opposing team by himself.

No player caught 600 passes at a younger age than Rice, who was thirty when he reached that plateau. He had a record 215 yards in Super Bowl XXIII and was the game's Most Valuable Player.

"Rice is a complete wide receiver," says Paul Warfield. "He has the capacity to catch possession passes consistently. He has a unique ability to be a gamebreaker consistently. And he's a great blocker for the running game."

Rice played college football in Division 1-AA obscurity at Mississippi Valley State. One Saturday in October 1984, 49ers coach Bill Walsh flipped on his TV to watch a college football game. Walsh saw Rice on the highlights and quickly took notice. "The hands, the body, the speed," Walsh recalled. "What an absolutely majestic football player." Most scouts wrote off Rice because he played against overmatched competition. But Walsh drafted him the first round in 1985.

Willie Brown, one of the greatest cornerbacks ever, said, "Rice reminds me of (Lance Alworth). So quick getting off the line, real fluid downfield, and then that extra gear, that overdrive and the leaping ability. Zoom, zoom, and it's all over. That's what fooled people about Rice coming into the pros. They didn't understand his speed. They went by the stopwatch, but he had competitive speed, football speed."

Rice was All-Pro 1986 to '90 and again in '92 and has played in every Pro Bowl since his second season. He has averaged 84 receiving yards per game during his career, far ahead of anybody else.

"They call Michael Jordan Jesus in tennis shoes," says Cowboys receiver Michael Irvin. "Jerry Rice is Jesus in cleats."

Rice's quarterback, Steve Young, might have put it best: "I think he believes that if they covered him with eleven guys, he should still be open and win the game."

But, when asked if he was the best receiver ever, Rice answered, "You're never going to hear me say that. If my peers say so, that's okay. But you're never going to hear me say that."

3. RAYMOND BERRY—"What Jerry Rice and I both have in common," says Raymond Berry, "is that we're probably the most fortunate receivers ever being able to play where we played—with a great, all-time quarterback [Joe Montana and Johnny Unitas] and a coaching situation that was stable."

Perhaps the finest possession receiver ever, Berry made himself into a great receiver, proving that dedication, concentration, and long hours of practice can compensate for limited athletic skills. What he lacked in speed and size, he made up for with an unusual jumping ability and fantastic hands. He retired in 1967 as the leading all-time receiver (with 631 receptions, a record that has since been broken several times). He will always be remembered for his 12 catches for 178 yards in the 1958 championship game. Berry was inducted into the Hall of Fame in 1973, his first year of eligibility.

"He had a great feel for running patterns on defensive backs and setting them up with his outs and corner patterns," says Paul Warfield. "Tom Landry called him a 'move man.'"

Berry said he had exactly eighty-eight moves, and he used to practice all eighty-eight of them each week in his relentless drive toward perfection. He gained 9,275 yards re-

RAYMOND BERRY

ceiving, the third-highest total when he retired, despite the fact he was a medium-gain specialist instead of a long-range threat. He led the NFL in receiving from 1958 to '60 while scoring 33 touchdowns. He fumbled only one time in his entire career.

A twentieth-round future draft choice in 1954, Berry played thirteen seasons. He was All-Pro three times and played in five Pro Bowls. When it came to the mechanics of catching the ball and reaching one's potential, Berry is the best ever. He was 6-foot-2, 187 pounds, and wasn't much of a threat to run with the ball—he just caught it again and again. He and Unitas used to spend hours after practice developing exact pass patterns.

"All Ray had going for him was a bottomless capacity for work, a burning desire for self-improvement and unlimited patience," said Unitas, who teamed with Berry for over 600 receptions. "He simply devoted himself to catching footballs."

4. STEVE LARGENT—Steve Largent was selected in the fourth round of the 1976 draft by Houston, then traded to Seattle before the start of the season for an eighth-round pick. It was one of the greatest trade robberies in NFL history.

When Largent retired from the Seahawks after the 1989 season, he was on top of the NFL's receiving charts in the three most important categories: He had caught 819 passes for 13,089 yards and scored 100 touchdowns. He had broken Don Hutson's records of half a century before, and although all three records had since fallen, it took three players to break them.

Largent wasn't a speedster, and he didn't have great moves. He just caught the ball. He's often compared with Raymond Berry.

"There are a lot of similarities between our styles," Berry admitted. "We both had an exceptional ability to get sophisticated with fakes and moves. But

STEVE LARGENT

Steve had more speed and quickness. I was a craftsman."

"Largent looked tremendously slow, but, if a defender let him get even, he'd burn you," says Bobby Mitchell.

"He had the characteristics I appreciate—change of pace, setting up a defender with a move," says Paul Warfield, another member of the Hall of Fame, where Largent will be someday. "Year in and year out, he caught a minimum of sixty passes. And he put it in the end zone. He caught a lot of passes, but his touchdown-to-reception ratio is very high."

Largent was only 5-foot-11 and 190 pounds, but he had near-perfect instincts and concentration and he rarely dropped a pass. He caught passes in 177 consecutive games—every one from 1977 until '89. He had ten 50-catch seasons and eight 1,000-yard seasons, and he led the Seahawks in receptions and yards each of their first twelve seasons.

The Raiders' Lester Hayes used to try to cover Largent. "Steve is the master of tomfoolery," he said. "He has run pass routes on me that I've never seen or dreamed about."

Mike Haynes, the Raiders' other cornerback, added, "It's almost as if the quarterback says to him in the huddle, 'Do whatever you want. Just get yourself open and I'll throw to you.'"

About his records being broken, Largent says only, "They're all great people and great receivers and they deserve it. They all worked hard to eclipse the records I set. To be honest with you, it was something I enjoyed a lot, and I hope they enjoy it as much as I did."

5. PAUL WARFIELD—Paul Warfield was a disciplined player who ran precise patterns, and the running teams he played for required just that. He didn't catch as many passes as most other top receivers, but he kept defenses honest because he averaged more than 20 yards a catch (20.1, which is better than any other Hall of Famer) and scored once every fifth reception over his career. He was elected to the Hall of Fame in 1983.

Warfield played for running teams (1964–69 and 1976–77 in Cleveland and 1970–74 for Miami), and didn't have the ball thrown to him very much. But he sure did a lot with it.

Former Dolphins teammate George Mira once said, "He's the only one I ever saw putting on moves when he's just walking."

"He could control his speed and cut on a dime," says Raymond Berry. "He had great faking ability, and not all speed receivers are good at doing that. It's a rare combination."

"All of the great receivers have great speed and great hands," says Elroy Hirsch. "But it's the speed you have to respect. Warfield could catch with his speed, and with his elusiveness he could get off a long gain."

"If Warfield had ever been the featured offensive weapon, there's no telling what he could've done," says pro football historian Jim Campbell.

But Warfield was also a key to his teams' running attacks because opponents couldn't stack against the run. And he was a devastating blocker on runs, too.

PAUL WARFIELD

Nobody knows what kind of numbers Warfield could have put up had he played on passing teams. As it was, he caught 427 passes for 8,565 yards and 85 touchdowns. He never caught more than 52 passes in a season, and that was as a rookie. He caught only 29 passes in each of 1972 and '73, when Miami won two Super Bowls. He was named All-Pro five times and played in eight Pro Bowls.

"Even though we won a lot in Miami, I had a feeling of great frustration," he admits. "The Dolphins threw the ball in very few situations, and there were games where Bob [Griese] only threw five passes."

Earl Morrall quarterbacked Miami to ten of its seventeen victories in 1972. "I've thrown to a lot of receivers in my time. Warfield definitely ranks right at the top," Morrall said. "He has fluid moves, and anytime he gets one-on-one, he's gone. He is the complete player. He never makes a mistake."

6. LANCE ALWORTH—Lance Alworth's nickname of "Bambi" was as appropriate as "Bronko" Nagurski or "Bulldog" Turner. He had great speed and moves and tremendous leaping ability.

"Waist down, he looked like a stevedore," says Jerry Magee, the longtime *San Diego Union* sportswriter. "Waist up, he looked like a ballet dancer. He gave the game a delicacy few were able to lend."

"That guy had just incredible natural athletic ability," says Raymond Berry. "He could score from anywhere once he caught the ball."

Like most of the early AFL stars, Alworth's career is sometimes overlooked because of the competition he faced. But he was the first AFL player inducted into the Hall of Fame, and he rightfully belongs.

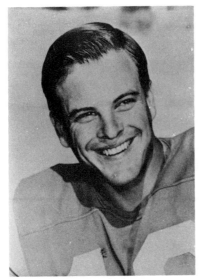

LANCE ALWORTH

"He was probably the prettiest and most graceful wide receiver I've ever seen," says Joe Horrigan. "In full stride, he was so smooth. He had an acrobatic style like Lynn Swann."

Sports Illustrated's Paul Zimmerman named Alworth to his All-Time Dream Team in 1992. "Alworth was, simply, the finest deep threat ever to play the game," Zimmerman wrote.

With his burst of speed and his leaping catches, Alworth (6-foot, 184 pounds) was as explosive as the lightning bolt on the side of his Chargers helmet. He was the AFL's show-piece receiver with a baby face and sandy crewcut, and he was instant box office for a new league seeking to establish itself through the pass.

Alworth put together seven straight 1,000-yard seasons from 1963 to '69, a feat that has never been duplicated in pro football. In 1965, he gained 1,602 yards, the second-highest total all-time, and averaged 23.2 yards per catch. The ultimate escape artist, his average per catch of 18.9 yards ranks second among Hall of Famers behind only Paul Warfield. He is the only player in pro football history to come anywhere close to Jerry Rice's average of 84 receiving yards per game. Alworth averaged 72 yards a game.

Sid Gillman was Alworth's coach early in his career. "In the history of the game, very few have been equal to his talent," Gillman said. "He had the greatest hands I have ever seen. Nobody could jump and catch the ball as Lance did."

The Raiders' Willie Brown covered Alworth for over a decade. "Hunger, he always had that great hunger for the ball," Brown remembered. "Shoot, in today's system, with all those zone coverages, Lance would have over a hundred catches a year easy."

7. ELROY HIRSCH—One of the most spectacular big-play receivers ever, Elroy "Crazylegs" Hirsch was one of the first ends moved out wide and made a flanker. He teamed with receiver Tom Fears and quarterbacks Norm Van Brocklin and Bob Waterfield to set records that still stand today.

In 1951, he might have had the greatest single season any pass receiver ever had, with nine of his 17 touchdown catches going for 44 yards or more (44, 47, 53, 70, 72, 76, 79, 81, and 91 yards). That year he caught 66 passes for 1,495 yards and 22.7 yards per catch.

"He produced at a rate that no one has been able to match," said Raymond Berry. "I always wanted to catch passes like that."

Hirsch got his nickname because of his unusual running style—his muscular legs seemed to gyrate in six directions at once—but it was a very deceptive one. "I liked the post or corner patterns—the deep stuff," he said. But Hirsch could do more than just outrun defenders. He was also an elusive runner with the ball and a top blocker.

In nine NFL seasons, Hirsch caught 343 passes for 6,299 yards and 53 touchdowns. Before starring for the Rams from 1949–57, Hirsch had a difficult transition from halfback, which he played for three years in the All-American Football Conference and one in Los Angeles. But in 1969 he was named the flanker on the NFL's all-time team of its first fifty years. Don Hutson, Hirsch's boyhood idol, was the other receiver.

8. ART MONK—Art Monk is now pro football's all-time leading receiver with 847 catches. He's a big semi-tight end with the skills of a wide receiver, though not a deep threat.

"You have a tendency to overlook a guy who is just consistent," noted Paul Warfield. "Art doesn't bring attention to himself. He just goes about his work quietly."

His quarterback, Mark Rypien, called Monk "a real professional who is quiet about his work and very loud about his results." And teammate Gary Clark says, "He's always talking about how none of this means anything to him."

And he has been doing it that way since 1980. "Just being drafted was a surprise to me," Monk says. "I knew I had some ability, but I didn't know I could compete on this level. To hang around as long as I have is pretty surprising." Of his talents, he adds, "I guess I'm more of a possession receiver; that's my role."

Monk is 6-foot-3 with a long, fluid stride, a pair of sure hands, and a talent for making fearless catches in perilous traffic over the middle. But he's also sublimely graceful and seems to float through defensive backfields. Monk's signature play is a 5-to-7-yard route called "The Dodge," in which he simply fires off the line of scrimmage, finds a seam and gets there before the defense can react. His 106 catches in 1984 was the single-season record for eight years, and he has the third-longest streak for consecutive games with at least one reception (148).

Dallas safety Bill Bates, who has covered Monk for years, says, "A lot of times you think you have him shut out for the whole game, and in the fourth quarter he catches six passes. He makes adjustments better than any receiver I've ever seen in the NFL."

"He is not your typical receiver who goes out there and runs patterns in air and space and catches the ball," said former Redskins coach Joe Gibbs. "Art's the strongest outside receiver I have ever coached, and he has caught a lot of balls inside and taken the hit. He's big. He's strong. He's intelligent. He has everything. You don't get the whole package very often."

9. BOBBY MITCHELL—Bobby Mitchell started his career as one of the top running backs and ended it as one of the top receivers. From 1958–61 he played halfback opposite Jim Brown in Cleveland, where he was one of the best-kept secrets in pro football, rushing for 2,297 yards in four seasons. Then, in 1962, he was traded to Washington, where he was switched to flanker. In his first two seasons with the Redskins, Mitchell caught 141 passes for 2,820 yards (leading the NFL in receiving yards both years) and averaged more than 30 yards per kickoff return.

"He really terrified defensive backs," Paul Warfield says of his longtime rival. "He was one of the best run-and-catch receivers I've ever seen. If a defender tried to stay with him and run with him, he'd be wrong."

Mitchell was almost in Gale Sayers' class as a runner, with great speed and moves. After an eleven-year career, he retired as the No. 3 receiver in NFL history with 521 catches, second in all-purpose yards (14,078), tenth in kickoff return average (26.4 yards), and fifth with 91 career touchdowns (18 on runs, 65 on receptions, 3 on punt returns, and 5 on kickoffs).

Mitchell, who was inducted into the Hall of Fame in 1983, had exceptional speed, uncanny faking ability, and superior balance, which made him one of the best catch-and-run players in the game.

"You've got to go out there with confidence," he said. "If you come hesitating, that defenseman, he has you in his back pocket. You got to aim at him with authority and make him worry about you, and not you worry about him."

And few did it better than Mitchell.

10. CHARLEY TAYLOR—Charley Taylor was pro football's leading receiver when he retired. He was prolific, catching fewer than forty passes in a season only once during his career (1964–77).

At 6-foot-3, 210 pounds, Taylor had deceiving size, but he was a good open-field runner. He formed a strong tandem with Bobby Mitchell.

"A lot of receivers get what the quarterback gives them," said Mitchell. "Charley could take a five-yard pass and turn it into sixty yards."

"He was an extremely intense pass receiver," says Paul Warfield. "He had a tremendous desire and was an artful executor of pass patterns. And he was a good blocker."

A halfback-turned-receiver, Taylor finished in the top eight in both rushing and receiving as a rookie. He led the league in receiving in 1966 and '67. He finished with 649 catches for 9,140 yards and 79 touchdowns, and played in eight Pro Bowls.

Roger Wehrli, a cornerback on the Cardinals, says, "Charley Taylor is one of the toughest receivers I faced over the years. Of course, you remember he was a veteran who was in his prime when I was only a rookie. He was big and strong

[with] good moves. And he had good quarterbacks who got the ball to him, Sonny Jurgensen and Billy Kilmer."

Charlie Waters, the Dallas cornerback who covered Taylor late in his career, said, "He's a helluva competitor. We'll jaw back and forth at each other; he's always trying to psych me out. He's one guy who talks a good game and can also back it up."

11. FRED BILETNIKOFF—Fans best remember Fred Biletnikoff with loose sleeves flying off his No. 25 jersey, socks hanging down below his boney knees, long blond hair flowing out of the back of his helmet, stick 'um on his socks, and black under his eyes. Balding, frail, and unassuming are the words that best describe Biletnikoff's looks. But competitive, gutty, and skillful are the words that fit the way he played football.

Biletnikoff had little speed, but he would use a change of pace to outrun defensive backs. He was a dedicated practice player who was fearless across the middle.

"He probably had the best hands of any receiver I've seen in the modern era," says Paul Warfield. "He could make a great, difficult catch in a key ballgame."

Biletnikoff's Raider coach, John Madden, agreed. "He could catch anything he could touch. That's no accident—some receivers would catch fifteen or twenty passes in practice. Fred would catch a hundred."

His quarterback, Ken Stabler, said, "He's the greatest pass receiver of all time. He caught almost 600 passes, and I think he caught half of them standing on his head. I threw him some terrible passes, balls I flat gave up on. Somehow he caught them. The greatest thing about Fred is his consistency. In big games, he made more clutch catches in the playoffs than any receiver in the league."

Biletnikoff retired ranking first in receptions and receiving yardage in playoff history, and his 10 touchdowns was second. He finished his career with 589 receptions for 8,974 yards and 76 touchdowns. He was the Most Valuable Player in Super Bowl XI and was enshrined in the Hall of Fame in 1988.

12. TOM FEARS—Like any of the great receiving duos, Tom Fears and Elroy Hirsch benefited because teams couldn't double-team one of them. Fears was a precise pattern runner with speed and power, the perfect complement to Hirsch.

"He was as fine a third-down receiver as anyone in the league," remembers Hirsch, his longtime teammate. "He loved third-and-ten. He'd run the out-and-hooks."

Fears played with the Rams from 1948–56 and was an instant success story, leading the NFL in receiving each of his first three seasons. Nobody since then has been the league leader three consecutive years. He caught 84 passes in twelve games in 1950, a record that stood for a decade, and his 18 catches in the final game that season is still a record. In ten seasons, he caught 400 passes for 5,397 yards and 38 touchdowns. He was inducted into the Hall of Fame in 1970.

"Fears was one of the first receivers after Don Hutson to catch a great number of passes," says Bob Carroll.

He was also part of the first three-end offense ever attempted on a regular basis in pro football. Interestingly, Fears was considered to be a defensive specialist when he was drafted by the Rams in the eleventh round. But after intercepting two passes in his first pro game, he was shifted to offensive end. He was a precise route runner who made up for a lack of speed with a fierce determination. He specialized in the button-hook pass.

Fears wound up his career by playing tight end when he weighed barely 215 pounds. "And I was big for a tight end then," he said.

13. DON MAYNARD—Don Maynard was the NFL's all-time leading receiver when he retired, but he's often overlooked because it took fifteen years after his retirement for him to make the Hall of Fame.

Maynard was undisciplined and didn't run the patterns as they were drawn up. But he turned catching a ball into a science.

Drafted by the Giants in 1958, he went to Canada for one year. In 1960, he was the first player signed by the New York Titans. Maynard played with twenty-five different quarterbacks during his career.

In one game against the Raiders, the Jets were backed up to their one-yard line. Joe Namath threw 51 yards to Maynard. "He came back to the huddle," remembered Namath, "and I said, 'Hey, Don, how you feeling?' He said, 'Shoot, Joe, I'm just fine.' I said, 'You think you can do it again?' He said, 'Hey, you go ahead and lay it on out there. I'll go get it.' The next play was good for 48 yards and a touchdown. Two plays for 99 yards and a score."

After a fifteen-year career, Maynard retired in 1973 with more catches (633) and more yards (11,834) than any receiver, although his records have since been broken, and he ranked second with 88 TD catches. Maynard's average per gain of 18.7 yards was third of all Hall of Fame receivers when he was inducted, and his fifty 100-yard games was also a record.

At Maynard's Hall of Fame ceremony, Namath said, "He was the man our opponents worried about, the knockout punch. Lightning in a bottle. Nitro just waiting to explode. I mean, he could fly, but with the grace of a great thorough-bred. He gallloped through the best of the very best football players of the world."

14. JAMES LOFTON—No receiver in NFL history has caught passes for more yards than has Lofton, who has accumulated 13,821 yards on 750 receptions (which ranks third) since 1978.

Although he had his best seasons in the early 1980s with Green Bay, Lofton had a strong finishing kick in Buffalo after barely seeing the ball in 1988 and '89. He has also caught 75 touchdown passes to rank fourteenth on the all-time receiving list. He has played in eight Pro Bowls and has an average of 18.4 yards per catch. He's had six 1,000-yard seasons and was the oldest to do so.

"I've never been a guy who's caught a lot of passes," said Lofton. "I remember when Art Monk caught 106 passes, I think I caught 62 passes and I had more yardage than him."

Lofton is a smart, tough, and durable player who has scored a touchdown in three different decades. Now the NFL's oldest starting wide receiver, Lofton is, amazingly, still one of its best deep threats.

"God made James Lofton a great receiver because he gave him all the physical attributes that, if you had to put a receiver together, he has many of those attributes," said Buffalo offensive coordinator Nick Nicolau.

Redskins safety Brad Edwards said two attributes stand out: Speed and savvy. "That is definitely the scariest combination because just an all-out fast guy who doesn't have any brains is going to make mistakes sooner or later," Edwards observed. "[Lofton] is the type of guy who isn't going to make any mistakes. He knows how to trick people and give them different looks. He uses his mind."

FOUR

TIGHT ENDS

*The only other group I've dealt with who struck me as being
essentially meaner than politicians are tight ends in pro football.*
HUNTER S. THOMPSON

Tight end is the one position in the NFL that seems to go through an evolution every decade or so.

Three decades ago, the term "tight end" was just starting to come into vogue. The early tight ends were third tackles who made the off-tackle play and sweep work (they were, in fact, called "loose tackles" for a while). Within ten years, tight ends were multipurpose weapons who started to catch the ball more, which made them more valuable, and some were even deep threats. Another ten years after that, they started to catch the ball a lot, almost like a third wide receiver.

Today, the tight end has come almost full circle. In most cases, he's a good blocker who doesn't catch the ball much. On some teams, the tight end has been diagramed out because of the evolution of four-wide-receiver offenses and the fullback/tight end hybrid position known as the H-back.

As Ozzie Newsome, who caught more passes than any tight end ever, put it, "At the peak of my career, I was a threat on every down. But during the end of my career, a tight end was lucky to be in for 60 percent of the snaps in a game."

A tight end is one of the most physically demanding jobs in football, and a great one has to be a combination of all the styles. He has to be a great blocker like Ron Kramer, the first tight end; a great receiver like Kellen Winslow, the most prolific ever; and a scoring threat, like John Mackey.

But the tight end grew out of the game's normal evolution. "We developed the first tight end as a pressure valve," said Sid Gillman, the Hall of Fame coach and recognized master of the passing game. "In the American Football League, you knew you were going to throw and you had to get the middle open to take some pressure off the outside."

"Tight ends used to determine the strength of the offensive formation," says former Bengals Pro Bowler Bob Trumpy. "When we went to the right, the strength of the offense went with us. What a wonderful responsibility to have on your shoulders.

"The tight end used to be a hybrid, the one true hybrid on the field . . . not fast enough to be a wide receiver and not big enough to be an offensive lineman. Now, when you want somebody to catch the ball deep, you bring in a little wide receiver and you call him a slotback. When you want a blocker, you bring in a bigger guy. You have two guys trying to do the job that one used to do and neither doing it very well. You don't get it in one package anymore. All things in the NFL are cyclical, and, when the defensive backs started getting smaller, tight ends became useless."

Billy Devaney, the Chargers' player personnel director, agrees. "I don't think there will ever be a classic tight end again," Devaney says. "The position really is extinct."

No tight end made the Hall of Fame until Ditka in 1988. Said Mackey, "I was happy when he [Ditka] went in. I never looked at who goes in first. I was glad to see somebody break the ice."

But Trumpy says of Ditka and Mackey, "They're our Hall of Famers. Unfortunately, they'll probably be the last two tight ends to get in."

1. JOHN MACKEY—When

Mike Ditka learned in 1988 he had become the first tight end voted into the Hall of Fame, he reacted with genuine astonishment. "You've got to be kidding. I'm thrilled beyond words. But you guys have got to get John Mackey into the Hall. He belongs more than anybody."

But Mackey wasn't inducted until 1992.

"I used to get so much fan mail— 'Why aren't you in?'" Mackey said. "I couldn't believe it. Ten, fifteen years later I was still getting it."

In comparison with Ditka, Mackey had a better combination of power and

JOHN MACKEY

speed. He got off the line of scrimmage better, and he was the first of the great tight ends to roam downfield. He wasn't just an outlet, like most tight ends. Mackey would go one-on-one with linebackers who couldn't cover him, and he was a threat to score on a bomb. Anytime he caught the ball, that is, because his hands were sometimes made of stone. He counters that knock with, "[Johnny] Unitas used to say I dropped the one in my hands and I caught the one I should've dropped. I made up for the drops."

Former Detroit Lion Ron Kramer said Mackey was "the best deep receiver, and maybe the best runner of all the tight ends." But another football observer said, "I never saw anybody go from the penthouse to the outhouse quicker. Mackey lost it in a year."

As a rookie in 1963, Mackey caught 35 passes for 726 yards, a 20.7-yard average per catch and seven touchdowns.

"We weren't sure what to do with him because he was such a great talent," Don Shula said of Mackey's rookie season when Shula was the coach of the Colts. "We weren't sure whether he should be a running back or a tight end. But the more we got to know John and the more we worked with him, tight end seemed to be his natural position."

In 1966, Mackey scored six of his touchdowns on plays over 50 yards (lengths of 51, 57, 64, 79, 83, and 89 yards). He was a three-time All-Pro and played in five Pro Bowls. In 1969, he was voted the tight end on the All-Pro team of the first fifty years of the NFL. His career average of 15.8 yards per catch on 427 receptions is very impressive for any receiver, let alone a tight end.

Mackey called himself "a lineman who could run and catch the ball." But he also loved to block, especially on traps. "My job was to wipe out the defensive end and go get the linebacker," he said. "Man, that's what I loved. I ran over a lot of those guys."

Dick Bielski, his position coach at Baltimore, said one time, "Once he catches the ball, the great adventure begins. Those people on defense climb all over him. The lucky ones fall off."

The greatest compliment a tight end of the nineties could possibly receive would be for his coach to comment, "He plays just like John Mackey."

"When I was playing," he said, "it was never in my mind that I was revolutionizing the position or anything like that. I just thought it was a natural thing. I played with Unitas, and Unitas would come to me if I was open."

2. MIKE DITKA—Mike Ditka was a bull, a rugged, tough player with tons of desire who could do it all. At 6-foot-3 and 230 pounds, he could block, catch, break tackles, and score from anywhere on the field. And he didn't just split defenses—he attacked them.

"He was going to fight you all day long and knock the hell out of you," recalls Ron Kramer. "He was magnificent, a guy with great determination."

Says Bob Trumpy, "He was a bruising guy. He'd run over linebackers, defensive ends, defensive backs—anything in his way."

Ditka was the first tight end to be elected to the Hall of Fame, in 1988. He was also the first tight end who caught a lot of passes. In 1961, his first season, he had 56 receptions for 1,076 yards and 12 touchdowns and was named the Rookie of the Year. The next two years he caught 58 and 59 passes, and then in '64 he had 75 receptions, a record for the position that lasted until 1980 when teams started playing sixteen games. He played for the Bears from 1961–66; during that time he was a four-time All-Pro and a member of four

MIKE DITKA

Pro Bowl teams. He moved to Philadelphia for two seasons and then on to Dallas from 1969–72. In the five seasons from 1966 through '70, Ditka caught only 96 passes. But in '71 he caught 30 balls as well as a touchdown in Super Bowl VI, which the Cowboys won. When he retired, his 427 catches was the record for tight ends.

"I could care less about being All-Pro," he said. "The Super Bowl victory and being a part of it is the big thing."

Ditka was the prototype tight end as the position evolved. Until he came along, tight ends were viewed primarily as blockers. He was one of the first to move away from the offensive tackle on many alignments. Ditka had a fierce straight-arm move that fended off many would-be tacklers.

"It was Ditka who made football people realize the importance of tight ends," said Cooper Rollow of the *Chicago Tribune*. "He was a dominating force."

The trademark of Ditka's career was a catch-and-run he made in a game against Pittsburgh in a 1963 game played the day after President Kennedy was assassinated. With the Bears trailing 17–14 in the third quarter, Ditka caught a pass over the middle and proceeded to break six tackles while racing 63 yards to set up a game-tying field goal. The tie enabled Chicago to win the division. "To this day, I believe that if Mike doesn't make that play, we don't win the championship," said Bears defensive end Ed O'Bradovich.

For all his many accomplishments, Ditka is best remembered as a fierce competitor who played with a fervor seldom matched (the same goes as a head coach, too). "I just try to hit the other guy before he hits me, and if I hit hard enough, maybe he won't hit me back. I like contact," Ditka said. "And I don't mind getting hit myself."

KELLEN WINSLOW

3. KELLEN WINSLOW—If

another tight end is going to be inducted into the Hall of Fame, it will probably be Kellen Winslow. He was the first in the position's just-past evolution—a big wide receiver disguised as a tight end. Winslow wasn't much of a blocker, but he wasn't asked to block. For a pure pass-receiving tight end, Winslow is the one.

He was usually split wide, but sometimes Winslow was put in motion, lined up in the slot, or even in the backfield. "He was what a wingback used to be," said ex-Lions tight end Ron Kramer.

During a career that was cut short by a knee injury (1979–84), Winslow caught 488 passes for 42 touchdowns. He led the NFL in receiving in 1980 and '81. In 1981, Winslow became the only tight end to catch five TD passes in the same game. He broke Mike Ditka's record for most receptions by a tight end.

"He could run, he could catch, he could do all the things necessary as a receiver and blocker," says former Dolphins tight end Larry Seiple, now the team's receivers coach. "He was the best receiving tight end to come along in a long time."

He was the twelfth pick in the '79 draft, causing Chargers owner Gene Klein to say, "It isn't often that you get the best player in the draft without your team having the worst record."

Winslow's number of pass receptions were, in order, 25, 89, 88, 54 in the 1982 strike season, 88, and 55 passes during his career. Early in his career, he once looked at Charley Taylor's old record of 649 catches, and said, "Kel, if you stay healthy, you can do this in eight or nine years."

He caught more passes in his first five years than any other NFL receiver, even though he missed nine games in his rookie season with a broken leg.

But Winslow's career was cut short by a serious knee injury midway through the 1984 season. At the time, his 55 catches through eight games put him on schedule to catch 110 in sixteen games. He came back in 1985 mostly as a blocker, playing ten games but catching only 25 passes, a tremendous comedown.

He retired as the twelfth all-time leading active receiver and thirty-fifth overall with 424 catches in only six seasons. Only three tight ends had caught more when he retired (Ozzie Newsome, Jackie Smith, and Mike Ditka).

After he was injured, Winslow said, "I like to think of myself as one of the better ones. I loved to play. It's that simple. When a ball is coming in my direction, it's mine. Plus, it helps to be 6-5, and weigh 248 pounds.

"What I've done in the past might or might not be good enough to get me into the Hall of Fame, and if I had never been able to play another down I'd still feel good about the career I had. But I wanted to be noticed that I worked hard to come back."

It was, but, as with Gale Sayers, Billy Sims, and many other players, it's a shame that Winslow's career was cut short. But he'll still always be remembered as one of the best ever.

4. JACKIE SMITH—Forget the pass from Roger Staubach he dropped in the end zone in Super Bowl XIII—Jackie Smith was one of the greats. He was a good receiver and blocker who followed John Mackey as a prototype tight end. He could go long, and he was consistent year after year.

JACKIE SMITH

Although he was 6-foot-4 and 235 pounds, Smith rarely lined up tight, so it was obvious he was going to be a pass receiver. Still, he was a target that teams couldn't stop often. "On down-and-ins and post patterns, he was as good as anyone," said Ron Kramer. "And he dropped *only* one pass."

Smith's former teammate, Cardinals quarterback Jim Hart, agrees. "He's got all the stats in the world," Hart says. "All everyone remembers is the pass he dropped. Look at Jackie Smith at tight end, and look at his stats. Mike Ditka is a good friend of mine, but does he have the stats of Jackie Smith? Mike's in the Hall of Fame, and Jackie never seems to make the finals."

Smith played from 1963–78 and caught 480 passes. In 1967, he caught 56 passes for 1,205 yards, an enormous total for the position. He not only has better statistics than both Ditka and Mackey, but his yards-per-catch average of 16.5 was better than two wide receivers who made the Hall of Fame finals in 1992, Lynn Swann and Charlie Joiner.

Smith's former coach, Wally Lemm, said, "Once he caught the ball he set sail for the end zone and nothing was going to stop him. He was just a bull to bring down."

"I always thought Jackie Smith was the finest tight end I ever watched," says John Steadman, the esteemed writer for the *Baltimore Sun* and a member of the Hall of Fame electorate. "He played sixteen years. The fact that he dropped one pass should have nothing to do with it [not getting into the Hall of Fame]."

5. DAVE CASPER—Another tight end who could run deep was Dave Casper, who was nicknamed "the Ghost to the Post." He wasn't fast, but he was smart.

Casper caught 378 passes over eleven seasons with 52 touchdowns. But, like too many athletes, Casper might have played a year or two longer than he should have.

"He started out great. He was unbelievable," says former Detroit tight end Charlie Sanders, now the team's receivers coach. "He went downhill after he left the Raiders. Sometimes a tight end fits a system, and he did that with the Raiders."

Casper was one of the tight ends who could do it all—he had speed and agility, could block well, and seemed to catch everything that came his way. Also nicknamed "Big Ox" and "The Ghost," Casper played for the Raiders from 1974–80, and the Oilers from '80 to '82. He went to the Vikings in '83 and then finished his career back with the Raiders in 1984.

Casper played in five Pro Bowls from 1976–80. He caught at least 48 passes each of those five years, and he scored 10 touchdowns in 1976 and nine in '78. He got his famous nickname in the 1977 playoff game against Baltimore when he caught a 42-yard pass that set up the tying field goal before the Raiders won in overtime.

As John Madden once said of Casper, "He's so big and wide that not only can defenders not get around him to the ball, sometimes they can't see it coming. It would be fair to say he's one of the best blocking tight ends in football."

6. OZZIE NEWSOME—Ozzie Newsome caught 662 passes in his thirteen-year career, ranking fifth all-time and first among tight ends. He was actually too big to play wide receiver and too small for tight end. But the numbers he compiled can't be overlooked.

"He never has received the notoriety of a Mackey," said ex-Lions tight end Charlie Sanders. "He has just quietly done his job and gotten the stats."

Newsome was also a pretty good blocker and a strong scoring threat earlier in his career. In each of the '83 and '84 seasons, he caught 89 passes. No other tight end has ever caught more. He also caught passes in 150 consecutive games, second on the all-time list behind Steve Largent's streak of 177.

"It gives me a lot of satisfaction that players like Kellen Winslow and I helped define the position of tight end," said the humble Newsome. "We were a part of the game when a tight end was an athlete who was asked to do a lot of things. Now it's going back to the John Mackey-type of tight end."

Newsome caught 50 or more passes in six seasons, something only ten players have done, and he had two 1,000-yard seasons, which is extremely rare for a tight end. From 1979 to '85 he caught 464 passes. He played in three Pro Bowls.

7. PETE PIHOS—Who's Pete Pihos? He is perhaps the most unrecognized member of the Pro Football Hall of Fame.

If one goes back before Ron Kramer and Tom Fears, one could trace the earliest evolution of the position to Pihos, who starred for the Eagles from 1947 to '55. He finished with 373 catches and 61 touchdowns.

"Pihos was closer to what today's tight ends are," says pro football historian Jim Campbell. "He blocked and caught extremely well."

Pihos missed only one game while playing both offense and defense most of his career. Nicknamed "The Golden Greek," he was named All-Pro at end in 1948 and '49 (no platoons were named then), at defensive end in 1952, and then back on offense from 1953–55, when he led the league in receiving all three years. He also played in the first six Pro Bowl games.

He didn't have great speed, but, as former NFL commissioner Bert Bell said, "Any defender who battles Pihos for a pass is bound to get the worst of it physically. He plays it clean but very hard and, after he catches the pass, you would think he was a bulldozing fullback."

8. RUSS FRANCIS—Russ Francis had one of the longest careers of any tight end, thirteen years (1975–88, except for 1981 when he "retired"). In that time, he caught 382 passes for 40 touchdowns. He was a big player who could make the tough catch, and he might have been the best blocker of the largely pass-catching breed of tight ends. Francis was also fast enough to play wide receiver, and he rose to the occasion in clutch games.

"He had as much potential as any tight end," said Charlie Sanders. "But he wasn't utilized much after he left the Patriots [and went to the 49ers]."

At 6-foot-6 and 240 pounds, Francis was once called "a league leader in the Greek God department." He was also one heckuva football player who, unfortunately, had to play injured too many times during his career.

"This man's got more talent than six of us put together," said O.J. Simpson. And Bert Jones added, "If you asked Aladdin to bring you the perfect tight end, he'd bring you Russ Francis."

Chuck Fairbanks, Francis' coach early in his career at New England, once said, "This guy is the most remarkable pure athletic talent I've ever seen."

9. RON KRAMER—Ron Kramer was the pioneer, and the first tight end was a blocker. "Kramer was a great blocker," said Mike Ditka. "He had no peer."

Kramer was a key to Green Bay's famed power sweep, blocking down on a defensive end or a linebacker, with either Fuzzy Thurston or Jerry Kramer and then Jim Taylor and Paul Hornung hot on his heels.

Former Bengals tight end Bob Trumpy remembers, "Kramer was big enough [6-foot-3, 234 pounds] for the offensive line, but he had too much athletic ability."

"[Vince] Lombardi said I was like a twelfth player," said Kramer.

But, while he was big, he could also catch the ball. In ten seasons with Green Bay and Detroit he caught 229 passes for a 14.3-yard average with 16 touchdowns. He was once described as "a runaway beer truck when he tears into defensive backs."

"They didn't throw to me a lot," he recalled. "But then, with that ground game, they didn't have to."

10. CHARLIE SANDERS—Charlie Sanders patterned himself after John Mackey (he also wore the same No. 88), and was even called "Little Mackey."

Fast for a tight end, Sanders caught 336 passes for 31 touchdowns over his career in Detroit (1968–77). He was a better pass receiver than a blocker, and early in his career, he took advantage of zone defenses, going against linebackers until teams adjusted to him.

"I was a possession receiver. I was going to get the ball on third down," Sanders said, "and everyone knew it. Especially the eleven guys on the other team."

Sanders was a first-down-getter, not a deep threat, although he could run over people. He played in seven Pro Bowls and retired as the Lions' all-time leading receiver. He had all the tools for a top tight end, especially great concentration.

In 1973, then-Lions coach Don McCafferty said, "I was associated for years in Baltimore with John Mackey. . . . And I think Sanders is just as good."

OFFENSIVE LINEMEN

*I've compared offensive linemen to the story of Paul Revere. After
Paul Revere rode through town, everybody said what a good job he
did. But no one ever talked about the horse.*
GENE UPSHAW

Offensive linemen are usually unseen and always underappreciated. All they have is their own self-satisfaction, and that has to make do. The media reports when somebody runs fifty yards for a touchdown, but it rarely tells who made the blocks. The offensive linemen know who sprung him; in fact, everybody on the team knows who made it possible. After all, the skill-position players can't go very far without the offensive linemen.

"The fans will jump up and carry a guy on their shoulders because he has run forty yards," said Bob St. Clair, a Hall of Fame offensive tackle for the 49ers. "Meanwhile, nobody comes out to the three or four linemen—who knocked themselves out to spring the back loose—to help them out of the mud."

"The stars get most of the newspaper space," admits ex-Ram Tom Mack. "Frustrating? Sure it is. You can have a great game and never read a word about it the next day. But you learn to live with it."

"To be an outstanding offensive lineman . . . a man must be a self-starter," said Paul Brown, the late head coach of the Browns and Bengals. "He must be able to motivate himself and he must take pride in his performance. He can't be a man who needs glory."

As ex-Cardinal Dan Dierdorf once said, "Any offensive lineman that has to have a lot of recognition won't be an offensive lineman for long."

For an offensive lineman, personal goals are secondary to unit goals. Having a back run for 1,000 yards or allowing the fewest sacks in the league is a line's satisfaction.

But that doesn't mean offensive linemen aren't good football players. "Don't ever use the term 'skill positions' around me," Dierdorf retorts. "That infers that the others are the unskilled positions. There's more preparation in the offensive line than any wide receiver ever experiences."

The anonymous offensive linemen are in a precarious position. All game long, they beat up on defensive linemen, and then once, just once, a defender slips through and gets the quarterback. And then everyone wants to know who blew the block, who got beat. And they are embarrassed in front of millions of people.

But some aren't embarrassed often. Some of them dominated their position and dominated defensive linemen so much that they *were* noticed.

Football fans will always debate whether Jim Brown or Walter Payton is the greatest running back ever, or whether Johnny Unitas or Otto Graham or Joe Montana is the best quarterback of all time.

But, when it comes to offensive linemen, there is no debate. The best ever is Jim Parker.

Mike Webster was a dominating center. Dwight Stephenson was the quickest center. John Hannah was a devastating run blocker. Forrest Gregg was called "the perfect player" by Vince Lombardi. Anthony Munoz has been the best lineman for the last decade no matter the position.

But Parker, a Hall of Famer who played eleven years at guard and tackle for the Colts, was the greatest, and the consent is nearly unanimous.

1. JIM PARKER—Jim Parker of the Baltimore Colts was the first lineman elected to the Hall of Fame exclusively as an offensive performer. He played five and a half seasons at left tackle, then he switched to left guard in the middle of the 1962 season, which is where he stayed for the last five and a half years of his career. During that period, he was voted All-Pro eight consecutive seasons—four at tackle, three at guard, and one (1962) at both.

Parker was quick and agile, and equally dominating at either position. He was a great run blocker both in-line and on sweeps, and he could control speedy defensive ends on pass plays. Some people called him the best pure pass blocker who ever lived. He wasn't overly aggressive, but he had great balance and was like a rock on the offensive line with a shoulder block better than anybody ever. And he was rarely beaten by a defensive lineman.

"I idolized Jim Parker when I was a kid," said Hall-of-Fame Dolphins guard Larry Little. "I tried to be the guard he was."

"He's the best I ever saw," said former Viking Ed White. "I've seen film of him—he was absolutely devastating. I don't think I've ever seen anyone as devastating as Parker."

"My goal was to be the best offensive lineman ever," Parker said. "I kept that in the back of my mind; I never mentioned it to anybody."

Parker had a philosophy that was unlike most offensive linemen. "You can't wait for the quarterback to make something happen," he said. "You start it at the line of scrimmage. You had to think you were the most important person on the field, that you were the best on the field. That's the way I thought."

JIM PARKER

Gene Brito, one of pro football's best defensive linemen ever, once told Parker, "I'm sure glad I never had to play against you." Brito played on the opposite side of the field from Parker.

But Andy Robustelli, the Giants' Hall of Famer, did have to go up against Parker. "I used to think that I could outmaneuver any big tackle, but that Parker can stay with anybody. He sure could move with me. The only way you can beat him is to make him move his head. But he is too strong and too good and too smart to do that."

Parker was 6-foot-3 and 275 pounds, which was big in his day. He could trap and pull and even cave in a whole side of a defensive line. But his most remembered assignment was to protect Johnny Unitas' blind side. "We're just the butter. He is the bread. Look, if I break my arm, I can still play. If he breaks his, we're dead. It didn't take me long to learn the one big rule: 'Keep 'em away from John,'" he said. "I remember coach [Weeb] Ewbank telling me my first summer in camp: 'You can be the most unpopular man on the team if the quarterback is hurt.' How could I ever forget that?"

Offensive Tackles

As the game of football has evolved, the positions have changed, and it's hard to compare players of different eras. It's even more difficult with offensive linemen, because the rules have changed so much. Today's linemen can extend their arms and use their hands; twenty-five years ago, they had to keep them close to their bodies.

It's also difficult to rate the two-way players. For example, former Bears Hall of Famer George Connor would be rated among the top three two-way tackles of all time. But, strictly as an offensive tackle, he doesn't rate in most people's top ten (Connor was a pretty good linebacker, too).

Cal Hubbard, who played for the Packers and Giants from 1927 to '35, was voted the tackle on the NFL's all-time team picked in 1969, but, in those days, linemen were noted more for their defensive play.

But, when it comes to playing offensive tackle, it has never been an easy job no matter when the era.

As Hall of Famer Ron Mix once said, "Offensive tackle is probably the worst job in professional sport. On every play, I don't care what it is, even if it's in a controlled scrimmage, the tackle makes contact. It's pound, pound, pound. Nobody knows except you, the guy you are pounding and maybe a coach."

Bob Brown, one of the great offensive tackles ever, agreed with the physical aspects of the position. "It's a simple issue of me-him," Brown said. "Who's the strongest, who's the most determined. Who has the highest threshold of pain."

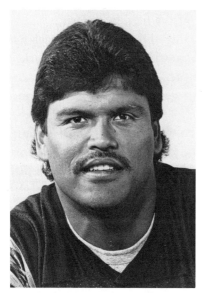

ANTHONY MUNOZ

2. ANTHONY MUNOZ—During a lull in a *Monday Night Football* game in 1991, the ABC broadcast crew started to talk about the Bengals' Anthony Munoz. "I think he's the best of all time," said Dan Dierdorf. "I know he's a contemporary player, but when you think of the Forrest Greggs and the Rosey Browns, this guy is the best. What sets him apart is sheer athleticism. People speak of him in a reverent way."

Frank Gifford then added, "I think if you asked Forrest Gregg and Rosey Brown, they'd say the same thing."

Munoz was an All-Pro selection in eleven of his thirteen years, more than any player of that time, and he played in the Pro Bowl every season except his first and last. He was big (6-foot-6, 285 pounds), strong, fast, durable, and consistent with great feet and balance. While most players have a fault or two, Munoz had none. He is closing out his career with the Buccaneers.

Before he was drafted in the first round of the 1980 draft, Munoz was scouted at the Rose Bowl by Paul Brown and his sons, Mike and Pete. "The three of us sat there and laughed out loud," Paul Brown said. "The guy was so big and so good it was a joke."

Hall of Famer Mike McCormack called Munoz "the epitome of what an

NFL offensive tackle should be. I've never, ever, seen one better."

Chicago defensive end Richard Dent called Munoz "the best I've ever faced."

And Hall of Famer Ernie Stautner, now the Broncos' defensive line coach, said, "He's been a very dominating player over the years. He matches up with any defensive end in the league. He's a very physical player and overpowering at times."

His line coach, Jim McNally, once observed, "Anthony's one of the few guys I've seen who can drive a guy back fifteen or twenty yards. I have to think it takes an opponent a full week to get mentally prepared for him."

Munoz was the best in the NFL at what coaches call "pancakes," which is when an offensive lineman drives a defender off his feet and onto his butt. Munoz got half a dozen a game, at the least.

Raiders defensive end Greg Townsend said, "He has a defensive mentality on offense. He has this killer instinct to get his man and put him away. He's the best tackle I've ever seen."

And he was the best pro football has seen in a quarter of a century.

3. FORREST GREGG—Vince Lombardi once called Forrest Gregg "the finest player I have ever coached"—and that's saying a lot when you consider that Lombardi coached more than a dozen Hall of Famers. Gregg played in nine Pro Bowls in the sixties and was even named All-Pro at both guard (Associated Press) and tackle (United Press International) in 1965 when he took over for Jerry Kramer.

Gregg was tremendously consistent and a great technician and finesse player during his fifteen-year career with Green Bay (1956–71). A master of the dance, he made people go where he wanted them to. He also played some guard, making Pro Bowl there, too. Versatile and disciplined, Gregg "wasn't as big as the others," said John Sandusky, the longtime offensive line coach for Baltimore and Miami, "but he was just as rangy."

Gregg played in a then-record 188 consecutive games—never missing a game. He says he watched film of Jim Parker and Roosevelt Brown when he was a rookie. "That's the only way a fellow with a little ability can become a good tackle," he pointed out. "And that is through hard work."

FORREST GREGG

At 6-foot-4, 249 pounds, Gregg wasn't big enough to overpower the defensive ends he faced, so he beat them with finesse. In the 1960 NFL championship game, Gregg faced Joe Robb, the Eagles' pass-rushing specialist. "I tried everything against that Gregg," said Robb. "I just couldn't get a good rush. He'd be four yards deep, still blocking on me before I could set up. You just can't throw him. He's the greatest tackle I ever faced."

Gregg was inducted into the Hall of Fame in 1977, the first year he was eligible. "It's awesome to think that, as a player or coach, your tenure is only temporary," he said. "But election to the Pro Football Hall of Fame is permanent. It's something that can never be taken away."

"Hey, Lombardi said he was the best football player he ever coached," says pro football historian and author Bob Carroll, "and I'm not going to argue with that."

ART SHELL

4. ART SHELL—Art Shell was what is called a straight-ahead tackle, which fit into the Raiders' "keep-it-simple" method of football. With ideal size at 6-foot-5, 285 pounds, Shell exploded off the line of scrimmage along with his guard mate, Gene Upshaw. They formed one of the best sides of an offensive line ever in the NFL.

"He was a knock-'em-dead football player," said John Sandusky. "He came off the ball and would get into you."

Shell played fifteen years (1968–82) and, along with Upshaw, made the weakside run work for the Raiders.

"I was always told that I wasn't mean enough," says Shell, who is now the Raiders' head coach. "I describe the way I played as controlled aggression."

Overshadowed by more dynamic personalities on the Raiders, Shell was All-AFC from 1973–78 and All-NFL three of those years. He played in eight Pro Bowls and twenty-three postseason games. He was inducted into the Hall of Fame in 1989.

"He was one of those quiet leaders who commands respect just by being a great player," said his former coach, John Madden. "He never, ever, acted like a tough guy. But, whether you were his teammate or an opponent, you knew this was a man who deserved your deepest respect."

Never were Shell and Upshaw any better than in Super Bowl XI against the Vikings, when, in the first half alone, the Raiders ran 27 of 33 running plays toward Minnesota's Alan Page and Jim Marshall. Oakland gained 266 yards rushing that day in a 32–14 victory. Marshall, who was Shell's primary blocking target that day, had no tackles and no assists.

"When somebody told me I had a perfect game," Shell recalled, "I was shocked because I had no idea Marshall had not been in on even one play. I was too busy to keep track."

5. RON MIX—In the sixties, the Chargers had the best offensive line in the AFL, and it was built around Ron Mix. He was a big, strong player who also used finesse, and he was known as the strongest offensive lineman of his day. He could move and get in front of the Chargers' explosive backfield of Keith Lincoln and Paul Lowe.

RON MIX

Dubbed "The Intellectual Assassin" (he went to law school while playing football), Mix had only two holding calls made against him in ten seasons. He was All-AFL nine times and was named to the all-time AFL team. Mix was inducted into the Hall of Fame in 1979, only the second player from the AFL to be enshrined (Lance Alworth was the first).

"He made his reputation in a league that wasn't known for having a lot of blocking," says Bob Carroll.

His former coach, Sid Gillman, calls him the best blocking offensive tackle ever.

Joe Madro, who was his position coach in San Diego, once said, "The greatest I ever saw for getting himself prepared was Ron Mix. He was absolutely fantastic. Before a game, he would sit in a locker room and just stare at the floor for a long time. He'd sit there just silent and staring. Then he'd get up and go out on the field, and no man was ever more ready than Mix."

And he made it easier for everybody around him to play. As Lowe once said, "When you're running behind Mix, it's like you're a little kid and your big brother is protecting you from the wolves."

6. ROOSEVELT BROWN—One of the NFL's most notable "sleeper" draft picks, Rosevelt Brown lasted until the twenty-seventh round of the 1953 draft. He made himself into a great tackle, starting for the Giants the next fourteen seasons. In 1975 he became the second offensive linemen to be inducted into the Hall of Fame.

An All-Pro eight straight years from 1956 to '62 and member of ten Pro Bowl teams, Brown was quick rather than overpowering and was one of the first tackles to pull on sweeps. Old films of the Giants will often show him out in front of Frank Gifford and Alex Webster. He specialized in cut blocks and could knock defensive linemen flat. But he was also an excellent pass blocker.

"I guess I was quicker and faster than most tackles," Brown said. "I used more smarts than anything else, because I didn't have the strength of [somebody like Jim] Parker. I let my guy think himself out of the play."

The Giants drafted Brown after glancing at a weekly black newspaper, the *Pittsburgh Courier*. He had been named to the Black All-America team in 1952.

"We had nothing to lose," Giants president Wellington Mara would say years later.

Nothing to lose, and a whole lot to gain.

7. AL WISTERT—Al Wistert is the favorite of several football historians, who think he should be in the Hall of Fame. And his credentials certainly merit his consideration.

He made at least one All-Pro team every year he played, from 1943 to '51—something no other player can say. The lead blocker for Eagles Hall of Famer Steve Van Buren, Wistert is known for having pioneered the shoulder block in an era when other players were using the cross and body blocks, but he was also very fast.

Since Wistert played during the war years, when many of the NFL's best players were in the service, it's hard to make a judgment on him. But he certainly was better than his contemporaries.

"He may have been the first to have made a name as an offensive tackle, because he was known as a blocker," says pro football historian Jim Campbell. "He's one of the glaring omissions in the Hall of Fame. He was the best or second-best tackle during his time."

When he retired, Wistert said, "Pro football's a great game as long as you're able to give more than you receive. In the past few years, I've reached the point where the receiving is getting the edge. Therefore, it's time to quit."

8. BOB ST. CLAIR—Twenty-seven years after retiring from the 49ers, Bob St. Clair was elected to the Hall of Fame in 1990. At 6-foot-9 and 265 pounds, he was an oddity—a big man who could run.

Former Colts defensive end Gino Marchetti says St. Clair was the toughest lineman he ever faced. Sam Huff agrees, calling St. Clair "a big python. I couldn't get around him. He was the finest offensive lineman I ever played against."

St. Clair has been called a prototype of the crusher-type tackles. But he wasn't awkward and he didn't just overpower defenders. "It was a game of wits," St. Clair said. "You had to use techniques."

In an eleven-year career (1953–63), St. Clair was one of the most eccentric individuals to ever play in the NFL (he eats raw meat), but also one of the best. He provided protection for some of the game's finest backs, such as Y.A. Tittle, Joe Perry, Hugh McElhenny, and John Henry Johnson.

He was voted All-Pro in just one season, 1955, but he played in five Pro Bowl games. "He never got the credit," Jim Parker commented, "but he was the only man I ever saw cut-block [Gino] Marchetti. Marchetti never could beat St. Clair."

9. MIKE McCORMACK—One of the unsung members of the Hall of Fame, McCormack was a six-time Pro Bowler in a ten-year pro career that was spent mostly in Cleveland. He was inducted into the Hall of Fame twenty-two years after retiring, when he became the fourth modern offensive tackle to be enshrined.

McCormack was a very good middle guard for two seasons until switching to right tackle, where he was as adept at opening holes for Jim Brown as he was at protecting Otto Graham. He was aggressive—an offensive tackle with a defensive player's temperament.

Former Cleveland coach Paul Brown, who acquired McCormack in a fifteen-player trade in 1953 while he was still in the service, said McCormack was the team's best offensive lineman in the fifties. "He was an excellent pass protector, but he could also blow people out of there," Brown said. "It is only justice that he is in the Hall of Fame."

10. BOB BROWN—Bob Brown played ten years, from 1964 to '73, and he could be as good as anybody—sometimes. But Brown didn't always give it his best, which is what has kept him out of the Hall of Fame (he has made the final 15 list in the past).

"I'm not a finesse linemen like a lot of tackles in this league," Brown once said. "I'm about as fancy as a sixteen-pound sledgehammer. I'm basic. From the opening kickoff on, I beat on people. I do it because I want to see some results by the fourth quarter. Those finesse guys are all right except that in the last quarter their opponent is still trying to get around them. With me, the opponents don't have quite as much left. They're not so sure they want to keep coming at me no more."

But former Colts center Dick Szymanski said Brown was "too aggressive. He always wanted to kick the s— out of you."

Brown played in six Pro Bowls and was named to the All-Pro team of the sixties. He was extremely quick and agile for his nearly 300 pounds, especially on sweeps. He was All-Pro five times and was named to six Pro Bowls (three as an Eagle, two as a Ram, and one as a Raider).

Don Shula once said of Brown, "He is a great—I mean great—football player." John Madden echoed those thoughts: "He's just the most devastating football player I've ever seen. He's a super superstar."

11. DAN DIERDORF—Early in his career, Dan Dierdorf set a goal to "be the best lineman who ever played football." Well, he wasn't the best, but he is certainly one of the best ever.

Dierdorf was an intimidator, an enforcer every bit as violent and aggressive as the men across the line from him. In a career that stretched from 1971 to '83, Dierdorf was All-Pro five times and played in six Pro Bowls. He has been one of the final 15 candidates for the Hall of Fame in the past—and many football people think he belongs there.

"Does John Hannah deserve to be in [the Hall of Fame] before Dan Dierdorf?" asks Jim Hart, the former Cardinals quarterback. "Give me a break. No way he should be. And why will Dan be any more deserving next year than he is now?"

Jack Buck, the Hall of Fame voter from St. Louis, agrees. "Too Tall Jones chewed everybody up when he played defensive end for Dallas," Buck says. "Dierdorf handled him like a pup."

In seventy plays, if Dierdorf was not dominant on sixty-eight of them, he was disappointed. At 6-foot-3, 280, he possessed size, speed, quickness, intelligence, and the consistency to become an ideal offensive lineman. He anchored a line that led the NFC five straight years in fewest sacks allowed.

12. CAL HUBBARD—Cal Hubbard was the archetype of the football gladiator, a giant ahead of his time and the prototype for all future pro tackles. He was voted the tackle on the NFL's all-time team chosen in 1969 and was a charter member of the Hall of Fame. He's also the only person who is a member of both the Pro Football and the Baseball Hall of Fame (he also achieved fame as a baseball umpire).

Former NFL coach Bo McMillan once said, "Hubbard was the greatest football player of all time."

He was the most feared lineman of his era and one of the few early pros who was as large as today's players (6-foot-5, 250 pounds). Hubbard played both offense and defense from 1927 to '36, mostly with the New York Giants.

Historian Bob Carroll specializes in the early days of pro football. "Hubbard was big for his time. He was a terror when he was with the Giants, and he was still opening holes like crazy for Green Bay in '35. He was certainly the best offensive tackle of that period."

Hubbard was mobile, aggressive, and a hard hitter. "I played hard and rough," Hubbard once said, "but I made only one dirty play in my life."

13. JACKIE SLATER—Jackie Slater has played tackle for seventeen seasons with the Rams, longer with the same team than all but four players in NFL history (Jim Marshall, Jim Hart, Jeff Van Note, and Pat Leahy). And his 238 games played ranks thirteenth on the all-time list and fourth among offensive linemen.

But Slater is more than just a player who saw a lot of action. He's a great technician with superior pass-blocking ability because of his long arms. He was selected to six consecutive Pro Bowls from 1985–90 and seven overall. The NFL Players Association named him Offensive Lineman of the Year three times.

"Jackie Slater has every move that every tackle will ever have in this league," says John Madden.

The oldest active player in the NFL in 1992, some people thought Slater was cruelly overlooked on the NFL's Team of the 1980s.

Offensive Guards

The position of offensive guard is simple, unadulterated violence. Their objective is to physically dominate the guy across from them—totally and completely. In order to do that, they have to keep hitting a defensive lineman repeatedly, harder and harder. It's better to give than to receive.

After the snap, it happens so fast—it's a world of constant movement— it becomes almost instinct. It's something ingrained in a guard. But that's the measure of greatness.

There are no statistics for a guard, and Jerry Kramer's famous block in the 1967 Ice Bowl is the only play by a guard you'll ever hear mentioned. Guards tend to be better run blockers than tackles. They used to be the players that provided the clue as to where a play was going to go. Today, however, guards are just as involved in misdirection plays, such as traps.

A guard's job is fourfold: drive-block straight ahead, do a short pull to execute a trap block, get outside on a sweep or screen pass, and hold his position on pass plays. But he must have quick feet and he has to be able to think on the move in the ever-changing battle in the line.

But guards in pro football today don't play very much like the position's description. "It's just five tackles playing the game now," laments Hall of Famer Gene Upshaw. "They don't sweep as much as they used to. It's more solid-line blocking."

"It's kind of a mushing game," admits Ed White. "The more skilled people go to the other side of the ball. They [coaches] don't consider us skilled people. We're just big people."

JOHN HANNAH

2. JOHN HANNAH— When you think of a pulling guard, you think of John Hannah. A thirteen-year veteran with the Patriots, he is quite possibly the best run blocker in pro football history. Hannah was named All-Pro every year from 1976 through 1985 and also played in nine Pro Bowls.

Hannah was big and tenacious with great speed and quickness. He was inducted into the Hall of Fame in 1991, his first year of eligibility. He is the only Patriot—player, coach, or administrator—to be enshrined and only the second player ever who played his entire career at guard. Although he was a great run blocker, he wasn't respected as much when pass-blocking.

"He wanted to kill the [defensive] guy all the time," remembers Hall of Famer Upshaw. "And that got him into trouble on pass protection."

However, the NFL Players Association, of which Upshaw is the executive director, did vote Hannah the Offensive Lineman of the Year from 1978 through '81.

At 6-foot-2 and 285 pounds, "Hog" Hannah was bigger than guards of his day. He has been compared to Jim Parker. "When they hit you, they hurt you," said John Sandusky, who coached Parker with the Colts.

The fourth pick in the 1973 draft, Hannah had to make the adjustment from blocking in a wishbone offense at Alabama—where Bear Bryant once called him "the best offensive lineman I ever coached"—to the pro technique of dropping back rather than charging out.

In 1978, largely with Hannah leading the way, the Patriots rushed for an NFL-record 3,165 yards.

When Hall of Fame center Jim Ringo was the Patriots' offensive coordinator, he once said, "John has better pulling speed than Jerry Kramer and Fuzzy Thurston, even though he is twenty pounds heavier than either of them."

Like most offensive linemen, Hannah, the son of a former Giants player and the brother of Charley, who played for the Raiders and Buccaneers, didn't toot his own horn. When he retired a few months after playing in Super Bowl XX, he said, "I guess I just want to be remembered as a player who did the best that he could with what he had."

3. GENE UPSHAW—Gene Upshaw played in Super Bowls in three different decades. He played more games than any other Raider and was only the second guard inducted into the Hall of Fame (and the first to exclusively play the position). The story goes that Raiders owner Al Davis drafted Upshaw so he would have somebody to block Kansas City's Buck Buchanan.

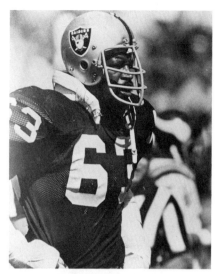

GENE UPSHAW

"I figured if Buchanan was going to play for the Chiefs for the next ten years, we better get some big guy who could handle him," Davis recalled. "So we got Upshaw. Those two guys put on some stirring battles over the years."

Upshaw, at 6-foot-5, 255 pounds, was the first of the big, tall, strong guards, as opposed to the short, fireplug type. He prided himself on his speed, and he was especially effective pulling and taking on defensive backs downfield.

"He always seemed to rise to the top in big games," remembers Larry Little. "He had great speed for an offensive lineman."

Upshaw was named All-AFL, All-AFC, or All-NFL his first six seasons and eight times altogether. He teamed with another Hall of Famer, Art Shell, to give the Raiders perhaps the strongest left side of an offensive line ever seen in pro football. Upshaw was famous for leading sweeps around left end year after year. "That's my play," Upshaw said. "A wide receiver wants to catch a long touchdown pass. A defensive tackle wants to break through and sack the quarterback. I get my satisfaction from pulling to lead those sweeps. That's when it comes down to just me and the defensive back. If I get him clean, we're going to make a big gain. If I miss him, we don't get a yard."

However, when Upshaw was drafted, he didn't want to play guard, nor did he want to play for the Raiders. "He thought they were renegades," admitted Davis.

They were renegades, to be sure, but the Raiders were winners, too. Upshaw played in twenty-four postseason games, including three AFL and seven AFC championships and three Super Bowls. He was a team captain for nine years.

4. JERRY KRAMER—Jerry Kramer is mostly known for "The Block," the one he threw in the 1967 "Ice Bowl" championship game in which Bart Starr sneaked over for a touchdown to beat Dallas. Although he isn't in the

JERRY KRAMER

Hall of Fame, Kramer was voted to the all-time NFL team picked in 1969.

He was at his best leading the Packers' famed "power sweep," pulling with Fuzzy Thurston—the most publicized pair of guards in NFL history—just ahead of Jim Taylor or Paul Hornung. The play remains among the most famous the game has known.

Although he wasn't as big as other guards, Kramer was strong and quick and a powerful drive blocker. More than any other guard, Kramer brought offensive linemen out of the trenches into the spotlight—in no small part due to his best-selling book, *Instant Replay*. It's also that publicity that occasionally causes some of his peers to downgrade him.

But not Larry Little, the ex-Dolphin. "He wasn't that big," Little said. "But, for what Green Bay did, he was great for that offense."

In eleven seasons with the Packers (1958–68), Kramer was named All-Pro in 1966 and '67 and played in three Pro Bowl games. He played in six NFL championship games—winning five times—and in the first two Super Bowls.

In the 1962 NFL championship game, Kramer kicked three field goals, which was the difference in the Packers' 16–7 victory.

But he still hasn't been inducted into the Hall of Fame. "I'd be less than candid and less than honest if I said I wasn't a little troubled by that," he admits. "I felt that I was the best guard that had played. I don't think anybody will argue that I was the best drive blocker in the game at that time."

5. LARRY LITTLE—Larry Little is the lineman who made Miami's run-oriented offense work in the seventies. He was a great pass protector and an excellent pulling guard, and it took a lot of speed to get ahead of halfback Mercury Morris.

Little was a complete guard, excellent at all three main phases—run blocking, pass blocking, and pulling. He has been compared to Jim Parker because their size was similar.

"Now there's a great football player," says Howard Mudd, the former Cleveland guard who now coaches the Chiefs' offensive linemen. "Chicken [Little's nickname] could run out in space, knock guys off the ball and finish people."

"Consistency is what I look for," says Ed White. "Little was real consistent, and he was a good athlete."

Little was All-Pro six times and played in five Pro Bowls during his fourteen-year career (1967–80). He is a member of the All-Pro team of the seventies. Along with Jim Langer and Bob Kuechenberg, Little helped make the Miami running game one of the most successful in NFL history. The Dolphins rushed for a record 2,960 yards in 1972. But Little and his cohorts also prided themselves in not allowing quarterback Bob Griese to be sacked.

Former Miami running back Jim Kiick once said, "With Larry blocking, I don't have to run over anyone; I can run around. When Larry's leading the sweep for me and he comes around the corner, I can see the fear in the eyes of the defense."

LARRY LITTLE

6. TOM MACK—How a player can make eleven Pro Bowls and not get into the Hall of Fame has perplexed football observers ever since Tom Mack retired following a thirteen-year career with the Rams in 1978. Mack never missed a game in his career and was noted for his consistent performance.

"He could do it all," said Larry Little. "He was a great pass blocker and run blocker."

"He's definitely one of the great football players," commented Gene Upshaw.

Football historian Beau Riffenburgh calls Mack "the perfect guard. He did everything, and he was really good for a long time."

Mack has been a finalist for the Hall of Fame. He played in 184 consecutive games. He was voted All-Pro three times and All-NFC eight times. George Allen once said of Mack, "There's not a better blocker on sweeps."

He was a dedicated, dependable team player, and was vastly unrecognized on a team that included Deacon Jones, Merlin Olsen, and Roman Gabriel. In fact, Mack was even called "Tom Who?" by his teammates.

The second player chosen in the 1965 draft, Mack was only the second rookie to start for Allen. At 6-foot-3, 250 pounds, he had a rare combination of size, speed, and strength.

7. DICK STANFEL—The Bears' offensive line coach for many years, Dick Stanfel was the seniors candidate for the Hall of Fame in 1993, and he was certainly deserving. Stanfel played with distinction for Detroit and Washington in the fifties, although his career lasted only seven years. He made five Pro Bowls and four All-Pro teams and played in three title games. He was the Most Valuable Player in the 1953 NFL championship game.

"He was one of the greatest pulling guards ever," says John Sandusky, who played for the Browns at the time. "He was a tall, lean guy who could run and cut people down."

"Stanfel was top of the heap at the time he played," asserts Jim Campbell. "None better."

A first-round draft pick who was remembered as the first of the big guards, the 6-foot-3, 236-pound Stanfel was a great finesse and position blocker. Most of the guards at the time were short, stubby guys, but Stanfel could run and pull better than the rest.

8. GENE HICKERSON—The lead blocker for Jim Brown and Leroy Kelly, Gene Hickerson played for the Browns for fifteen years. He played in every Pro Bowl from '66 to '71 and was named to the All-Pro squad of the 1960s.

"He was the consummate guard," says Howard Mudd, a 49ers guard at the time. "He's much overlooked, a high-quality football player for a long time. When I came into the NFL, I said, 'Wow! That's the guy I want to be like.'"

Gene Upshaw even went so far as to say Hickerson was "overlooked for the Hall of Fame. Look at those guys he was blocking for."

Hickerson responds, "There is no one in the Hall of Fame who has a better record than I have as a player."

A seventh-round "future" draft pick in 1957, Hickerson was powerful, athletic, and could pull and run.

9. STAN JONES—In 1991, Stan Jones became only the fourth guard in the Pro Football Hall of Fame when he was voted in twenty-five years after retiring.

Probably the heaviest guard in the NFL during his time (1954–65 with Chicago and '66 in Washington), Jones was one of the first players to use weightlifting as a way of adding strength. He was named to the Pro Bowl every year from 1955 to '61, starting four times. He was selected either first- or second-team All-Pro by major wire services more than any other guard during that time.

Jones excelled at in-line blocking and trapping. Look at any old film of Rick Casares or Willie Galimore and you'll usually see No. 78 out in front.

In 1963, because of injuries, the Bears shifted Jones to defensive tackle. Chicago won the NFL championship that year, and Jones stayed on defense for a few more years.

10. JOE DeLAMIELLEURE—Reggie McKenzie got all the press because he pulled on the sweeps and was "O.J.'s buddy," but Joe DeLamielleure was the better player, say most of their contemporaries.

"He was never around when they took the pictures. Reggie was," remarked Gene Upshaw. "He was a solid guy who just constantly did his job."

"Joe D" is a solid candidate for the Hall of Fame, a strong run blocker and an excellent technician and trap blocker during his twelve-year career with Buffalo and Cleveland. He played in six Pro Bowls (compared with McKenzie's none) and was named to the All-Pro team of the 1970s along with John Hannah.

11. DANNY FORTMANN and GEORGE MUSSO (tie)—The Bears' starting guards half a century ago are both Hall of Famers who gained their reputations on offense as well as defense. Both players helped the Bears win several NFL championships.

"Danny Fortmann is truly an old-timer who played good offense," says historian Jim Campbell.

Fortmann was the last pick in the NFL's first draft in 1936 when he was only nineteen years old. He was small (6-foot, 207 pounds), quick, and rugged, and he called signals for the linemen. He was named All-Pro the last six of his eight seasons from 1936 to '43.

Musso really impressed Joe Horrigan, the Hall of Fame historian who watched some old Bears film with Bronko Nagurski's son a few years ago. "I was really impressed with Musso," Horrigan said. "He threw lead blocks, got off the ball in a hurry, and he just exploded into defensive linemen—he didn't wait for them."

Musso was big for his day—6-foot-2, 270 pounds. He was the first player to be voted All-Pro at two positions—at tackle in 1935 and at guard two years later. He played eleven seasons (1933–44) and had to wait thirty-seven years after retiring to be selected to the Hall of Fame.

"He was one of the real early speed-and-size guys—and mean. That's putting it nicely," says ex-Eagles guard Bucko Kilroy.

Centers

The best centers all played in the last three decades, because, before that time, players like Mel Hein, Bulldog Turner, Alex Wojciechowicz, Chuck Bednarik, and George Trafton were noted more for their defensive play, and all are deservedly in the Hall of Fame.

There are actually three eras of centers. The first played against five- and six-man fronts in which a center went against a middle guard. Then came the four-man defensive fronts, when centers either double-teamed defensive tackles with a guard or attacked the middle linebacker. Since the early seventies, most centers have faced 3-4 defenses, with a nose tackle head-on. In the fifties and sixties, a center's main responsibility was cutting off the middle linebacker. Today it's going head-to-head with a nose tackle.

It's an unnatural position. The center snaps the ball backward at the same time he is charging forward—and getting clubbed by a defensive lineman or two. Here are the best ever.

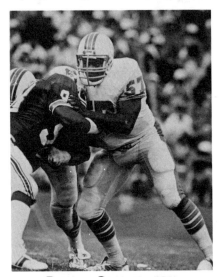

DWIGHT STEPHENSON

1. DWIGHT STEPHENSON—
Jim Langer is already in the Hall of Fame. But he's not even the best center to play for the Dolphins. Dwight Stephenson is.

Stephenson's career was cut short after eight seasons in 1987 because of a knee injury. He had incredible quickness, balance, and hand-use. He was All-Pro from 1983 to '87.

"I saw Stephenson in the Senior Bowl," recalls Jim Ringo, "and you could see all the ingredients he had. He had an amazing amount of strength."

"He would get on the [defensive guy] before he knew what the hell was happening," remarked Dick Szymanski, another Pro Bowl center. "He made it look effortless; he just had it all."

Stephenson had natural strength and was quick, strong, smart, and athletic with blinding speed off the ball. Unfortunately, he didn't last as long as others. As Dan Dierdorf once said, "He is the finest center I ever saw. I can't help but remember the night in 1987 when his career ended."

Stories about Stephenson are legendary, especially about some of his devastating blocks. There was the time he knocked a San Diego lineman out of the end zone. The team got a good laugh out of that one watching film the following Tuesday. Then there was the time he knocked out two New England blitzers using one forearm for each.

Former teammate Woody Bennett put it this way: "I just sit there and laugh because I cannot believe a player can dominate the way Dwight does. You're laughing, but you know the other guy is hurting—hurting bad."

Another ex-Dolphin, running back Tony Nathan, said, "He makes it look so easy. Sometimes you forget about Dwight during a game. Then on Tuesday you remember. You watch him manhandle a player and you can't believe he is the same size as Dwight."

Fred Smerlas used to play head-on with Stephenson. "If I never see that Number 57 again, I'll be real happy," Smerlas said. "He's a load and a half."

Teammate Bob Baumhower never had to face Stephenson in a game, but he had to go against him in practice. "Dwight is a bear. He's the toughest guy I've ever played against, and that made it so much easier for me on game day," Baumhower said. "The thing that makes Dwight so special is that he doesn't run his mouth off like a lot of guys. He just goes out there and kicks tail. And that's all there is to it."

Any more questions about who's the best center? Let Don Shula settle it. "I've never seen anyone better," Shula once said. "If I can tell a young player to learn from one of my veterans, to follow around and copy one player, that player would always be Dwight. He knows what to do in every situation. He's the best. There's little doubt about that any longer."

2. MIKE WEBSTER—Mike Webster played in nine Pro Bowls for the Steelers, more than any center, before finishing his seventeen-year career in Kansas City in 1990. He was a self-made center, a little short at 6-foot-2 and weighing 260 pounds. But Webster had tremendous strength and could cut-block better than anyone else.

MIKE WEBSTER

"He loved the game," said Jim Ringo. "He was a smart, tough person who had a lot of durability."

Webster made excellent line calls and was the key to the Steelers' running game in their Super Bowl years in the seventies and the last of them to retire. A Paul Bunyan look-alike, he was drafted in the fifth round of the 1974 draft along with Jack Lambert, Lynn Swann, and John Stallworth. He played in 177 consecutive games during one stretch of his career and didn't miss a play for six seasons. He holds the Steelers' records for seasons and games played and was named All-Pro six times.

Fred Hoaglin, a veteran center with the Giants who is now that team's offensive line coach, called Webster "a great one. He wasn't as big as Jim Langer, but he played longer."

Toughness personified Webster more than anything. Hal Hunter, one of his offensive line coaches, once said, "Webby is intimidating. He'll knock you down and then pick you up and tell you what a great job you did. That's disarming."

Webster was considered the strongest man in the NFL when he played, and he credited his strength to why he stuck in the pros. He also was the master of the cut block. He was strong enough to handle nose tackles and very intelligent on his line calls.

Craig Wolfley, a former teammate, told of another of Webster's unique talents. "He'll recognize a defense and turn around and suggest an audible," Wolfley said in a tone usually reserved for the Pope. "You don't see that very often."

JIM OTTO

3. JIM OTTO—At 6-foot-2 and 255 pounds, Jim Otto was smaller than most centers of his day (he started his career at 205 pounds), yet he compensated for his size with great range. He was the only All-AFL center in the league's history and an institution for the Raiders.

His longtime teammate, quarterback George Blanda, said, "Jim loved to win. He led by example and he set the tempo. He gave the Raiders an image of hard discipline, of hard work and of hard-nosed football."

Otto put in fifteen seasons from 1960 to '74. After making All-AFL for ten years, he was named All-AFC from 1970 to '72. He was a sure snapper with good speed and range. He overcame numerous injuries—including ten broken noses and nine knee operations—to play 308 games, counting exhibitions, all-star contests, playoffs, and Super Bowl II. He played in 210 consecutive regular-season games and was elected to the Hall of Fame in 1980 in his first year of eligibility.

Number Double-Zero had the ability to seek out targets far beyond the limited area usually expected of a center. He called the line plays, and, in one season, he was judged to have been wrong only three or four times in about 650 plays.

Much has been made of the fact Otto has undergone nearly a dozen operations on his knees and that he can barely walk these days. "I would do it again," he says without any hesitation. "If I could fix my knees up now, I'd try to play." If Otto's knees took a beating during his career, so did the defensive linemen he took on for those fifteen seasons.

4. JIM LANGER—The first Miami offensive lineman in the Hall of Fame, Jim Langer was quick, smart, and strong, especially with a man on his nose. He opened the holes for Larry Csonka in Super Bowl VIII, causing Vikings assistant coach Neill Armstrong to say he had never seen a better blocking center. Langer could also pull and lead on sweeps.

At Langer's induction into the Hall of Fame in 1987 (in his first year of eligibility), Dolphins coach Don Shula said, "Jim was the anchor of our great offensive line. It was the combination of his skills and leadership that enabled us to play exceptional ball-control football. . . . Jim had a way of playing his best against the best in the biggest games."

A free agent, Langer was a durable power-drive blocker and an excellent pass protector who played center like a guard. He got very few holding calls. He played every down during the Dolphins' perfect season of 1972. "One of the amazing statistics that year in grading out his blocking, out of 500 blocking assignments, he needed help on only three plays," said Shula.

Ex-Eagles linebacker Bill Bergey recalled, "Jim Langer of Miami, he overpowers you. A lot of centers will come out and give you a good shot when the play is at their point of attack. If it's not their side, they'll fall back and just go through the motions. Jim Langer is one man who hits you no matter what. He has something I've never seen a center do: He will snap the ball, pull, and trap off tackle. That's just an amazing feat."

"Strength was his great asset," said Mick Tingelhoff, who was the NFL's best center during most of the sixties. "He was a great blocker with a guy on his nose."

5. JIM RINGO—At 6-foot-1 and weighing only 235 pounds, Jim Ringo wasn't big but he compensated with his speed, finesse, and intelligence, making him the classic undersized overachiever. In fifteen seasons (1953–67) he played in ten Pro Bowls—seven with Green Bay and three with Philadelphia. At thirty-six years old, he was the oldest offensive lineman ever to play in a Pro Bowl when he saw action in the 1968 game. He started in his final 182 games—from 1954 to '67—a league record at the time.

Ringo specialized in cutting off a middle linebacker on straight-ahead plays. But he could pull, too, catching the onside tackle on sweeps. He became an All-Pro center with Green Bay in the fifties before the great Lombardi-era teams. As one observer remarked, "When Lombardi built the Packers, he started with his only All-Pro, Jim Ringo, and filled in the other all-stars around him."

Lombardi viewed Ringo this way: "A bigger man might not be able to make the cut-off blocks on our sweeps the way Jim does. The reason Ringo is the best in the league is because he's quick and he's smart. He runs the offensive line, calls the blocks and he knows what every lineman does on every play." Not bad for somebody who played alongside Forrest Gregg, Fuzzy Thurston, and Jerry Kramer for much of his career.

The last of a vanishing breed of linemen, Ringo said, "Small as I was, I had to be quick." He was inducted into the Hall of Fame in 1981.

6. MICK TINGELHOFF—Mick Tingelhoff was named All-Pro every year from 1964 to '70 and played in six Pro Bowls during his seventeen-year career with Minnesota. Many people think he deserves a spot in the Hall of Fame, but playing on four teams that lost in the Super Bowl has hurt his chances so far, although he replies that he had his string of All-Pro years before the Super Bowls.

"I can't understand why he's not in the Hall," said Jim Ringo. "He played so long and did a fabulous job. I guess there are oversights."

"Like [Jim] Langer, he was a nondescript guy," says John Sandusky. "Others got the notoriety, like the Purple People Eaters and the quarterback [Fran Tarkenton]. But, in Miami, the defense didn't get the publicity; the offensive line did."

Tingelhoff was a cerebral lineman, very quick and tenacious. "He was as tough as any football player I've ever seen," says Sid Hartman of the *Minneapolis Star-Tribune*. "You never could get him out of the lineup."

So true. Tinglehoff played in the final 240 games of his career. He did everything a good center was supposed to do, only better. Durability was his trademark, and he was one of the fastest men off the mark in the league, always cutting down a middle linebacker or cutting off a tackle almost at the same time he had to snap the ball to the quarterback . . . or at least that's the way it seemed.

His former coach, Bud Grant, once said, "He plays and plays well every week. Like most players, he is very durable and he doesn't let the little injuries slow him down."

7. FRANK GATSKI—At 6-foot-3, weighing 240 pounds, Frank "Gunner" Gatski was one of the biggest centers of his era. He played in eleven championship games during his twelve-year career with Cleveland and Detroit (1946–57), with his team winning eight times. He was inducted into the Hall of Fame in 1985, twenty-eight years after his final start.

He was an exceptional pass blocker and never missed a game from high school through the pros, in an era in which he played both ways and when middle guards played over the center. He was All-Pro four times.

"Gatski had the perfect personality for a center," says Joe Horrigan. "He was unassuming and did his job. He'd just snap the ball and protect the quarterback."

The Eagles' Chuck Bednarik went against Gatski twice a year for many years. "He was the best and toughest I ever played against," Bednarik said. "As a linebacker, I sometimes had to go over the center, but Gatski was an immovable object."

Another Browns Hall of Famer, kicker Lou Groza, commented, "Gunner was the best center the Browns ever had. He was the only center who ever pulled on the trap play. He was also the strongest guy on our team."

8. MEL HEIN—Mel Hein was All-Pro eight consecutive seasons (1933–40). He was the NFL Most Valuable Player in 1938 and is still the only offensive lineman to be so honored. A fifteen-year fixture at center for the Giants, Hein was a tower of strength in the middle of their line. The Giants won two league championships and seven division titles with him at center.

Longtime New York sportswriter Harold Rosenthal called Hein "the greatest two-way player in Giants history."

Solid at 6-foot-2 and 225 pounds, Hein was an extremely durable snapper (to tailbacks in the single wing) and a crushing but skillful blocker. He was also a terrific linebacker who excelled at pass coverage (he used pass-jamming tactics not commonly used until decades later) and was a deadly tackler.

After winning All-American honors in 1930, Hein had to write three NFL teams offering his services. The Giants had the high bid with an offer of $150 a game.

DEFENSIVE LINEMEN

Going after the quarterback is like playing king of the mountain.
When you get to the quarterback, you're on top of the mountain. He's
the brains of the team. I learned along time ago that if you killed the
head the body would die.

JOE GREENE

In the NFL today, players get nicknames like the Smurfs or the Three Amigos.

Two decades ago, there were names such as the Fearsome Foursome, the Purple People Eaters, the Steel Curtain, and the Doomsday Defense. Those all referred to defensive lines that were manned by great defensive players. If there was ever a time of great defensive lines in the NFL, it was the sixties.

Football today is a high-scoring game, with the air filled with balls and a dozen or more runners a year gaining a thousand yards on the ground. It didn't used to be so.

Not in Deacon Jones' day.

"Quarterbacks try to get their teams into the end zone," Ex-Rams defensive end Jones says. "But the defensive line is the number-one determining factor who gets into the end zone. And the sixties was the greatest period of defensive linemen ever."

Jones is right. Although the NFL today is filled with a lot of very good defensive linemen, most of them star for a few years and then slip into the roles of good players who get the job done. Those with high profiles are known for their pass-rushing skills more than anything because football today is a passing game. It used to be that the big defensive linemen just sat in one place and waited for the play to come to them. But some players are so great that fans have become acutely aware of defensive linemen.

Joe Namath once said, "Football is a struggle between the front four and the quarterback." And that's why the first role of defensive line play is to get the quarterback or just collapse the pocket and crowd the passer into inaccuracy.

"We're the heat men," said Jones. "We put the heat on. That's our job. A great defensive line can control an entire football game."

"It's the quarterback you have to beat," Cowboys Hall of Famer Bob Lilly pointed out.

Which is why defensive linemen dislike quarterbacks, and quarterbacks dislike defensive linemen.

"I hate quarterbacks," said former Jet Joe Klecko. "They stand between me and success."

Defensive Ends

Defensive ends are the players most responsible for providing the pass rush that usually is the difference between a good defense and a great one. Even great defensive backs can't cover receivers forever; they need someone putting the heat on the passer.

The best defensive ends get off the ball and are headed at the quarterback before the offensive tackle is even set. They are more finesse than tough, and they have to play under control. Many defensive schemes are set up to allow the defensive end to get at the passer.

"I played defensive end for eighteen years in the pros," said Hall of Famer Doug Atkins. "It's not the same as being a kicker or backup quarterback. A defensive end, if you don't cut it, you're on your butt in a hurry. I loved it."

As former 49ers coach Bill Walsh once said, "A pass rush late in the game is the key to NFL football."

Here are the men who did it best.

1. GINO MARCHETTI—Gino Marchetti is the prototype defensive end of any era. He was 6-foot-4, 245 pounds of rugged brawn, but he proved that speed could be coupled with size at his position. He was selected as the best defensive end of the NFL's first fifty years, played in ten Pro Bowls in an eleven-year stretch (missing in 1960 because of an injury), and was named All-Pro every year from 1956 to '62.

Marchetti was the first of the great pass rushers, and he laid the ground-work for modern-day defensive end play. He was often double- and triple-teamed (which just made the rest of the Colts' rush line more effective), and he

GINO MARCHETTI

was just as strong against the run. He became the first defensive end specialist in the early fifties at a time when teams were phasing out two-way players.

"He's the best I've ever seen," said Hall of Famer Bob St. Clair. "We came from the same college [San Francisco], and we had a great rivalry. He was so far ahead of everybody else . . . second place is way down the ladder compared to him."

Hall of Fame center Jim Ringo put it simply: "Oh, my God . . . who's better than him?"

Ringo went on to say the Packers used to look forward to facing the Colts just for the confrontations between Marchetti and Forrest Gregg. "They had a helluva match against each other for a lot of years," he said.

"Marchetti was relentless," remembers Marion Campbell, the former Falcons and Eagles head coach who was a lineman for the Eagles in the fifties. "He had obvious talent, but he went way beyond that. He batted down a lot of balls with his height."

If Marchetti had a peer as a pass rusher, it was Deacon Jones. But even Jones called Marchetti "one of my idols."

Marchetti didn't have to think much—football was a game of reaction to him. He read offensive linemen very well, and it seemed as if he could look in a player's eyes and see if he was going to set up for a pass or blow out on a running play. He was quick and relentless and he knew all the tricks in an offensive lineman's book.

Few players were more terrorizing on third downs than Marchetti, and he played all out all the time. Bobby Layne once compared what it was like to be overwhelmed by Marchetti on a pass rush to "running into a tree trunk in the dark."

Marchetti played defensive end in an era in which they didn't have the supporting cast of linebackers they do today. He was years ahead of his time, although it wasn't long before other teams went looking for players like him. So far, nobody has found anyone like him yet.

2. DEACON JONES—A fourteenth-round draft pick out of Mississippi Valley State, Deacon Jones was credited with coining the term "sack," and was one of its most successful practioners. If Marchetti was the NFL's first pass rusher, Jones elevated it to pre-eminence. He was All-Pro five times and played in eleven Pro Bowls.

Jones and Merlin Olsen formed the best left side of a defensive line in NFL history. "We were lucky enough to blend so well," Jones said. "We put pressure on the quarterback every play."

During their heyday, Olsen once said, "Sometimes I make a terrific move on my man, slip past the guard and get by the blocking back and think, 'Boy, I'm really going to unload on the quarterback now.' Then, when I get there, Deacon's already knocked him down."

Occasionally called "The Secretary of Defense," Jones was fiery, the fastest defensive linemen in the league in the sixties. He played in an era in which a lineman could

DEACON JONES

head-slap his offensive opponent, and nobody did it better than Jones.

"He had great quickness off the ball, with a great head slap," said Dick Modzelewski, who retired in 1990 after thirty-six years in the NFL as a player and coach. "But, if you tried to run at Deacon, he'd stand you [the blocker] up and make the tackle."

"Deacon was an exciting football player," remembered former Chiefs defensive tackle Buck Buchanan. "He would just explode past blockers."

From 1961 through 1974, Jones was noted for his innovative and flamboyant play. He was a unanimous All-Pro choice from 1965–70 and the Defensive Player of the Year in 1967 and '68.

Jones analyzed his style once. "I might be blocked forty out of forty-one times," he said. "but I must keep coming because I know that one time when my opponents break down, no matter how tired you are, no matter how hurt you are, you must keep coming. . . . I'm getting double-teamed and triple-teamed. It's like trying to fight my way out of a cage. If I'm blocked, I'll claw my way in. If I'm knocked down, I'll crawl. If I get through to that man with the ball, I'll hit him high and try to make him fumble."

And, more often than other players, Jones would get through to the man with the ball. Packers quarterback Bart Starr recalled one game when Jones knocked him down four times: "He got in on me so quick I thought he was one of my own backs," Starr said.

Starr's Hall of Fame tackle, Forrest Gregg, faced Jones for a decade. "You just can't power out at him. You fire out hard and he's gone, slipped around you," Gregg said. "You have to be controlled, keep your balance, and try to move with him."

WILLIE DAVIS

3. WILLIE DAVIS—Another low draft pick (seventeenth round), Willie Davis was All-Pro five times and played in five Pro Bowls during the Packers' glory years in the sixties.

At 6-foot-3 and 245 pounds, Davis wasn't as big as other defensive ends of the day, but he was quick and he added the dimension of intelligence to a position that was noted more for brute strength. Davis learned the pass-rush moves of his opponents and was able to diagnose plays better than most ends. Before Davis, players would try to bull-rush a blocker over. But Davis used his hands to get rid of a blocker.

"I think he was the first real fast guy at defensive end," said Art Daley, a long-time Green Bay sportswriter. "He'd take off like a shot."

Y.A. Tittle, a Hall of Fame quarterback with the 49ers and Giants, once said Davis is "always towering over you, coming, coming all the time."

Davis was a team leader with size, speed, agility, and dedication. He never missed a game during his twelve seasons (1958–69). He played in six NFL championship games and the first two Super Bowls. At the time he retired, he had recovered 21 opponents' fumbles, just one shy of the all-time record.

He started his career in Cleveland, going back and forth between offense and defense. Upon being traded to Green Bay, Davis was told by Vince Lombardi, "Your reactions are just incredible. We feel with your quickness, you can be a great pass rusher."

And that's exactly what he was. As the final gun sounded at Super Bowl II, Raiders offensive tackle Harry Schuh reached out to grab Davis by the jersey. "You're the best I've ever gone against," Schuh said to Davis.

Davis' peers recall his ability to make things happen. "When a play had to be made," says Marion Campbell, "he just said, 'I'm going to make it,' and he did."

4. REGGIE WHITE—Widely regarded as the best defensive lineman in pro football today, Reggie White has tremendous size, power, and speed. After eight seasons with the Eagles, he now plays for the Packers.

"He dominates his position. He can turn games around," says Marion Campbell, who coached White for his first two seasons. "Quarterbacks are always thinking where he's at, and it makes them jittery."

"If you make a model of a defensive end, he'd be a great one," says Torgy Torgeson, a former lineman and now the Redskins' defensive line coach. "He can run with great speed."

After an All-Rookie season in 1985, White has started in the Pro Bowl the last seven seasons and has started 120 straight games. He has more sacks than any active player, and he's the only player ever to have more sacks (124) than games played (121).

"Reggie is definitely the best defensive end in pro football today, maybe of all time," says Dale Haupt, the Eagles' defensive line coach.

Ron Heller, an Eagles tackle who faced White in practice, notes, "People are so worried about [Reggie's] speed that they forget about his strength. They try to get out there and set up before he beats them with speed, so they're a little off balance and then he'll just throw them over. I've seen him put 300-pounders on their butt a bunch of times. No one guy can block him consistently. I mean, he's human, people can block him, but . . . it's inevitable he's going to beat you several times a game. You just know you're in for a real long afternoon and a potentially embarrassing one."

REGGIE WHITE

In August 1992, White and his Eagle teammates visited the Hall of Fame in Canton, Ohio, prior to the team's exhibition game against the Jets. It was his first visit to a place where he will probably be enshrined someday. "I don't think about that," he said. "It would be an honor to be elected into the Hall. I have more important things to think about, but as far as individual honors go, the Hall of Fame is the ultimate."

5. GENE BRITO—Who's Gene Brito? Perhaps the most overlooked player of all time at any position. Brito's nine-year NFL career was cut short by myasthenia gravis, a muscle disease. Brito played on some bad Redskin teams in the fifties before going to the Rams. He has been nominated for the Hall of Fame in past years.

Brito wasn't very big at 6-foot-1, 230 pounds, but he made up for it with quickness. "I thought I was quick off the ball," said Dick Modzelewski, "but I thought he was offside all the time, he was so quick."

Dick Stanfel, a former All-Pro guard with the Lions and Redskins, called Marchetti and Brito the two best defensive ends of the fifties. Brito was named to the Team of the Decade.

Brito was just a tough, hard-nosed football player who threw his body around and came hard every play. For ten years, he was one of the most volatile pass rushers in pro football.

Long-time NFL executive Don Klosterman said, "He was one of the most intense players I've ever seen. He was called 'Mean Gene' Brito for years, and yet he never had an unnecessary roughness penalty called on him his entire football career. He was incredibly tough, but no cheap-shot artist."

Former Bears quarterback Bill Wade commented, "It used to amaze me how he could play defensive end as well as he did. Actually, he wasn't big enough for the position. He made up for his size with his quickness."

But there's no better story about Brito than the one about a Steelers quarterback who was being eaten alive by Brito in a game and said to one of his linemen, "I can't take much more of Brito. I don't care if the referee's looking, if you can't keep him off me, hold him." The offensive tackle responded, "You kidding? I've *been* holding him."

6. ANDY ROBUSTELLI— Another small defensive end (6-foot, 230 pounds) of the fifties who was picked late in the draft (nineteenth round, from tiny Arnold College), Andy Robustelli started as a two-way end before settling in on defense, which led him to the Hall of Fame. He was All-Pro with the Rams twice and the Giants five times, and was an intelligent, quick, strong, durable player and inspirational leader who missed only one game in fourteen seasons. In 1962, Philadelphia's Maxwell Club selected him NFL Player of the Year, a rarity for a defensive lineman.

Robustelli used finesse on his pass rush and used his hands a lot. Because of his short size, he would rip underneath a blocker to get to a quarterback.

"He had surprisingly deceptive strength and great hands, and was always a guy who would come up with the big play for you," said Hall of Fame linebacker Sam Huff.

Robustelli says he could still play today, no question. "I don't think the size was any different," he says. "I played against some big men then, as big as today's players. I mean, there's never going to be a tackle in pro football as good as Jim Parker.

"You've got to know when to rush. Over-anxiety can hurt you. Knowing when comes with experience, and nothing else. There is only one way to play this game, and that is as hard and tough as you can."

Years ago, Giants coach Allie Sherman put it this way: "Watch Andy on a field and you'll be studying a real master. Terrific speed of mind, hands, and feet make him the best. But without his burning desire and his extra determination he'd be just an average football player."

7. DOUG ATKINS—"*There* was a terror." That's what Hall of Fame offensive tackle Bob St. Clair said of Doug Atkins, a 6-foot-8, 275-pounder who played for the Browns, Bears, and Saints from 1953 to '69.

"He could hurdle blockers," Torgy Torgeson said. "And for a big guy like

Doug to do it, it was something. When he got fired up, he was as good as anybody."

The knock against Atkins was that he played only when he wanted and wasn't consistent. "I don't know where he got that knock," said Dick Modzelewski. "He always played hard on Sundays. Teams always had to be very, very concerned about Mr. Atkins."

Atkins combined almost inhuman strength with size, skill, agility, and aggressiveness. "I have three moves," he once said, "inside, outside, and right over him."

He played in eight Pro Bowls in a nine-year span (1958 to '66) with the Bears, then turned in three strong seasons with the expansion Saints. Atkins was a devastating pass rusher who inspired terror over a long period and for more games (205) than any other lineman when he retired. He was inducted into the Hall of Fame in 1982.

The stories about him are legendary. Former Colts and Jets coach Weeb Ewbank said, "Atkins was the most magnificent physical specimen I had ever seen."

Ex-Colts quarterback Johnny Unitas used to say, "One of his favorite tricks was to throw a blocker at the quarterback."

And Jim Parker, one of Unitas' blockers, said, "I played against some mean ones, but I never met anyone meaner than Atkins. After my first meeting with him, I really wanted to quit pro football. He just beat the hell out of me. He rammed me back there so hard the only thing I could do was wave to Johnny (Unitas) as I went by. It was awful. Finally, my coaches convinced me that not every pro player was like Atkins." That's the greatest offensive lineman of all time, mind you.

They weren't. As Tom Fears, his coach in New Orleans, said, "They threw away the mold when they made Doug. There'll never be another like him."

8. LEN FORD—A fine two-way end who broke in with the Los Angeles Dons of the All-American Football Conference, Len Ford was All-Pro from 1951 to '55 after the Browns were merged into the NFL. He was also named to four Pro Bowls.

Ford was known for his pass rush, and, like Doug Atkins, he often leaped over blockers to get to a quarterback. Ford was an intimidating pass rusher who was one of the first defensive players whom fans found exciting to watch.

"He was a big guy who didn't have the quickness, but you couldn't move the guy out," recalled Dick Modzelewski.

Ford had great size (6-foot-5, 260 pounds), speed, strength, and great hands. He was the first Cleveland defensive player to be inducted into the Hall of Fame. In the 1954 NFL championship game, he intercepted two passes from his position on the line, returning one of them for a 46-yard touchdown in the

Browns' 56–10 victory over Detroit. When he retired after one final season with Green Bay in 1958, he held the league record for opponents' fumbles recovered with 20.

Perhaps a Detroit Lions scouting report from the mid-fifties best explains the respect all Cleveland opponents held for Ford. The report read: "LEN FORD—Really blows in. Does a lot of jumping over blockers. Does not predetermine this—if he sees a fellow going very low to block, he will jump over. Plays inside very tough. Must be blocked or he will kill the passer. He claims there is no one in the league who can take him out alone."

9. JACK YOUNGBLOOD—Merlin Olsen once paid Jack Youngblood the perfect compliment by calling him "the perfect defensive end."

Olsen wasn't far off. In fourteen seasons with the Rams (1971–84), Youngblood was named All-Pro five times and played in seven Pro Bowls from 1974 through '80. He has been one of the fifteen finalists for the Hall of Fame and should get in someday.

Youngblood, who was somewhat small for a modern-day end at 6-foot-4, 245 pounds, never missed a game during his career, playing in 202 straight. In 1979 he played in the NFC championship game and Super Bowl XIV with a stress fracture in his left leg, which he had suffered in the divisional playoffs.

Youngblood attributes his tenacity to Olsen. "Merlin taught me to play each play as if it was the only one in the ballgame, to go all out on each down as if it were the most important ever. Total commitment on every play."

And that's just what Youngblood did. John Robinson, his last coach with the Rams, said, "I think Jack Youngblood is the best football player I've ever been around. He is truly special. [He] has worked harder than any player I've ever seen to achieve greatness."

Longtime Vikings tackle Ron Yary said, "I'd have to say Jack Youngblood has always been the toughest [I ever faced]. It's his quickness, his intensity, plus he's smart. If he takes a chance, he takes it at the right time. He's so quick, he's not afraid to take an inside move when he still has outside responsibilities because he's quick enough to adjust."

10. HOWIE LONG—When Howie Long is healthy, he's among the best ever. In the mid-eighties, he was the most intimidating lineman in the league. He played in five consecutive Pro Bowls from 1983 to '87 and again in '89. He was named to the team of the eighties, and is heading into his thirteenth season.

Long went from a little-known rookie to a starter on one of the league's most respected defenses in one year. He has all the attributes of a model lineman—size (6-foot-5, 270 pounds), speed, explosive quickness and tremendous intensity. He draws double-teams regularly, which is the key to the Raiders' high sack totals of the last decade. Yet Long consistently ranks near the top of the league in sacks. And he also plays the run equally well, something that is rare for defensive linemen today.

"As an inside rusher, he has outside speed and quickness," said Chicago head coach Dave Wannstedt.

"When he was healthy, back in the mid-eighties, he was as good as they come," says football historian Jim Campbell.

Long also has a great rip move to get past blockers, and he is versatile enough to play anywhere on the line.

11. CARL ELLER—One of the mainstays of the Vikings' Purple People Eaters, Carl Eller, at 6-foot-6, 247 pounds, was an intense player and an imposing threat to quarterbacks from 1964 to '79. He was named to six Pro Bowls and was All-Pro from '68 to '71. He's been among the Hall of Fame's final fifteen candidates in the past.

The heart of the Minnesota defense, Eller became a regular as a rookie and held the job for fifteen years (he ended his career after one season in Seattle). He was a major factor in his team's long-term success at left end. He was extremely quick and mobile, excellent on rushing defense, and super as a pass rusher. In the three-year span from 1975–77, he had 44 sacks. By the time he had retired, he had recovered 23 opponents' fumbles, then the third-best mark in NFL history.

"He was a great pass rusher," said Marion Campbell. "He had as much leverage as anyone, and he used it."

Eller's first coach in Minnesota, Norm Van Brocklin, once said, "Things come easy to him. When he stretches out and gets after people, nobody can hold him."

12. L.C. GREENWOOD—Often overlooked on a defense that led Pittsburgh to four Super Bowl victories and included four current Hall of Famers, L.C. Greenwood had a reckless, free-wheeling style. He was known as a pass rusher, but he also played the run well.

He had the game of his career in Super Bowl IX, deflecting three passes and helping hold the Vikings to 23 yards rushing. A year later, he had three sacks of Roger Staubach in Super Bowl X. In thirteen seasons (1969–81), Greenwood played in six Pro Bowls and was named All-Pro two times.

Shortly before he retired, Greenwood said, "I believe that I've had the natural strength to do some things. And I've always had the outside quickness, that good, strong, first-penetration step. That's how I got to the quarterback nine times out of ten."

He was the last remaining player from Chuck Noll's first draft in 1969. At 6-foot-6 and 250 pounds, Greenwood looked more like a basketball player than a defensive end, although most of the offensive linemen he went up against were bigger than him. He led the Steelers in sacks six times.

13. HARVEY MARTIN—Ed "Too Tall" Jones got the press, but Harvey Martin was the Cowboys' most feared pass rusher in the seventies. The sack was Martin's trademark. He led or co-led the team in sacks (the Cowboys used to call them "traps") ten consecutive years from his rookie season in 1973 until '82.

In 1977, Martin had one of the finest seasons of any defensive player ever—a league-high and team-record 23 sacks, two fumble recoveries in the NFC championship game, co-MVP with teammate Randy White in the Super Bowl, and the NFL's Defensive Player of the Year. But that was the only season in which he was named All-Pro.

"Harvey is the guy who gets the front four going," said former Cowboy defensive back Dennis Thurman. "He's the leader, the catalyst. When he's going good, those linemen are unstoppable."

A tough, intimidating player who was a fiery competitor and an emotional leader, Martin missed only one game in eleven seasons (1973–83). He was a four-time Pro Bowler (1976–79).

14. LEE ROY SELMON—Lee Roy Selmon was the first Tampa Bay Buccaneer to be named All-Pro. In 1979 he also was the league's Defensive Player of the Year, helping to take his team—only in its fourth year of existence—to the NFC championship game, one step from the Super Bowl.

That year, Detroit coach Monte Clark commented, "He is simply amazing. Watching him is like watching a grown man at work among a bunch of boys."

In a nine-year career from 1976 to '84, Selmon was named All-Pro three times. He was named to six Pro Bowls (1980–85). His line coach at Tampa Bay, Abe Gibron, said, "Lee Roy has no peers at his position. If it were just a matter of putting him up against a single blocker, it would be no contest."

One of those single blockers was the Bears' Ted Albrecht. At halftime of one game against the Bucs, Albrecht remembers pleading to his line coach. "I said I never wanted to be buried at sea. I never wanted to get hit in the mouth with a hockey puck. And I didn't want to go out and play the second half against Lee Roy."

Defensive Tackles

At most positions, one or two names stand out as the greatest players ever. But at defensive tackle, a strong case can be made for any one of a handful of Hall of Famers. Bob Lilly, Merlin Olsen, Joe Greene, and Alan Page were all superior football players who played for many years and were named All-Pro a number of times. They also beat many quarterbacks into the ground.

As one current NFL scout, who wanted to keep his anonymity, said, "If I had to see a difference between [Lilly and Olsen], I would have to say that at their primes, Lilly was slightly better than Olsen, but that Olsen maintained that highest possible level for a longer period."

Others, like former Steelers coach Chuck Noll, liked Greene the most. "He's the best I've seen. He set the standard for us. There will never be another Joe Greene."

A defensive tackle is double-teamed much of the time. "It can be very discouraging," said Olsen. "I mean, you beat the guard and you feel like you're home free, and all at once the center pops you in the ribs."

Even the best defensive tackles are neutralized most of a game. They are usually run stuffers. Once in a while they get a sack.

"You can't get to the passer every time. If you reach him two or three times in a game, you have done a good job," said ex-Lion Alex Karras. "But, if you can occupy a blocker, or sometimes two blockers, maybe someone else will get by him and reach the passer."

1. BOB LILLY—Bob Lilly was amazingly quick and agile for someone his size (6-foot-5, 260 pounds), and his pursuit was so intense that some teams found it best to run straight at him. From 1964 to '72, he was named All-Pro every season except 1970, and he was named to eleven Pro Bowls in fourteen seasons.

"He's number one, without question," says Ed White, the former Vikings guard who faced Lilly many times.

"He knew before the snap where the ball was going all the time," noted former Eagles and Falcons head coach Marion Campbell. "He was a big-time playmaker who made things happen."

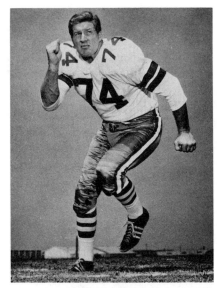

BOB LILLY

Stan Jones, a former All-Pro lineman for the Bears who is now the Browns' strength coach, said, "Lilly probably didn't have measurable strength, lifting-wise, but he was strong on the football field. He was able to dominate a blocking situation."

And former Dallas coach Tom Landry put it more simply: "A player like Bob Lilly comes along once in a coach's lifetime. He is something even a little bit more than great. Nobody is better than Lilly."

The keystone to Dallas' Doomsday Defense, Lilly was the Cowboys' first-ever draft choice (1961), their first player selected to a Pro Bowl (1962), the first to be named All-Pro (1964), and the first in the Hall of Fame (1980). Big, fast, and durable, he missed only one game in fourteen seasons. And, while defensive tackles aren't supposed to score touchdowns, Lilly scored four of them.

No defensive tackle was ever triple-teamed as much as Lilly. Outwardly intense, he was so upset after losing Super Bowl V that he broke his helmet by throwing it at the field. It was once said of Lilly: For his size, speed, and achievement, he might have been the greatest all-around athlete in pro football.

Hall of Famer Ernie Stautner, who was Lilly's position coach, said, "I didn't consider myself in Lilly's class. He could do things I could never do. He was the best defensive tackle I ever saw. I never realized just how strong Bob was until I was grading films one day. I watched the guards set up to take him, and then Bob made his move. He grabbed a guard by the shoulder pads and threw him bodily off to the side. This is really something, because an offensive lineman sets up awfully strong. . . . The people who play against him try to get set for his quickness. They think they know what to expect from studying films or even from playing against him before. But then they go up against him, and most of the time Bob's by them and into the backfield before they can get off the dime."

Known as "Mr. Cowboy," Lilly was once asked to define his philosophy of football. "Until you run over a few people, your moves or nothing else are going to work," he said. "You've got to stomp your guys into the ground a few times to get their respect."

MERLIN OLSEN

2. MERLIN OLSEN—In fifteen seasons, Merlin Olsen was selected to play in fourteen consecutive Pro Bowl games, more than any other player. He was extremely consistent and complemented Deacon Jones well. Olsen was a combination of Bob Lilly and Leo Nomellini—big and fast, although he used a thinking man's approach to the game. He's been called the prototype defensive tackle.

Outwardly gentle, he didn't often show that fiery kind of emotion that others did. But the biggest difference between the 6-foot-5, 270-pound Olsen and the rest of the great defensive tackles is that his Rams teams made the playoffs only six times and never made it to the championship game.

"Oly was two different players—strong and one of the smartest players I've ever been around," said Marion Campbell. "He had a strong upper body. Every time I see him do those flower commercials on TV, I say to myself, 'Is that the same old guy I used to head-butt out there?' "

Torgy Torgeson, who played and has coached in the NFL since the fifties, said, "Merlin had some of the best techniques of any lineman ever. He had great leverage and balance, and never was in a bad position. He was always ready to make a play."

Olsen, who was the Maxwell Club's Player of the Year in 1974, was a charter member of the Rams' Fearsome Foursome. "Until we came along, most fans only looked to the offensive players, primarily the quarterbacks and running backs, for excitement," he said. "The emergence of our line brought some attention over to the defense. We took great pride in our accomplishments. Knowing that we could influence the entire sport was very gratifying. We were innovators. We tried things like stunting and looping that no one dared try before. We could intimidate certain teams. Players got pysched out by the Fearsome Foursome label, and we thrived on it. It was fun knowing that every time we went on the field we were the guys who were going to make something happen."

Roman Gabriel, the Rams' quarterback during most of Olsen's career, said, "Merlin has great physical ability, but it's his dedication that amazes me. He works very hard every week, he plays hurt and he never says a word. He does not have bad games. He does not have bad practices. He is the best influence I can imagine for a young lineman. He pushes them; usually it's the other way around."

One of those young linemen was Jack Youngblood. "I remember one time a guy stepped on Merlin's hand with all those nylon cleats, ripped it wide open," Youngblood recalled. "He came back to the huddle holding it. I looked over and I could see all the bones. I almost fainted. Merlin said, 'Ah, it's all right.' "

George Allen, who coached Olsen for five seasons, said, "We never had a bad game from Merlin Olsen. You always got a good game from Oly, and, more often than not, you got a great game."

3. JOE GREENE—The first player drafted by Chuck Noll in the Steelers' rise to the Super Bowl, Joe Greene was All-Pro five times and played in ten Pro Bowls in thirteen seasons. Maybe no defensive player in the history of the game was so instrumental in turning a team around or had the long-term impact on his team as did Greene. A player like him is the difference between a good football team and an excellent one, or between an excellent one and a great one. He made everybody on his defense play that much harder.

Greene had a unique stance, lining up on an angle between the center and guard to disrupt the opposition's blocking assignments. He might have been the quickest lineman off the snap, and he was very agile, with great strength as his main asset.

"MEAN" JOE GREENE

"He was a tackle who had some of the attributes as a pass rusher of those guys on the outside," said Buck Buchanan, another Hall of Fame defensive tackle. "And he was kind of nasty. They didn't call him 'Mean Joe' for nothing."

"He's the one who made it go [for the Steelers]," said Torgy Torgeson. "He was quick and strong and awful hard to handle."

The heart and soul of the Steel Curtain defense that led Pittsburgh to four Super Bowl victories in the seventies, Green was the fourth overall draft choice in 1969, an unheralded player from North Texas State. That year, even though the Steelers finished 1-13, Greene was named the NFL's Defensive Player of the Year by a runaway margin (that honor came again in 1972 and '74). It didn't take long for one of his teammates, Andy Russell, to say, "Joe Greene is the most intimidating man in football. If he's angry, if he sees somebody take a cheap shot at a teammate, he's liable to do anything. The sight of that would strike fear in anyone."

At 6-foot-4 and 260 pounds, Greene could dominate a football game. He was a big, strong player with speed who hustled like crazy.

Jim Langer, the Hall of Fame center for Miami, once said, "You don't handle someone like Joe Greene. You don't even think of knocking him down. All you hope to do is neutralize him long enough so he can't jam up the play."

"Going after the quarterback is like playing king of the mountain," Greene once said. "When you get to the quarterback, you're on top of the mountain. He's the brains of the team. I learned a long time ago that if you killed the head the body would die."

Maybe that's why Noll, at Greene's Hall of Fame induction, said, "The thing that sets Joe aside from everybody is his attitude. . . . One of the other ones is he didn't like to lose."

4. ALAN PAGE—In 1971, Alan Page became the first interior lineman and first defensive player to be named the NFL's Most Valuable Player. He disrupted offenses in a manner seldom seen in pro football. Nine times he was voted All-NFC or All-Pro, and four times he was voted NFC Defensive Player of the Year.

"I have never seen a player have a year like he did," recalled former Chief Buck Buchanan of Page's 1971 season. "He was annihilating people. It was the kind of season you dream about as a player."

The most honored defensive lineman of his time, Page played off the line, almost like a linebacker in a three-point stance, and he read plays before reacting—sort of like his own flex defense—as opposed to most tackles who charge hard at the snap. Despite that, he had the power and quickness to get into the backfield before a play had developed.

ALAN PAGE

"Page has remarkable reaction to the snap of the ball. Most of the time he's into the blocker before the man can set up," said Bud Grant, his head coach.

The worst possible thing to try to do was run away from Page because he would hunt down a ballcarrier before he could get to the line of scrimmage. He could also run down the pass, and he was an excellent kick blocker. He blocked 28 punts or placekicks and recovered 23 opponents' fumbles.

"What I remember about him were his great inside moves and pursuit," said Hall of Famer Leo Nomellini.

Arguably the best pass-rushing defensive tackle ever, Page redefined the position of defensive tackle. In fifteen seasons, he made 173 sacks. Intelligent and hard-working with that amazing speed, quickness, and pursuit, Page made tackles sideline to sideline. He was born in Canton, Ohio, where he returned in 1988 to be enshrined into the Hall of Fame.

The best member of the famed "Purple People Eaters" defensive line, he played twelve and a half years with the Vikings. The 6-foot-4 Page, who usually played at 278 pounds, was waived in the middle of the season. He finished out his career at 220 pounds with four years in Chicago.

Neill Armstrong, who was his position coach in Minnesota and his head coach in Chicago, said, "One thing about Page that always impressed me is that I can never remember a game where he didn't give us his absolute best."

5. LEO NOMELLINI—Leo "The Lion" Nomellini was one of the most fierce players ever. He had a tremendous physical presence and might have been the strongest player of the fifties. He also probably equaled Alan Page's quickness. Nomellini was named the defensive tackle on the all-time All-Pro team picked in 1969.

"He was super strong. He could throw people around," recalls Marion Campbell, who both played and coached against Nomellini. "When he was fired up, I don't think anyone could block him."

"Determination was what I had," Nomellini said. "I took care of my position first, and then I went to help others."

In fourteen seasons Nomellini was named to the Pro Bowl ten times and played in 174 consecutive games. He is one of the few players ever to be named All-Pro on both offense and defense—as an offensive tackle in 1951 and '52, and then as a defensive tackle in 1953, '54, '57, and '59.

His debut with the 49ers was delayed by military service until 1950, when he was twenty-six years old. But he played the next fourteen years, and in that time didn't miss a game—including preseason, regular season, playoff, and Pro Bowl games, 266 in all. He was inducted into the Hall of Fame in 1969.

The first draft pick of the 49ers after they merged into the NFL in 1950, Nomellini was also a professional wrestler during his playing days. A native of Italy who became the adopted son of San Francisco's North Beach area, he drew record crowds for his world championship matches with Lou Thesz in the fifties.

Unbelievably strong at 6-foot-3, 265 pounds—he said his boyhood idol was Bronko Nagurski—Nomellini used to move offensive linemen around like they were so many paper dolls. When he was playing, there wasn't any question about a quarterback being "in the grasp," because when Nomellini latched on to someone, that quarterback went down.

"Fact is," said former 49ers teammate Gordy Soltau, "he was so quick, he never got his pants dirty. He was like a cat moving around in the middle of the line."

6. RANDY WHITE—In fourteen seasons, Randy White went to nine straight Pro Bowls (1978–86) and had a Cowboys-record eight consecutive All-Pro selections. He was co-MVP with Harvey Martin in Super Bowl XII and the Defensive Player of the Year in 1978. At his peak in the late seventies and early eighties, White was the NFL's best defensive lineman. He was extremely strong and quick.

"He capitalized on strength and speed," said Deacon Jones. "He was able to come off the ball real fast."

A star pupil of Ernie Stautner, White was the best defensive tackle of the last twenty years. He had better movement off the ball than any of his contemporaries, and he spent an unimaginable number of hours in the weight room trying to make sure that there was no lineman in the league stronger than he was. And, at 6-foot-4, 250 pounds, he was lighter than most of them.

"We've never had a player, and I've never seen a player, probably other than Ernie Stautner, who could match Randy's intensity from game to game," said ex-Dallas coach Tom Landry. "When Randy White lines up on you, he doesn't care if you're an All-Pro or if you're a rookie. You're going to get the same treatment. That makes him unique in this game. There is no doubt in my mind that he'll be in the Hall of Fame. He is a great competitor with a great heart, one of the really special ones I was fortunate to coach. He's in that group with the Roger Staubachs and the Bob Lillys."

White's nickname was "Manster"—half man, half monster. It was a nickname that fit, because he reduced the game of football to "seek and destroy." As Drew Pearson said, "I'm not talking people fear him just the day before the game. I'm talking all week long."

7. ERNIE STAUTNER—Ernie Stautner was small (6-foot-1, 235 pounds), but he gave the losing Steelers teams of the fifties a reputation as a tough group. Stautner could play anywhere on the line, and he roamed all over the field with excellent mobility and burning desire.

Stautner was the classic case of a superstar playing for a team that simply couldn't win. In fourteen years with the Steelers, he only once played on a team that won more than seven games or finished higher than third place. Yet he was selected to nine Pro Bowls and was inducted into the Hall of Fame in 1969, his first year of eligibility.

"He was small but quick," recalls Dick Stanfel, an All-Pro guard with Detroit and Washington in the fifties. "You came out with a bruise after you played him."

" 'The Horse' was unbelievable," says Jim Campbell. "If you had four of him, you'd have a championship team—he could make that much of a difference."

"He was great with his hands," said Dick Modzelewski, another longtime player and coach. "He'd use a head slap, his forearm, everything."

Stautner exemplified toughness. Although he wasn't big, he was aggressive, agile, and incredibly persistent. He would beat on a player until he would eventually wear him down. Few players ever played the position with more toughness, desire, or determination that Stautner, and few have had his results. When he retired, Stautner had tied the league record with three safeties and was third with 21 fumble recoveries.

Hall of Famer Jim Parker said, "That man ain't human. He's too strong to be human. . . . He's the toughest guy in the league to play against because he keeps coming head first. Swinging those forearms wears you down. That animal used to stick his head in my belly and drive me into the backfield so hard that, when I picked myself up and looked around, there was a path chopped through the field like a farmer had run a plow over it."

8. ART DONOVAN— "The best one I ever played against was Artie Donovan," said Jim Ringo, the Hall of Fame center for the Packers and Eagles. "He was a tough SOB."

"He knew the art of kicking ass in the NFL," said Deacon Jones.

Donovan was one of pro football's original big men. He was All-Pro four straight years, played in five consecutive Pro Bowls and was the first Colts player inducted into the Hall of Fame (1968). He stayed home and gave teammate Gino Marchetti free reign to rush the passer.

"If you took a look at Artie in his uniform, he looked like a football clown," said Dick Modzelewski. "He didn't have great quickness, but you couldn't run against him."

"And he was one helluva pass rusher, too," recalls Leo Nomellini. "He had an uncanny way of putting pressure on the quarterback if he was man-on-man with a guard."

The lovable Donovan was one of the most popular players in NFL history. He was a mainstay of Baltimore's defense throughout the fifties. He always appeared as if he were just a big, fat slob (6-foot-3, 270 pounds) whom the offensive linemen could out-quick. But then he would whip their butts with an amazing show of strength and surprising quickness. He just wanted to make mincemeat of anyone he faced, and he usually did.

Former Colts teammate Dick Szymanski said, "He was probably the most popular guy ever to play in Baltimore, and I'm talking about a town that loves guys like Johnny Unitas and Gino Marchetti."

Alex Karras, the All-Pro defensive tackle for Detroit, commented, "Artie Donovan is the best defensive tackle I've seen."

9. BUCK BUCHANAN—Buck Buchanan was the prototype for the tall, speedy defensive tackles in the game today. He played for the Chiefs from 1963 to '77, and at 6-foot-7 and 274 pounds, he always seemed to be where the ball was.

Hank Stram, Buchanan's former coach, said, "A big guy will be strong, and he might be quick, but he is rarely fast. Or sometimes he's strong and fast but not quick. But Buck had it all—big, strong, fast, and quick. Plus, he had a great attitude."

A six-time All-Pro, Buchanan had a remarkable combination of strength and quickness and durability. From 1963 to '75 he played in 181 of 182 games. He was inducted into the Hall in 1990.

"He revolutionized the game," says former Raiders coach John Madden. "Guys that size usually played on the outside. Buck was the first tall guy to play the inside. When a tall guy with his type of speed is rushing, he takes a couple of steps and then—boom—he would be on the quarterback."

Raiders owner Al Davis drafted Gene Upshaw in the first round of the 1967 draft for the express purpose of neutralizing Buchanan. Upshaw admits he didn't always get it done. "I was big, but Buck was bigger and stronger and turned me every which way but loose. When you played Buck, you couldn't sleep the night before a game," Upshaw said. "You don't imagine a guy 6-foot-

8, 300 pounds being so quick. You'd go to hit him, and it was like hitting a ghost."

The first player picked in the 1963 AFL draft, Buchanan made the first sack in a Super Bowl, and he helped lead the old AFL into respectability by the way he intimidated passers. He could overpower a defender or fake him and go around with tremendous quickness. As Buchanan once said, "Hell, I'm bigger by twenty or thirty pounds than just about anybody I go against. Sometimes I go straight at them just to let them know I'm there. But there's no way I can count on just overpowering my man. Just no way. Those dudes are big and they're strong, and the good ones are smart. I take pride in my quickness. No one makes All-Pro if he's not quick."

10. ARNIE WEINMEISTER—Arnie Weinmeister played only six seasons (1948 to '53), and the first two were in the All-American Football Conference. So it was a tribute that he made the Hall of Fame despite playing only four years in the NFL. He ended his NFL career to return to his native Canada and play in the CFL.

Weinmeister was one of the first defensive players to captivate fans the way an offensive player could, making him the first superstar defensive lineman in pro football. Weinmeister was big (6-foot-4) and aggressive, although he weighed only 235 pounds.

"He was an ex-fullback, and he came through the line like a knife through butter," says Bob Carroll. "Nobody could stop him. He was devastating."

Weinmeister could read plays so well, the story goes, that offensive players would look around in the huddle to make sure he hadn't sneaked in there with them. He was a tremendously agile performer who was All-Pro four seasons, when he was the key to the Giants defense.

"Arnie was bigger than most who played at that time, and he had great speed," said Tom Landry, then a defensive back with the Giants. "He could go sideline to sideline because he was probably the fastest lineman in the league. He could outrun most of our big backs."

Buck Shaw, the former coach of the 49ers, called Weinmeister "the best defensive tackle in pro football. Unless two men are assigned to him, he'll mess up the play every time."

When he was elected to the Hall of Fame in 1984, one voter said, "He was to the defensive tackle spot what Gale Sayers was to halfbacks—in a class by himself."

11. ALEX KARRAS—Although Alex Karras never made the Hall of Fame, he is still well-remembered among his peers. In his twelve-year career with the Lions, he never played in a championship game, but he was All-Pro in 1960 to '62 and again in '65 and played in four Pro Bowls.

He hurt his chances of making the Hall of Fame because he liked to laugh and downplay his abilities, like Artie Donovan. But he was as good as anyone for a long period of time.

"He did things I always wanted to do as a defensive tackle," commented Buck Buchanan. "He was very mean and very quick."

"He was the first of the 'jukers'—a guy who gave you a move to get around you," recalled Deacon Jones. "He didn't just come over the top of you."

Sports Illustrated's Paul Zimmerman said, "He's so identifiable as an actor that people forget how great a player he was, and for how long. He combined a tap-dancer's moves with a vicious hand-fighting technique."

At 6-foot-2, 250 pounds, Karras was small for a defensive tackle, but he was enormously strong for his size. He didn't get much national attention until he was suspended for gambling in 1963, but he was certainly known by then to NFL offensive linemen. He was a devastating package: incredibly talented, fanatically intense, and unsparingly aggressive.

In the sixties, former Lion teammate Les Bingaman said, "Karras doesn't want anybody to get the best of him on a football field. He's the best pass rusher in football, bar none. He's awfully quick on his feet and quick with his hands. That, plus he's mean and tough."

Nose Tackles

After the middle guard was phased out with the advent of the middle linebacker and the 4-3 defense in the fifties, nobody lined up over the center on a regular basis until the seventies. That's when the position of the nose tackle was born, one defensive lineman taking on two and three blockers at a time. By the mid-eighties, twenty-three of the twenty-eight NFL teams had switched to 3-4 defenses, but now teams seem to be switching back to the 4-3 defense because it puts more pressure on quarterbacks.

In pro football, there is no more frustrating position than nose tackle. It has been described as like trying to fight your way up the down escalator at a department store the day after Thanksgiving. A nose tackle is outnumbered on every play. He lines up across from the center, but once the ball is snapped, one or both of the guards slams down on him and he winds up wrestling with as many as three blockers, an unfair version of that old game, Odd Man Out. Few athletes can adequately play the position, and fewer even want to.

"The toughest part is psychological," said Curley Culp, who was the best nose tackle ever. "As a defensive lineman, your first instinct is to rush the quarterback. But nose tackles don't have the same chance to get a sack. You get off one blocker and there's another one waiting for you. You get off him and there's another. It's like that the whole game, so you just got to try and try and try. Part of the nose tackle's job is to tie up as many blockers as he can to free other guys to make the tackles. In a way, I'm almost a sacrificial lamb."

"Nose tackles are the key to 3-4 defense," says Marion Campbell, former coach of the Eagles and Falcons. "Most are great run defenders. Those guys get hit every play."

"They don't last very long," adds Howard Mudd, a former guard and current Chiefs offensive line coach. "They get beat up. Someone's always whacking at them."

So it takes a different temperament to play the position. And not all nose tackles think all the odds are against them.

"Most people think a nose tackle is there to take on two blockers and plug the hole," said the Bengals' Tim Krumrie. "I try to take on two blockers, plug up the hole, and make the tackle."

1. CURLEY CULP—Curley Culp played seven years for Kansas City, mostly as a defensive tackle lined up directly over the center. He went to Houston in 1974 and played in a three-man line for six more years. He could disrupt an offense that wasn't used to having a lineman play over center.

CURLEY CULP

"He had everything you would want in a nose tackle," says John Sandusky, Miami's long-time offensive line coach. "He was short, so he could get underneath a center. He was quick and strong. God put him on earth to play nose tackle."

"Nobody playing, then or now, is as good as Curley," agrees Buck Buchanan, his linemate with the Chiefs. "He had a knack for making big plays inside. He was incredible."

"Defensive linemen watch other defensive linemen for technique," says former Dolphin Bob Baumhower. "I used to watch him and Jim Langer go at it."

Larry Little, a Dolphins guard, used to go at it with Culp, too. He recalled a game in 1975 when "Curley hit me upside my head. I said, 'Damn, Curley, what are you trying to do to me?' He started laughing. I don't like to play in front of Curley. I can feel it in my entire body when I play in front of Curley. It's beaten up."

Former Pittsburgh center Mike Webster said, "Culp is awesome, he's so strong and quick."

Culp was built like a tree stump at 6-foot-1 and 270 pounds. He had a low center of gravity that enabled him to get under blockers and drive by them when they fired out. He was quick, strong, and vicious, and he reminded opponents more of a bear than a man. He also had enormous natural strength, which he developed tossing fifty-pound barrels on his father's farm. He also was an expert in the art of Greco-Roman wrestling. He was the NCAA heavyweight wrestling champion his senior season at Arizona State and was undefeated his last two intercollegiate seasons. He was a member of the 1968 U.S. Olympic wrestling squad.

However, Culp really preferred to play in a 4-3 defense. "I really don't care for the three-man front. It doesn't give you a chance to express yourself."

Former Houston defensive coordinator Ed Biles called Culp "the smartest defensive lineman I've ever been around. He knows formations, situations, what he's expected to do. If you need him to eat up two people to try and free up somebody one on one, he'll do it and not worry about the glory of a sack. He's a real pro."

BILL WILLIS

2. BILL WILLIS—From 1946 to '53, Bill Willis played middle guard (over the center in a five-man line), which is equivalent to a modern-day nose tackle. Although he would be too small to play today, he was fast and could get across the line and catch a runner in the backfield. He rolled off blocks rather than charging straight ahead.

"He was one of the original quick guys," remembers Dick Modzelewski. "He could get under the center's legs and get to the quarterback."

One of the first blacks to play in modern-era pro football, Willis was the hub of the Cleveland defense on a team that enjoyed perhaps the longest streak of success in pro football history. In the eight years he played, the Browns never failed to win a division title. They won four AAFC championships and one NFL title. He was named All-League seven of those years and was inducted into the Hall of Fame in 1977.

He weighed 210 but admitted "they listed me in the program at 225 pounds. It was a psychological thing. Paul Brown didn't want the other teams to know I was really that small."

Willis had great speed and agility and would often drop off the line to play what later would be middle linebacker. But it's on the line where he is remembered best.

Bears Hall of Famer Bulldog Turner said, "About the first guy that ever convinced me that I couldn't handle anybody I ever met was Bill Willis. They called him 'The Cat.' He would jump right over you."

3. BOB BAUMHOWER—Bob Baumhower was unusually tall (6-foot-5) for a nose tackle. Still, he was voted to five Pro Bowls in eight seasons before retiring over a contract dispute in 1985. Whereas most nose tackles tie up one or two offensive linemen and rarely get in on a play, Baumhower made an incredibly large number of tackles (556) in his first four seasons. He was one of the few nose tackles who played every down.

"He was tall and rangy and people could get up under him because of his long frame," remembers Curley Culp. "But he was cagey. He could do things from the way he lined up. He just set in there and took the pounding, although no one likes to do that."

Former Jets center Joe Fields said, "Baumhower was strong, but he would try to trick you more often. He would act like he was going to jump offsides one way and then go the other way, and then he'd use a head-butt and pull you."

4. FRED SMERLAS—Nose tackles don't usually last fourteen seasons, but Fred Smerlas isn't a typical nose tackle. A throwback to the old days, Smerlas was a tough, every-down player for eleven seasons with Buffalo (1979–89), starting a club-record 155 consecutive games and not missing a game for ten seasons. Since then, he has been a situational player for San Francisco and New England.

"He's one of the best," says Curley Culp. "He has a low center of gravity and good strength."

The 6-foot-4, 291-pound Smerlas was selected to play in five Pro Bowls, including four straight from 1980–83. He was never a great pass rusher, but he used his quickness to put pressure up the middle.

"He's real intense," said Bob Baumhower. "He has good size and quickness."

5. JOE KLECKO—Joe Klecko is the only player in NFL history to make the Pro Bowl at defensive end, defensive tackle, and nose tackle. From 1977–87, he was a force against both the run and the pass even though he played with two bum knees most of his career.

A four-time Pro Bowler with the Jets, he actually played most of his career at end and tackle. But he fit the nose tackle mold better than the other positions.

"Joe is a mutation," said former Jets teammate Joe Fields. "He has two things that cause the biggest problem for an offensive line: quickness and strength, an awesome combination."

LINEBACKERS

*Linebackers are the strangest guys of all. . . . They're people who just
plain love to run into things. They'll hit you as you go by them the
way other people shake hands.*
AHMAD RASHAD

Twenty-five years ago, the middle linebacker was the key player on any team's defense. It was the day of Dick Butkus and Ray Nitschke. They made the tackles because plays were funneled their way. Meanwhile, the outside linebackers were the unsung players, rarely noticed.

These days it's Lawrence Taylor, Derrick Thomas, and Cornelius Bennett who get noticed all the time. They're the key players on defense, rushing the passers and getting the sacks. And it's the inside linebackers these days who don't draw much notoriety. All they do is make a lot of tackles.

Football has evolved from five-man defensive lines to four-man and now three-man fronts, and the position of linebackers has changed with it. In the 1960s, outside linebackers dropped into pass coverage often. Today, outside linebackers are more like defensive ends in the five-man fronts of the fifties. They're pass rushers first and pass defenders last.

Linebackers have been called the best athletes on a football team. They have been called the meanest hitmen in the game. And they have been called the brains of a defense.

"Linebacker is one of the most difficult and challenging positions to play," said Hall of Famer Bobby Bell. "You have to worry about the pass, the run, man-to-man coverage, containing the play, screens and draws. It's a spur-of-the-moment position. There is a lot of thinking there and a lot of responsibilities."

"I think linebacking is the most difficult job on the football field," concurred ex-Packer Dave Robinson. "When you say a quarterback is out to fool the defense, what you mean is that a quarterback is out to fool the linebackers. The quarterback knows what the front four will do: rush. And he doesn't have time to fool the deep backs. He's out to make three linebackers think *pass!* Or he's out to make you think *run!* A lineman worries about stopping runs. A deep back worries about stopping passes. A linebacker's got to worry about stopping runs and passes."

Three decades ago, middle linebackers got all the ink. They were the glory guys, making 10 to 15 tackles a game. Now it's the same thing with the outside linebackers because they are the pass rushers.

Middle Linebackers

One word describes middle linebackers: intensity. But, as Maxie Baughan, a former Pro Bowl linebacker who's now the Buccaneers' linebackers coach, said, "You'd be intense, too, if you stood in the middle and got hit from both sides."

"To be a middle linebacker, you have to be like a lion out on the field," said Hall of Famer Chuck Bednarik. "You look for prey with a killer instinct. It's search and destroy."

"To me," said Mike Singletary, the just-retired Bear, "playing middle linebacker is like war. It is an opportunity to get out there and know what is happening on every play and meet the challenge to stop it from happening."

"Whether you're talking about Nitschke or Butkus or [Joe] Schmidt, you're repeating yourself," said ex-Falcon linebacker Tommy Nobis. "They're all out of the same mold. They're rough, tough guys who played aggressively, even when they're hurt. The linebacker is the prototype of a pro football player."

"It comes back to the basics," agreed Schmidt. "Linebackers have a higher, more intense level of competitiveness. They don't like to lose. That's what separates them. The mentality is, 'I have to be in on every tackle.' But it's an easy position to play. If you could read the fullback and have intuition, if you liked to be aggressive, that's what a linebacker is."

Middle linebacker is the No. 1 enemy of offense, and a good middle linebacker is in on two out of every three plays. He usually has two or three people trying to knock him down on every play. He has to fight them off and make the stop. The grind of being in the middle takes its toll, so it takes a rugged individual to play middle linebacker.

Said Chiefs Hall of Famer Willie Lanier, "Playing middle linebacker is sort of a science. The key factor is to make instantaneous response to a given stimuli. It involves mathematics, geometry, and angles. There is, it's true, great joy in exploding into a man, making a tackle they call the big hit. But you cannot do that on every play. So often you must control your own aggressiveness."

DICK BUTKUS

1. DICK BUTKUS—Dick Butkus is "the crown jewel of middle linebackers," according to former Eagles middle linebacker Bill Bergey. In nine seasons (1965–73), a career that was shortened considerably by injuries, Butkus played in eight Pro Bowls. He was also named All-Pro six times. He intercepted 22 passes and recovered 25 opponents' fumbles, a record at the time he retired. If records were kept of fumbles forced, Butkus would undoubtedly own the all-time mark. His resume is particularly impressive in light of the weak Bears teams he played on.

"Butkus played linebacker like it was meant to be played," says Tommy Nobis. "He was one of the most intimidating linebackers. He would take a guy down and then twist his head. He realized we were in the entertainment business before we did. He enjoyed what he was doing, and he worked at being the star."

By his own admission, he played every game as if it were his last one. Playing at 6-foot-3, 245 pounds, Butkus was hailed as the meanest linebacker to ever play the game. He had speed, strength, quickness, and an exceptional instinct for the ball. Teams didn't run on the Bears because of Butkus. The one complaint was about his speed, but not many people realized he was also excellent in zone pass-coverage.

Pro football historian Jim Campbell says, "Butkus may have been the best defensive player of all time. He had a great nose for the ball. He truly intimidated people, and that's scaring some pretty hard-nosed characters."

Russ Thomas, the late general manager of the Lions, once called Butkus "an annihilating son of a bitch."

But Butkus said, "I play the game the way I think it should be played, and if they think it's animalistic, well, they wouldn't be calling me God if I stood out on the field above everybody else, so they find another word for it. Still, and all, I must be doing something for them to be calling me things. It doesn't bother me."

Tommy Prothro, who coached the Rams late in Butkus' career, once said, "I never thought any football player could play as well as writers describe their play. But Butkus comes as close as anybody. He looks fat, clumsy and awkward, but he kicks the devil out of everybody. And if you pass, he's right there, too."

Late in his career, Butkus said, "My goal is to be recognized as the best. No doubt about it. Anybody and everybody makes one All-Pro team or another. You read magazines before the season starts and they're full of All-Pro this and All-Pro that. Everybody's All-Pro. But when they say middle linebacker, I want them to mean Butkus."

They did then and they still do.

2. JACK LAMBERT—Look up Jack the Ripper in an encyclopedia, and you'll see a picture of Jack Lambert. He had great speed, quickness, and extraordinary knowledge of opposing offenses. At 6-foot-4, he was tall—perhaps too tall—but he played at only 218 pounds, light for the position.

"That's a good weight for a linebacker," said Chuck Bednarik. "You don't need all that weight. You just need speed and guts. Lambert was an ornery guy."

"He was all-out, intimidating people," said Tommy Nobis. "When he put a lick on a quarterback or a running back, they knew who hit them."

Lambert was All-Pro seven times from 1975 to '83 for the Steelers, and he played in nine straight Pro Bowls, more than any other player of his era. He was the NFL's Defensive Player of the Year in 1976 and '79. He also intercepted 28 passes. The youngest star on Pittsburgh's great defensive teams in the seventies, Lambert was inducted into the Hall of Fame in 1990.

"Of all the great middle linebackers in the history of the game . . . what set Jack apart was his ability to defend against the pass," said Lambert's former teammate, Jack Ham. Another ex-Steeler, Andy Russell, said, "If you compare Lambert with Butkus or Nitschke, Lambert was comparable against

JACK LAMBERT

the run to them, although not as impressive. But he could play pass coverage in a way they never dreamed of."

Lambert made the comparison this way: "I try to get to the football, as opposed to the Butkus and Nitschke types who stood in the middle and dared you to knock them down. If I can run around a blocker and make the tackle, I'll do it."

Lambert is best remembered for his toothless snarl and his vicious tackling, but it was his quickness—the ability to get to the ballcarrier in the first place—that was the real secret to his success.

But Lambert didn't think he would be big enough to play middle linebacker. "I play the way that suits me best," he remarked. "I weigh around 218. Most of your middle linebackers go 230, 235. Some of them are 250. Because of my size, I have to be active and aggressive. But that's as far as it goes. I tackle somebody as hard as I can and then get up and go back to the huddle. I play clean if you play it clean. If you don't . . ."

Then he added: "We're *supposed* to be intimidators."

RAY NITSCHKE

3. RAY NITSCHKE—Ray Nitschke was the immovable force in front of opposing ballcarriers. He was also one of the hardest tacklers ever to play pro football. A real leader and the core of the Green Bay defense, he was named All-Pro only three times in fifteen seasons from 1958 to '72 with Green Bay. But Nitschke was voted the linebacker on the NFL's all-time team that was chosen in 1969 during the height of his career.

He will always be remembered as one of the greatest defensive players ever.

"He looked the part," said Tommy Nobis. "He was so damn ugly with his helmet on and the mask. He walked and ran like a football player, and sounded like one."

Former Eagles linebacker Bill Bergey agreed: "He was toothless, ugly. He would run through walls."

"Nitschke was so close to Butkus," said Joe Horrigan, the Pro Football Hall of Fame's historian. "The only difference was that Butkus called signals. But maybe Nitschke hit harder than Butkus. He threw more people than Butkus."

Nitschke was inducted into the Hall of Fame in 1978, the first Packers defender from the sixties to be enshrined. He was an excellent pass defender, as witnessed by his 25 interceptions. He was particularly fast, and he had amazing lateral quickness and mobility for someone of his size (6-foot-3, 235 pounds). But he made his name as a savage run-stopper.

"He hits harder than anybody I've ever seen," said former teammate Paul Hornung. "He likes to hit. He loves to hit."

Nitschke answered, "It's a violent game. It's a survival type of thing. You've got to like contact. If you're not willing to hit people, you don't belong on the field. You have to hit them before they hit you and hit them harder than they hit you. You want them to remember you're there."

Like most great players, he picked up some of his strengths from other stars. "I took parts from every one of them," he admitted. "The angles they took. The drops. They way they played the pass. Angles for sweeps. The way they attacked the blockers. You pick out each player's things they did well."

Former Rams great Les Richter said, "It's not so much his speed or even his quickness. In his case, it's a desire to make the play, an ability to get to the right spot ahead of everybody else. . . . As a leader, he is without a peer."

4. JOE SCHMIDT—A seventh-round draft pick who started his career at outside linebacker, Joe Schmidt moved into the then-evolving middle linebacker position in 1955 and immediately became an NFL institution. He was chosen All-Pro nine times in a career that spanned from 1953 to '65 with Detroit. He wasn't big or fast, but he had an exceptional knack for diagnosing plays and making tackles. He also had 24 career interceptions. Schmidt was the first great middle linebacker, a hard hitter and a team leader.

JOE SCHMIDT

"He used to hide behind [defensive tackles] Alex Karras and Roger Brown, and he was hard to get to," said former Vikings center Mick Tingelhoff. "He could run like a deer."

"He was always in the right place at the right time," said Ray Nitschke.

Schmidt said, "I was lucky to come along when the two-platoon era was still in effect in college ball. . . . It's instinctive. Why is Willie Mays a good hitter? What makes a good race car driver? You can teach an athlete certain things, but the natural instinct must be right there."

Buddy Parker was the Lions' head coach when Schmidt turned pro. "His style of play brought about the zone defenses, revolving defense and the modern defensive look in pro football," Parker said.

At 6-foot and 222 pounds, Schmidt was one of the smallest middle linebackers to star for a team. But he was strong enough to overpower blockers and fast enough to follow a run or drop back into pass coverage.

That's why, when Norm Van Brocklin, then the Vikings coach, was asked hypothetically to choose a player that he could start a team with, he answered, "I'd select Joe Schmidt to form the core of my team."

Former Lions teammate Wayne Walker, another All-Pro linebacker, said, "They don't get an extra yard when Schmidt tackles them—a pop, that's it."

And John Henry Johnson, another Hall of Famer, commented, "He's always in the way."

Schmidt's Lions teammates voted him the team's Most Valuable Player four times. He also served as Detroit's head coach for six seasons after he retired. He was inducted into the Hall of Fame in 1973.

MIKE SINGLETARY

5. MIKE SINGLETARY—Mike Singletary was the best middle linebacker of the last decade, matching the intensity of Dick Butkus and Jack Lambert. He was the NFL Defensive Player of the Year in 1985 and '88, and he played in ten consecutive Pro Bowls from 1983–92. He's a sure future Hall of Famer.

An incredibly hard hitter, Singletary was too small (6-foot) and too slow, but he was strong against the run and, especially early in his career, he could run with receivers on pass coverage. He has been called "Butkus with control."

"No one is more intense," said Tommy Nobis. "You can see it in his eyes. He's a little undersized, but he's a student of the game, and he approaches it like a coach does."

"He is totally focused on what he does," said Bill Bergey. "I'd love to have played next to him. Every bit of talent God gave to him, he has used to the utmost."

New York Giants general manager George Young said, "Singletary has really overcome his lack of height, and he deserves a lot of credit. He's had a great career for a guy that size."

Singletary practically willed himself to be great. The Bears' run-stopper, he was first or second on the team in tackles every year except his rookie season in 1981. He played the second-most games in Bears history.

The third in a line of great middle linebackers playing for Chicago the last four decades after Bill George and Dick Butkus, Singletary's play was infectious.

Butkus said, "Mike's been able [to dominate] as a player and a leader. A lot of guys play the game but don't show the enthusiasm as much, which becomes contagious to other players. That's a strong point in Mike."

Shortly before Singletary retired, Joe Schmidt, the Lions' Hall of Famer, remarked, "He is a throwback to the old days. He could play in any era. He should be rated right up there with any who have played the position. Great instincts, a great nose for the ball. And a great leader."

And one of the greatest middle linebackers of all time.

6. WILLIE LANIER—Think of Kansas City's Willie Lanier and you think of a powerful hitter. But, along with forcing a lot of fumbles (and recovering 15), Lanier was also a stellar pass defender—the best among middle linebackers, according to some—finishing his eleven-year career (1967–77) with 27 interceptions. He was named All-League or All-AFC eight times.

Ermel Allen, who was a longtime assistant coach with the Cowboys, once said, "You hear a lot about Dick Butkus and Tommy Nobis, but Willie Lanier is really the best middle linebacker in pro football."

He was certainly the AFL's best middle linebacker, although most people didn't recognize his abilities until he played in a Super Bowl. That's when people started to notice what a powerful performer he was. "I'm a pretty well-behaved guy all week," he said. "But something happens out there on Sunday. I put on a helmet and become a little schizoid. I go out to fight the war."

The first black to star at middle linebacker, Lanier was 6-foot-1 and 245 pounds, which gave him what it took for his often devastating hits. He wasn't nicknamed "Contact" for nothing. But he did his job with intellect as much as with his skills.

At Lanier's Hall of Fame induction in 1986, Chiefs owner Lamar Hunt called him "a forceful bear of a man whose strength and intensity and striking power set new standards for the game. He was the immovable rock who had to be avoided at all costs by the offense."

7. TOMMY NOBIS—Some people rate Tommy Nobis much higher and feel, if he had not played for an expansion team, he might be the all-time great.

"You're only as good as your front four," said Herb Paterra, a former pro linebacker and longtime NFL assistant coach. "Nobis was a great linebacker, but expansion teams never get the continuity you need."

"If he would have been on a better team with better legs, look out," says Jim Campbell. "He was everything you wanted in a middle linebacker. Nobody hit harder than Nobis."

But being the star of an expansion team (Atlanta, 1966–76) meant Nobis got the attention other Falcons didn't receive, almost as much as Butkus and Nitschke.

"I wasn't the strongest or fastest player out there," Nobis said, "but I was able to make plays with desire and the will to do so. Certainly, I would have liked to have been Jack Lambert and line up behind the Steel Curtain, or be Sam Huff and line up in New York behind those guys, or be Lee Roy Jordan behind Bob Lilly and those guys, but there's not a darn thing I can do about that. Loyalty meant something back then."

Nobis was named All-Pro only one time, his second season when the Falcons were 1-13. He played in five Pro Bowls. At 6-foot-2, 240 pounds, Nobis was faster than most of the great middle linebackers.

Don Perkins was one of the NFL's best fullbacks in the sixties. He recalled a game in 1967 against Nobis. "I got pretty sick and tired of reading about Nobis all week," Perkins said. "I knew the guy couldn't be *that* good. Well, he *is* that good. He's the toughest middle linebacker I ever played against. I got to block on him all day. Half the time I couldn't find him, and when I did find him, I wished I hadn't."

8. BILL GEORGE—Bill George invented the position of middle linebacker, or so the story goes. A middle guard for the Bears in the fifties, George took a step back from the line during one game, stood up and became a middle linebacker. Thus he was able to rush the passer, play the run, or drop back into pass coverage.

George played in eight Pro Bowl games and was named All-Pro as many times during his fifteen-year career (1952–66). He was strong at clogging up the middle, and was also one of the best inside blitzers ever. George was very intelligent. He went to the Rams after his skills had diminished and was still a very effective player. The 6-foot-2 230-pounder was inducted into the Hall of Fame in 1974.

Former Eagles and Browns coach Nick Skorich once said of George, "He's the fastest man off the ball in the league."

And Maxie Baughan, a nine-time Pro Bowl outside linebacker who played with George in Los Angeles in 1966, said that year, "I've never seen anyone like him. Bill and I watch a lot of game films together. When the offensive team gets set, Bill will sit in his chair and call the play. He's uncanny. He's right so often that it's frightening."

Abe Gibron, the former Eagles offensive guard, once said, "Bill George was the first great middle linebacker. He brought all the romance and charisma to the position."

9. SAM HUFF—Go just about anywhere in the country, except New York, and ask football people if Sam Huff belongs in the Hall of Fame and a lot of them will say no. "Don't quote me," said one Hall of Famer, "but it's that New

York press (that gave Huff all the exposure). In New York, they'll make you look like a god."

A half-hour CBS special in 1960, "The Violent World of Sam Huff," also helped, as did one championship and six division titles during his eight years with the Giants. But Huff was an excellent player, a tough, hard hitter who was All-NFL four times and made five Pro Bowls during a thirteen-year career that began in 1956 with the Giants and ended with the Redskins.

David Neft, a football historian and co-author of *Pro Football: The Modern Era,* put it this way: "Would he have been a Hall of Famer without Harland Svare and Bill Svoboda playing alongside him? If Ken Anderson had played for Bart Starr's team, who would have made the Hall of Fame?"

Another pro football historian, Bob Carroll, says, "Huff was a little over-rated because he played in New York, and he would sit on the bench if he was on the same team with some of those other guys. But he was *not* that overrated that he doesn't belong in the Hall."

Huff was quick, powerful, and durable, with a nose for the ball. He was noted for his hard-hitting duels with the likes of Jim Brown and Jim Taylor.

Huff once said, "If a man was destined for anything, I say I was destined to be a middle linebacker. I don't know any other position I could have played on a professional football team."

10. MIKE CURTIS—"Now we're talking about crazy men," laughed ex-Packer Dave Robinson when he was asked about Mike Curtis. "But I mean reckless abandon, not foolishness. Curtis was a short Hendricks or Lambert—you know, 'This is my turf; don't invade it.' When it was third-and-two, that's the guy you wanted in the trenches."

In one game, a Baltimore fan dashed out onto the playing field, and Curtis clubbed the man with his taped forearm. "The guy should have known better," said Curtis. "That's my turf. Keep off my turf."

Curtis played in four Pro Bowls during a fourteen-year career (1965–78) with Baltimore and Washington, playing slightly more at middle linebacker than on the outside. He was an outstanding blitzer who had a ferociousness about him.

"I used to watch and study Curtis," recalls Bill Bergey. "He had a knack of coiling, like a rattlesnake, and getting every bit of his 232-pound body into a ballcarrier."

Curtis was nicknamed "Mad Dog" and "The Animal," and he played his nicknames to the hilt. "When I'm on the field I feel like a Cossack. [But] I'm never out to hurt anybody. I'm just out to play hard and be aggressive and not make a mistake that costs a first down or touchdown. I like to be called aggressive rather than vicious because I'm a competitor, not a bully."

While everyone focused on Curtis' image, Green Bay quarterback Bart Starr was saying, "Mike Curtis is the most underrated linebacker I've ever faced."

And former pro center Bill Curry added, "What Mike Curtis is more than anything else is pure football player. Excellence is more important to him than acceptance by teammates or anyone else. He is a man apart; a purist, a totally dedicated football player obsessed by winning."

Outside Linebackers

Today, outside linebackers gain most of their renown as pass rushers. In the days of 4-3 defenses, they were just as likely to cover a receiver as they were to rush the passer. "I loved playing pass coverage," Hall of Famer Jack Ham said. "Some people think of a linebacker only as a guy who gets to the hole in a hurry and hits hard. To me, that's less than half of being a linebacker. You've got to do your job on pass coverage, or else you're a liability."

Hall of Famer Bobby Bell saw it another way: "I've played just about everything. I played on both lines and I played fullback and tight end. But my favorite spot is where I'm playing today—outside linebacker. You are involved in every kind of play. You stop runs and you stop passes. I love open-field tackles and I love to hit. It's a great position."

Outside linebackers play in both 4-3 and 3-4 defenses, although those in the 3-4 defenses are better known. They have very different roles, and the recent emphasis on pass defense and situational substitution has altered the position. Today, the position is such that there is not a lot of difference between outside linebackers and undersized defensive ends; both are primarily pass rushers. Historian David Neft said, "Lawrence Taylor plays a position that used to be a defensive end. Forty years ago, he would not have been an outside linebacker."

But all outside linebackers are supposed to be big enough to shut down power runners and be dominating on sweeps. And they have to be able to stay with receivers and backs out of the backfield on pass coverage.

As Dave Robinson said, "You need great peripheral vision. You have to see what's coming while looking ahead. You need quick lateral movement. In three-fourths of a second, you'll find yourself blocked."

1. LAWRENCE TAYLOR—Few players in the history of the game ever made the impact Lawrence Taylor did. He totally redefined the position of the outside linebacker, making one of its primary functions rushing the passer. But, in Taylor's case, it doesn't look like the man who set the trend will be surpassed by the greats who will come along after.

No outside linebacker has ever been more dangerous and more feared than L.T. More than any other player in football over the last decade, he could disrupt an offense. He was a combination of athleticism and brute force. He could do it all—sack a quarterback with one hand, catch swift running backs from behind for a loss, and run with receivers out in the open.

"Lawrence Taylor is the best outside linebacker who ever lived—bar none," says former Eagles coach Buddy Ryan. "Before him, nobody played the position that way."

Taylor was selected to ten consecutive Pro Bowls (1981–90) and was the only unanimous selection on the Team of the 1980s chosen by the Hall of Fame. In 1986 he became only the second defensive player to be named league MVP (along with Alan Page). He suffered torn ligaments midway through the season in 1992 and will return for 1993.

LAWRENCE TAYLOR

At his first press conference at Giants Stadium after being picked second in the 1981 draft, Taylor said, "I like to eat quarterbacks in the backfield." And for the next twelve seasons he stuffed his face with quarterbacks. He has 136.5 career sacks, tops on the all-time list (sacks weren't made an official stat until 1982).

"Lawrence Taylor, defensively, has had as big an impact as any player I've ever seen come into the game," said John Madden. "I think Lawrence Taylor changed the way defense is played, pass-rushing is played, the way linebackers play, and the way offenses block linebackers."

"It was the ultimate respect that teams thought about him when planning their offense," said David Neft. "If you were an offensive coordinator, you had to devote part of your game plan to L.T., and that made him a unique force."

Mike Singletary, like Taylor a sure Hall of Famer, said, "The biggest thing I've noticed about Lawrence Taylor is that his motor never stops. It's always the same—he's always going to the ball."

Fans think of sacks when they think of Taylor. But he was also great as a pass defender and he could control an offense's entire running philosophy. Teams learned to run at Taylor rather than away from him because he was so active. But the beauty of Taylor was that he could dominate a game while playing on the flank, as compared with the stars of previous decades who played in the middle.

"L.T. set the standard with his speed, his strength, his all-out play," says Larry Wilson, who was the best safety ever. "A lot of players have tried to copy his style, but there will never be another L.T."

JACK HAM

2. JACK HAM—Jack Ham was All-Pro for seven consecutive seasons from 1973 to '79. He played in eight Pro Bowls and was the NFL's Defensive Player of the Year in 1975. He also was the only unanimous choice on the NFL's Team of the Decade.

Ham based his game on speed and intelligence. He was smaller than most linebackers of his day (6-foot-1, 212 pounds) but he often played like a defensive back in pass coverage, as evidenced by his 32 career interceptions. He also recovered 19 opponents' fumbles.

Former teammate Andy Russell recalls that Ham "was the fastest Steeler for five yards, even including our wide receivers and running backs. He would come off the ball and explode into a player." After Russell retired in 1976, he noted how his life would change in one way: "Now I'll have to pay for the privilege of watching Jack Ham play football."

A second-round draft pick from Penn State, Ham wouldn't rip a player's head off like Butkus or Nitschke, but he could deliver a blow. As a rookie, he had a sensational training camp, and he clinched a starting job after intercepting three passes in the preseason finale. Along with Joe Greene and L.C. Greenwood, Ham was a key element in an exceptionally strong left side of the Pittsburgh defense during the team's Super Bowl years.

"I was pretty aware out there," Ham recalls. "You can make a lot of plays if you're a split-second ahead of somebody else."

"Ham was one of the first small, quick linebackers, and he turned the position into a threat to be an intercepter," said Dave Robinson.

"He was one of the more intelligent players to ever play the position," said Maxie Baughan. "He was able to diagnose plays. You couldn't ever fool him."

Near the end of Ham's NFL career, a celebrity roast was staged in his honor to aid a charity cause. Steelers coach Chuck Noll was asked to speak. Noll went to the podium and said only, "How do you roast someone who is perfect?"

A dislocated toe in his left foot caused Ham to miss Super Bowl XIV, and he never completely recovered during his final three seasons. "The films don't lie," Ham said at the time of his retirement. "There has been a drop-off."

Pittsburgh sportswriter Phil Musick put it this way: "The fact is that Jack Ham, circa 1972–79, was a Mona Lisa. The Ham of the past three seasons was, by comparison, a finger painting."

But the injury didn't harm his reputation. He was inducted into the Hall of Fame in his first year of eligibility in 1988.

3. BOBBY BELL—They say that Hank Stram's only problem with Bobby Bell was where to play him. Bell was 6-foot-4, 225 pounds, and he had the strength of a lineman, the quickness of a back, and the ability to play almost any position. He was All-AFL as a defensive end in 1964, then switched to left linebacker, where he was All-League the next six years. Then, after the AFL-NFL merger, Bell was All-Pro three more times. He finished his career with 26 interceptions and 8 touchdowns. Remarkably, he returned those 26 thefts for 479 yards—an average of 18.4 yard per return.

BOBBY BELL

And all that is why he was the first outside linebacker inducted into the Hall of Fame. Bell was the L.T. of his era—not as good a pass rusher, but probably more athletic and more active pursuing in the open field. He was one of the first big, tall outside backers. He was a spectacular intimidator because of both uncommon strength and remarkable quickness.

His former coach, Hank Stram, once said, "I don't want to get into any discussion about who are my best athletes. I think every man on our team is great. But I will say one thing: If there's a better athlete in football than Bobby Bell, I haven't seen him. You hear a lot about all-around football players, but you don't really see many. There isn't a job Bell couldn't do—and do well."

Raiders owner Al Davis, who saw Bell twice a year for twelve seasons, once said, "He makes the big play going the other way. He's always intercepting a pass and going sixty yards or something like that."

Dave Robinson, whose Packers faced Kansas City in the first Super Bowl, says, "Bell had catlike quickness. He used his hands better than any linebacker I've seen in a while."

Bell's greatness was his versatility. He was so quick, he could chase backs from behind before they reached the line of scrimmage. And he was so strong he could destroy offensive linemen if they tried to run straight at him. He was one of the few linebackers regularly double-teamed on running plays. Teams would hold in their tight end and single-block on the line in order to get two players on Bell.

He was one of the first outside linebackers in a 3-4 defense. In the mid-1960s, Stram pioneered the so-called "stack" defense, an alignment that called for Bell to drop out of the 4-3 formation and become a fourth linebacker.

Buck Buchanan, his longtime teammate, described Bell this way: "This guy is the best all-around football player I ever saw. He can throw a football eighty yards. He can center the ball farther and more accurately than anyone in the business. He's the fastest runner you'll ever see. He can block. And he's the best defensive end, corner linebacker, and anything else defensively in the whole universe."

TED HENDRICKS

4. TED HENDRICKS—Ted Hendricks had deceiving looks for a linebacker—he had a tall, lean, towering frame that masked long but strong arms. He was a great blitzer who also excelled on pass coverage. He played for three teams, each of whom he represented in the Pro Bowl, although his career did go through some ups and downs. He was All-Conference three times as a Colt, four times as a Raider, and once as a Packer. He played in eight Pro Bowls.

But the 6-foot-7 Hendricks—who was nicknamed "The Mad Stork"—always was different, both in size and demeanor.

And, as John Madden once said jokingly, "Ted's elevator doesn't always go all the way to the top." Hendricks' antics included the times he walked onto the practice field wearing a Nazi helmet, or when he wore a Halloween pumpkin with face bars carved into it. Another time, when Madden called the players to practice, Hendricks came charging onto the field on a horse, in full uniform, with a traffic cone for a lance.

"There's another dominating player," said Fred Whittingham, the Rams' linebackers coach. "He was an 'L.T.' with less athletic ability. Offenses never knew where he'd line up."

Hendricks was one of football's best kick blockers ever, deflecting 25 field goals and extra points. He recovered 16 fumbles and intercepted 26 passes, and he had a record-tying four safeties. He also scored five touchdowns on returns.

"He's something different," said Dave Robinson. "Because of his height, he was one of the great kick blockers, and he was also hard to throw over. He had a devil-may-care attitude. He sacrificed his body. If he was leveled by a guard but made a tackle for a one-yard loss, he didn't care."

Hendricks was the forerunner of the current breed of players who line up in a different place every down. He was one of the most difficult players for offenses to handle because he combined a totally independent, free-wheeling mentality with his unusual physique, and his attitude helped intimidate the opposition.

Hendricks was never better than when he was with the Raiders, who let him free-lance. He jumped around the line of scrimmage, blitzed when he felt like it, read the play, and then reacted. There was a structure to what he was doing, but no one knew what it was. As a result, offenses couldn't key on him.

As Charlie Sumner, his position coach, said, "At least once a game, he'll do something, and I won't know how he did it."

Hendricks never missed a game due to injury during his career. But some coaches never thought his career would go very far because of his weight (he weighed 214 pounds as a rookie on that 6-foot-7 frame) or his attitude.

"They didn't think I could play linebacker at 214 because no one else was playing the position at 214. Well, that is really quite silly. If you're good, you're good."

And Ted Hendricks was very good. Good enough, in fact, to be inducted into the Hall of Fame in 1990.

5. DAVE WILCOX—Dave Wilcox played in seven Pro Bowls in an eight-year period (1967–74) with the 49ers. "The Intimidator" was one of the biggest and toughest players of his day, with long arms and sharp elbows. In Wilcox's time, players on the West Coast didn't get the same publicity they got in the East. But he was as good in his time as any of his peers.

"Once that ball was snapped, he brought an intensity whether it was on a blitz, covering a man or making a tackle," said ex-Vikings quarterback Joe Kapp. "I have to say Dave Wilcox played the position as well as anybody who ever played the position."

"Wilcox is not in the same league as Ham or (Chuck) Howley in pass coverage, but he was a great strongside backer against the run," said Andy Russell.

Tight ends who ran patterns across the field were pet targets for Wilcox, who used to talk to himself on the field. It was once said that he hit fullbacks and tight ends like a misplaced steer wrestler, grabbing them at the top with both arms or by the jersey and slinging them to the ground.

"He dominated people," said former 49ers quarterback John Brodie. "Nobody could get off the line against him. If you talk to any tight end, he is the meanest, most ornery guy who ever played the game. I think he is the best outside linebacker who has ever played the game by a long way."

"What I do best is not let people block me," Wilcox once said. "I hate to get blocked. I don't give a bleep if the play goes the other way. Walt Garrison of the Cowboys once knocked me down three times in a game, and that made me mad."

Rams quarterback Roman Gabriel remembered, "Dave played the game from his spot as an outside linebacker like Dick Butkus played it for the Bears from the middle. Wilcox thrived on pressure. 'Don't run away from me. Come to my side. Challenge the best,' he'd say."

"I had an area, and I did not like people in that area," Wilcox said. "It was my spot, and nobody was welcome there but me. It was kind of like you're king of the hill and nobody's going to knock you off it."

6. CHUCK HOWLEY— Still the only player from a losing team to be voted the Most Valuable Player in a Super Bowl, Chuck Howley played thirteen years (1961–73) for the Cowboys after a two-year stint in Chicago, making six Pro Bowl teams. He was one of the stalwarts around whom the "Doomsday Defense" was built.

"Chuck Howley was awesome. He was my mentor," said Andy Russell. "I was just amazed at what he could do. He had unbelievable quickness and was a gambler. He could do things you couldn't coach."

Howley was a quiet, unassuming person who was once called "The Silent Majority's football player." He had superb physical talents (he lettered in five sports in college at West Virginia: football, wrestling, gymnastics, track, and diving), and one of his coaches once said he could have been an NFL running back. But his greatest asset was his unrivaled, intuitive understanding of what an offense was going to do and the ability to react without hesitation, frequently before the play had even started. A Cowboys assistant coach once said he was right about 90 percent of the time when he gambled. "I had better be," answered Howley.

"Covering backs coming out of the backfield was my specialty," he said. "But, in those days, you played the run first, then the pass."

On a team loaded with stars, Howley was the big-play man on defense, and he saved his biggest games for some of the biggest moments in Cowboys history. In Super Bowl V, he intercepted two passes, recovered a fumble, and roamed the Colts' backfield seemingly at will.

7. DAVE ROBINSON—Dave Robinson was overshadowed on a Green Bay defense that featured four future Hall of Famers—including Ray Nitschke, who played next to him—but he was aggressive against the run and a superb pass defender who picked off 27 passes during his career. One of the first in a long line of top-notch linebackers from Penn State, Robinson played in three Pro Bowls. He was extremely powerful and excelled in playoff games, and some say he is a legitimate Hall of Fame candidate.

"When I started in 1963, I was one of the biggest linebackers in the game at six-three, 240," he said, "and, at the end, I was the smallest linebacker in Green Bay."

Number 89 handled tight ends exceptionally well because he had the strength and quickness that are the keys to holding those players at the line and to delay their patterns. He also didn't get cut down when opposing teams cut down on a linebacker on off-tackle slants.

8. MAXIE BAUGHAN—How good was Maxie Baughan? Listen to former Steelers linebacker Andy Russell: "He went to nine Pro Bowls [in a ten-year period], and no other linebacker went to more [until Lawrence Taylor]. I think he belongs in the Hall of Fame."

Baughan played from 1960 to '74 with the Eagles, Rams, and Redskins, finishing his career with George Allen's "Over the Hill Gang." He had such mental strength that he pulled the defense together wherever he went. Baughan was the heart and soul of the Eagles after Chuck Bednarik retired, and he was the defensive leader of the Rams despite having Merlin Olsen and Deacon Jones on the same team. Finally, he was also an important factor in impressing the Redskins that, under Allen, they could actually win football games.

"He was excellent," said ex-Cowboy Chuck Howley, "but he never got the credit he deserved. You always have your unsung heroes who don't get the ink they should. Baughan was just consistent, and that's what you look for."

Indeed, Baughan was once named one of the seven most underrated players in the NFL in a *Sport* magazine article. It was once said that he was every bit as astute as Johnny Unitas or Bart Starr, the quarterbacks with whom he waged mental wars on Sundays.

9. CLYDE "BULLDOG" TURNER and CHUCK BEDNARIK (tie)—Turner and Bednarik were from the old school—two-way players who saw action for sixty minutes a game at center and linebacker.

Turner lived up to his nickname during his career with the Bears from 1940 to '52. As a linebacker blessed with halfback speed, he led the NFL with eight interceptions in 1942, still the only linebacker ever to do so, and he made four interceptions in the five championship games in which he played. As a center, he was a flawless snapper and an exceptional blocker.

Bears teammate Sid Luckman once called Turner, "Dick Butkus on defense and Jim Ringo on offense."

Bednarik, football's "Iron Man," was also All-Pro at both positions during his fourteen-year career with the Eagles, and he's best-known for playing fifty-eight minutes in the 1960 NFL championship game long after the two-way player had faded from the scene. He was a seven-time All-Pro.

"He had a real sense of the ball," remarked Hall of Famer Joe Schmidt, "and a real zest for the game—a killer instinct."

Bednarik made one of the most famous tackles in NFL history, when he stopped Frank Gifford in a 1960 game that paved the way for a Philadelphia league championship. It also knocked Gifford out of action for a year. Then, on the final play of the NFL championship game, Bednarik held on to Jim Taylor near the goal line to preserve the title.

"Bednarik and Turner were the two best center-linebackers of their period," said David Neft. "If they played in modern day and concentrated on one position, they would have been as good as anybody."

Inside Linebackers

There are no inside linebackers in the Hall of Fame, and it might be a while before there is one.

"From a standpoint of who makes the tackles, inside linebackers should stand out," says former Broncos inside linebacker Randy Gradishar, who is one of the best ever. "But the outside linebackers are more promoted. Even though inside linebackers get the tackles, fans like the attention outside linebackers get, because they create confusion out there."

Most inside linebackers are good, solid players who never get the credit they deserve. But teams can win championships with them.

Inside linebackers have been around for only two decades, and they have been acknowledged on All-Pro teams for less than ten years. They are better athletes than the middle linebackers of yesteryear—strong enough to stuff the run and fast enough to run with backs and tight ends on pass coverage.

Walt Corey, Buffalo's defensive coordinator, claims there are two kinds of inside linebackers—235-pounders who do it all and those who just plug the middle against the run.

But there haven't been a lot of great inside 'backers. "There are a lot of good ones," Corey says, "but we're still trying to find the great ones. To get to that next level, you have to be spectacular. That's what sets them off."

1. HARRY CARSON—Harry Carson played in nine Pro Bowls in thirteen seasons (1976–88) with the Giants, which tied the all-time record when he retired. The true mark of a standout player is how he plays in big games, and that's when Carson was at his best. In New York, Lawrence Taylor got the press, but Carson, who was often compared with Sam Huff, was the mainstay of the team's defense. He was one of the best run-stuffers in the eighties, a hard hitter.

A longtime captain of the Giants, Carson was big and burly at 6-foot-3, 245 pounds, and he could absorb the punishment dealt out in the middle.

A fourth-round draft pick from South Carolina State, Carson was a moody man who played with burning intensity. He couldn't accept defeat. And, as a rookie, he didn't want to accept the move from down lineman to inside linebacker. "I knew it was the glamour position because guys like Butkus and Nobis and Nitschke made it that," he said. "But in my mind I was not sure of it." Carson had to be convinced by Bill Arnsparger, then the Giants' head coach, and Marty Schottenheimer, the linebackers coach. That year he took over a starting job at midseason and made the All-Rookie team.

HARRY CARSON

"He was amazingly consistent," says football historian David Neft. "There are probably guys who had better games, but none at his level of intensity for a long period of time."

"Carson is one of the great ones," agrees Herb Paterra, the Lions' inside linebackers coach. "He was a big, strong guy who was able to take guards on and have the ability to get off them."

"You have to be disciplined to play inside," says Randy Gradishar, one of Carson's peers. "You don't just follow the ball. Carson was bigger [than most inside 'backers]. Coming straight ahead, he filled the hole well."

Bill Parcells, who coached the Giants to two Super Bowls, says Carson belongs in the Hall of Fame. "I might be prejudiced, but you're talking about one of the greatest guys ever to play the game. It's the big deal. You judge a trapper by his furs, and he's got some furs. In fact, his horse is loaded. You don't accomplish what he has without being someone special."

A couple of years before he retired, George Martin, another longtime Giants player, was asked about his teammate. "When they decide on the proto-typical [inside] linebacker, I'm not quite sure what he'll look like," said Martin. "But I know he'll be wearing number 53."

2. RANDY GRADISHAR—Randy Gradishar played in seven Pro Bowls during his ten-year career. He was the NFL's Defensive Player of the Year in 1978, and was the most honored player in team history until John Elway came along.

At 6-foot-3, 230 pounds, Gradishar was extremely strong against the run. He was the kind of player who was often overlooked but always seemed to make the tackle. In 1981 he made 258 tackles, a team record and one of the highest totals ever for any team (although tackles are an unofficial statistic). He had good lateral movement and was quick enough to get back into pass coverage.

RANDY GRADISHAR

Gradishar was a very intelligent player with the mobility of a middle linebacker.

Drafted in the first round in 1974, Gradishar started his second season and went to the Pro Bowl.

Former Cowboys running back Tony Dorsett remembers a 1980 tackle by Gradishar. "I ran a pass pattern and was wide open, but Danny White didn't see me. I go back to the huddle and tell Danny that I'm wide open. I ran the same route again, but this time I was nearly decapitated. My eyes were only partially open when I hit the ground. Trainers and doctors came running onto the field. Everybody thought I was dead. Hey, I thought I was, too."

Dorsett says Gradishar was "second to none in terms of preparation and competitiveness." He had to be because he didn't have the physical abilities of his peers.

As Gradishar himself once put it: "I just totally mess up the popular image of what linebackers are supposed to be. If you play linebacker, you're supposed to bite guys and lose teeth and start fights all the time. I'm not saying I have all the athletic ability in the world, but I believe I can play linebacker without resorting to all those things. . . . I wasn't a big hitter. I was never the biggest or fastest linebacker. I certainly wasn't the strongest. Honestly, I was more finesse [than physical]. That was my style. My only goal was to make the tackle, to find a way to get there."

And that's why he is one of the best ever.

3. KARL MECKLENBURG—Karl Mecklenburg is one of the most versatile defensive players ever, having moved from defensive end to inside linebacker to the outside and back inside in his ten seasons with Denver. He's been voted to five Pro Bowls and has lined up in as many as seven positions in one game, disguising his intentions until the snap.

"Mecklenburg plays all over the place," says Jack Paterra. "In his own way, he's a helluva linebacker."

"He doesn't play that position as a true position," says Buffalo defensive coordinator Walt Corey. "But you have to have a lot of ability to play a lot of different positions."

Not bad for somebody chosen in the twelfth round of the draft.

DEFENSIVE BACKS

It's a lonely man's position, and if I had it to do over,
I'd get me a set of golf clubs.
LESTER HAYES

The defensive back is the last line of defense. He waits for lightning to strike, and it often does quickly. If an offensive player gets past a cornerback or a safety, it usually means six points and sometimes means a loss.

In the early days of pro football, players went both ways, and defensive backs were also quarterbacks and running backs. In the late forties, when specialization started to come into vogue, full-time defensive backs sprung up. Among the first were Emlen Tunnell and Jack Christiansen, pioneers who are in the Pro Football Hall of Fame.

Football was no longer "three yards and a cloud of dust." Footballs were flying through the air, and defenses had to find a way to stop them. It wasn't long before some of a team's best and fastest athletes were put on defense as the last line.

And it wasn't long before the stars were born. They usually make their name by swiping passes, because people too often look at the interception lists to see who is the best defensive back. But that isn't so. Run defense is just as important.

"Coming up to stop the sweep is a bitch, pure and simple," said Packers Hall of Famer Herb Adderley. "Just put yourself in that position. Say you're playing the Dolphins. When they sweep to your side, you only have to contend with Larry Little, one of those big, fat, mean guards who are just looking for you. I mean, they dream about finding cornerbacks out in the open field and driving them about thirty rows up into the stands. And if you somehow avoid Little, you only have to stop Larry Csonka, who is plenty fast and weighs about 235 and loves to run over people. That's all you have to do. It's a wonder any of us survive."

Defensive backs range from very physical players to light guys who can run with receivers. They need to have sprinter's speed, no nerves, and no memory. And they have to be gamblers in the truest sense of the word.

Cornerbacks

Cornerback is the loneliest job on the field. If one makes a mistake, everybody sees it. Over the years, cornerbacks have run the gamut from big, physical players to small ones who can run like gazelles. It is a position of occasional gambles, but conservative play—not getting beaten—is, by necessity, still the priority.

"The best athletes you have on the team play at cornerback," said Joe Schmidt when he was coaching the Lions. "The receivers come at you one-on-one and you just can't hide."

Lem Barney, one of Schmidt's players, called cornerback "the lonesomest spot in the world." Dallas Cowboy Mel Renfro agreed. "I like making All-Pro at cornerback. But I really hate to play it. It's the loneliest job they have."

And if that's true, then left cornerback might be the hardest job in football, because that player covers what is usually the opponent's best receiver.

But cornerbacks can't look good unless the entire defensive backfield plays well, and rare is the All-Pro defensive back who plays on a losing team.

1. DICK "NIGHT TRAIN" LANE—Lane is one of the unlikeliest Hall of Famers, having played only a year of junior-college football and some service ball before going professional. He tried out with the Rams as an end in 1952 but was quickly moved to defensive back because future Hall of Famers Elroy "Crazylegs" Hirsch and Tom Fears were entrenched in starting jobs.

That season, Lane intercepted 14 passes in twelve games, a record that still stands. Two of those interceptions went for touchdowns (and he dropped three other passes that were in his hands). Those are phenomenal numbers for a player with very little experience.

Lane was a head tackler, until that practice was outlawed—like a vampire going for the kill. He broke up as many passes by stripping a ballcarrier as he did by knocking them down. He is often called the hardest hitter in NFL history.

"Night Train and Dick Butkus—they'd hurt you when they hit you," ex-Colts wide receiver Alex Hawkins once said.

He played fourteen seasons with the Rams, Cardinals, and Lions (1952–65). He was All-Pro five times and played in six Pro Bowls. His interception total of 68 was the second-most at the time he retired. He was voted the all-time NFL cornerback in 1969.

DICK "NIGHT TRAIN" LANE

Lane was the pioneer cornerback; in fact, he wrote the book on how to play the position. He was big (6-foot-2, 210 pounds) but fast, and fearless—a gambler who usually won.

"He was an interceptor," said ex-Cowboys coach Tom Landry, a former defensive back with the Giants. "He took chances and he made the big plays."

Lane himself agrees. "I was a gambler, yeah, but it was not so much a gamble as it was a setup," he said. "I would give him [the receiver] only one way to go. Then he had to guess with me."

Teammate Joe Schmidt said Lane "takes a lot of chances and he gets burned, but he comes up with the big play a lot of times, too. Percentagewise, he's way ahead of the game."

Lane had outstanding speed, exceptional agility and reflex action, and a fierce determination to win. Green Bay coach Vince Lombardi once told Bart Starr, "Don't throw anywhere near him. He's the best there is."

"Night Train Lane was the best defensive back to ever play the game," said Packers Hall of Famer Herb Adderley. "I tried to pattern my game after him because he was the best. He could have played any one of the four [secondary] positions. I've never seen a defensive back hit the way he hit—I mean take them down, whether it be Jim Taylor or Jim Brown."

2. HERB ADDERLEY—A first-round draft pick who at first had a reputation as an offensive player, Adderley soon turned his disposition around and became a defensive standout. He was rarely beaten for touchdowns, usually drawing the opposing team's best receiver. He played in five consecutive Pro Bowls and was named All-Pro five times during a twelve-year career (1961–72)

HERB ADDERLEY

with Green Bay and Dallas. During his years with Green Bay and Dallas, he played in four of the first six Super Bowls. He was inducted into the Hall of Fame in 1980.

Adderley was fast enough to play off a receiver, setting up deep and playing the ball. And, if his receiver did make a reception, he was one of the surest tacklers ever, delivering a strong blow.

"Tom Landry once said I was the best 'cluer' ever," Adderley said, "meaning I could recognize different things happening because I had played offense."

Landry still agrees. "He was a unique type of player, like Everson Walls. They play the ball with their instincts. When Herb came to us [in 1970], I thought he was a horrible defensive back in the way I tried to discipline him. He played off the ball so much, so loose, but he never got beat. I learned that you left him alone and let him do his job."

What many people remember Adderley for was his ability to keep opposing receivers out of the end zone. "You have to recognize that you are going to get beaten once in a while," he said. "You just can't dwell on it. You just have to concentrate on not letting the same man beat you again."

Adderley also was an excellent runner; in 1965, he returned three of his six interceptions for touchdowns. He intercepted a pass in his first start and stole 48 passes in all, returning them for 1,046 yards, a 21.8-yard average. He scored seven touchdowns on interceptions and two more on kickoff returns, and his 60-yard interception for a score was a big play in Super Bowl II.

Former pro coach George Allen once said, "Herb Adderley was the ideal defensive back. He would have been an outstanding offensive back, too. He was smart and quick, strong and tough. He had fast feet and good hands. Boy, did he have good hands! It wasn't a gamble when he went for the ball. When he went for it, he caught it."

"Herb took chances, and that's the thing you have to do," said Raiders Hall of Famer Willie Brown. "He wasn't afraid. He had a lot of confidence."

But he wasn't a braggart. "When people leave the stadium," he said, "I want them to say they've just watched one of the best cornerbacks they've ever seen in their lives."

3. MEL BLOUNT—Mel Blount played cornerback like a linebacker and might have been the best bump-and-run cornerback ever during his career from 1970–83 with Pittsburgh. He was gifted with great physical assets at 6-

foot-3, 205 pounds, and he was able to stick with receivers relentlessly with his long arms. He played off his man and closed quickly. A durable player who missed only one regular-season game, Blount's key interception at the goal line in Super Bowl X helped the Steelers defeat the Vikings 16–6. He duplicated that feat three Super Bowls later against Dallas. In 1975 he was voted the NFL's Most Valuable Defensive Player when he had 11 interceptions.

MEL BLOUNT

"He's in the same class as Night Train [Lane], as far as toughness goes," said Herb Adderley. "He intimidated—not that we didn't, but he made it part of his game."

Jack Butler, a former All-Pro defensive back with the Steelers and now head of the BLESTO scouting combine, said Blount "broke all the rules. He was too tall for a corner, but he had the quickness the smaller guys had."

Tom Landry agreed. "Mel Blount might have been the strongest cornerback we had to compete against," he said.

But Blount's goals were quite simple. "I didn't want to be second to anyone," he said. "I wanted to set the standards for my position." And he did, because he was enshrined into the Hall of Fame in 1989, his first year of eligibility.

He started his career returning kickoffs, and was burned repeatedly when he got into the lineup at cornerback. "Yeah, I thought about quitting," he admitted. "I thought a whole lot about it." But instead he thought about what he had to do to improve. The next year, 1972, he wasn't beaten for a touchdown.

Blount was named All-Pro three times and played in five Pro Bowls. He intercepted 57 passes, which is a Steelers record and was tied for seventh-highest when he retired in 1983. And he had at least one interception every season.

But, while interceptions are the mark by which most defensive backs are measured, Blount was measured on another scale. In fact, his skills at keeping receivers from getting off the line—he was a master at the bump-and-run—helped force the NFL to change the rules during his career. So Blount quickly adjusted to zone coverages and never skipped a beat.

Teammate Jack Ham once said, "When you create a cornerback, the mold is Mel Blount. I played in a lot of Super Bowls. I never saw a cornerback like him. He was the most incredible athlete I have ever seen. With Mel, you could take one receiver and just write him off. He could handle anybody in the league."

WILLIE BROWN

4. WILLIE BROWN—Free agents who get cut by their first pro team usually have a short enough career, but Willie Brown lasted all the way to the Hall of Fame. A sixteen-year veteran with the Broncos and Raiders (1963–78), Brown says he invented the bump-and-run method of covering receivers. He intercepted nine passes in his second season, 54 in all, and is the only player in pro football history to have intercepted at least one pass in sixteen consecutive seasons. He played in nine AFL or AFC championship games, nine All-Star or Pro Bowl games, and is a member of the all-time AFL team. Brown's 75-yard interception return for the clinching touchdown in Super Bowl XI is still a record.

"He frustrated receivers. He never gave an inch. He was on wide receivers like glue," says historian Joe Horrigan. "He hit 'em at the line and stayed with them stride for stride."

Ex-Packer Herb Adderley said that Brown "had all the attributes—quickness, straightaway speed, good hands. And he had the temperament, too, to play out there."

Dick LeBeau, a fine cornerback for the Lions in the sixties who is now the Steelers' defensive coordinator, remembers Brown as "a character player. He refused to not play well."

And when the NFL changed its rules so as to pretty much outlaw the bump-and-run, Brown didn't miss a beat. "They changed the rule so you can do it only in the first five yards [off the line of scrimmage]," Brown said, "but that's all I needed, anyway. That's all I wanted—one shot at the line of scrimmage. It doesn't matter that the rule has changed."

Brown was an end on a Grambling team that sent nine players to the pros. He struggled as a free agent with the Oilers, who converted him to defensive back and then cut him before the 1963 season began. But he was picked up by the Broncos, became a starter, and then was traded to the Raiders four years later. He became the premier cornerback at a time when AFL secondaries were trying desperately to equalize the offense-defense mismatch in the league. Oversized at 215 pounds, gifted with a burst of speed, and almost as explosive as the Chargers' Lance Alworth, the league's premier receiver, Brown made the Hall of Fame as soon as he was eligible.

Alworth remembers after a game in the sixties in which he burned Brown, then with the Broncos, for a touchdown, "Al Davis called me up after that [and] asked me about Willie, said he had a chance to trade for him. I said, 'Al, he's the best, no one's close.' He said, 'Well, what happened?' I said, 'Hell, Al, he was hurt.' The next year, there was Willie in Oakland. What a mistake I made!"

5. JACK CHRISTIANSEN—

Jack Christiansen was "the first quarter-back of the defense." He was so good that the Lions' secondary in the fifties was called "Chris' Crew" after him. He was one of the first defensive specialists to become a dangerous weapon, as teams passed and punted the ball away from him. Christiansen led the NFL in interceptions in 1953 and '57 on the way to a career total of 46. He was enshrined in the Hall of Fame in 1970.

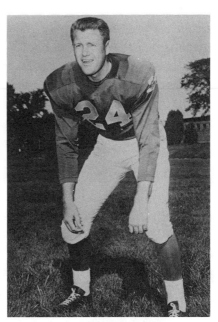

JACK CHRISTIANSEN

"He was one of what I call the 'hatchet men,'" said Herb Adderley. "They would hit."

And former Detroit general manager Nick Kerbawy once said of Christiansen, "He wouldn't be afraid if he were covering Satan himself."

Christiansen was extremely smart, big, and strong. He was also faster than most players of his time. His backfield mate, Yale Lary, said, "We knew what everybody was going to do because Jack called the signals."

A sixth-round draft pick in 1951, Christiansen returned four punts for touchdowns as a rookie, including two in one game. Both records still stand. But more on Christiansen's return abilities later in this book.

The Lions became immediate winners upon Christiansen's arrival, and they won three league championships with him, making them the best years in the team's long history. Detroit coach Buddy Parker later said, "I figure the difference in our 1951 and 1952 seasons was, simply, Jack Christiansen. He was instrumental in the overall development of our defense. He ran it, and he was the boss of the secondary."

He was one of the first great athletes to play on defense, and, as Joe Horrigan says, "He was not just an offensive player finding a spot on defense. He was used because of his talents there."

Christiansen played only eight years but was voted All-Pro six of them (consecutive seasons from 1952–57). He intercepted 46 passes, almost six per season, one of the highest averages ever. He scored 13 touchdowns, including three on interception returns and eight on punt returns.

"We had a standard rule when we played Detroit," said Cleveland All-Pro end Mac Speedie. "Don't throw in his area and don't punt to him."

6. JIMMY JOHNSON—Let Willie Brown tell you how good Jimmy Johnson was. "I remember the year I went into the Hall of Fame [1984]. I looked at the list of players who were eligible, and I saw my name next to Jimmy's, so I thought that I would not get in because they'd pick Jimmy for sure. In my mind, he and Mike Haynes are the two best corners who ever played. There's no question in my mind that he should be in the Hall of Fame."

"I can't understand that, either," said Herb Adderley. "He had the quickness and speed to close on receivers, and he had a great backpedal. John Taylor and Jerry Rice—they wouldn't be breaking on those hitches against a guy like Jimmy Johnson."

And *Sports Illustrated*'s Paul Zimmerman adds, "The two greatest corners ever are Johnson and Night Train Lane. Case closed."

Johnson played in five Pro Bowls during his sixteen-year career with the 49ers (1961–76). He was held in the utmost respect by teammates and opponents alike for his tough man-to-man coverage. Johnson credits his former 49ers coach, Jack Christiansen, for his development. Former Lions cornerback Dick LeBeau, who intercepted 62 passes himself, called Johnson "the first technique cornerback to play like they do now—drops, backpedal, that stuff."

As Johnson once put it: "There isn't a receiver in the league I can't cover."

He led the 49ers in interceptions only twice in fifteen seasons, because, as 49ers quarterback John Brodie put it, "The only reason he isn't leading the league is that he doesn't get a chance."

Mel Phillips, now the Dolphins' secondary coach, played with Johnson in San Francisco. "The problem was, nobody challenged him. What everyone looks at in a cornerback, he didn't get a lot of interceptions. Teams didn't complete balls on him. Very rarely. I remember once in a six-game span, teams averaged only two passes a game against him. And you have to get picks to get total recognition. Jimmy ranks up there with the best who ever played, like Mel Blount and Willie Brown. I think someday he'll be in the Hall of Fame."

7. LEM BARNEY—A year after Night Train Lane retired, the Lions had a new star at cornerback. Lem Barney made an immediate and lasting impression in his rookie season of 1967. He intercepted Bart Starr in the season opener and returned it twenty-four yards for a touchdown. In the season finale that year against Minnesota, he intercepted three passes in one quarter, returning one for a score. He tied for the NFL interception lead with 10, three for touchdowns, a first-year scoring feat that was matched only by Ronnie Lott in 1981. He was named the Defensive Rookie of the Year.

And that's only part of the reason the flamboyant speedster from Jackson State was inducted into the Hall of Fame in 1992, only the fifth cornerback to be enshrined.

A second-round pick, Barney played in seven Pro Bowls and was named All-Pro three times. His 56 interceptions is tied for eleventh all-time, and he returned them for 1,077 yards and a 19.2-yard average. However, he never played in a playoff game, let alone a championship game or a Super Bowl.

Joe Schmidt, who played with Lane and coached Barney, said, "Barney has the same thing Night Train had—a man gets a step on him, he has the quickness to get over to cover before the ball gets there."

And that's exactly how he played. Mike Weger, an old teammate, said, "He lays in the bushes . . . letting his man get two or three steps ahead of him, [then he] bursts in there for the interception."

A terrorizing defensive back, Barney had great physical strength, even against the run. But he was also a tremendous scoring threat. He scored 11 touchdowns—seven on interceptions, two on punt returns, one on a kickoff return, and one on a return of an opponent's missed field goal (which was legal back then)—and he set up countless other scores. He even punted for Detroit in 1967 and '69.

Former teammate Alex Karras said, "I think Lem Barney is the greatest athlete the Lions will ever have. He can do more things than any ballplayer I've ever played with on the Lions."

Another former teammate, Mel Farr, said, "If ever a man was made to be a cornerback, Lem is it. He's not overly fast, but he's quick, the fastest one in the game. And he's smart. He plays the position like no one else, maybe like no one else ever will."

"I left everything I had out on that 100-by-53⅓-yard field," Barney said. "Nothing was left in me."

8. MIKE HAYNES—Mike Haynes, who played fourteen years for the Patriots and Raiders (1976–89), was one of the best runners after making an interception. Like the great cornerbacks, Haynes could play man defense and not need any help.

Night Train Lane called Haynes "a super defensive back. He studied the game like I did."

"He was the thinking man's defensive back," says Joe Horrigan. "A Raymond Berry with speed on defense. He rehearsed his moves. He was never faked out. And he never gave a receiver a cushion."

Haynes played in nine Pro Bowls and intercepted 46 passes, a total that would have been higher had opposing quarterbacks not shied away from throwing to his side. At one point during the middle of the 1977 season, Patriots coach Chuck Fairbanks said, "Mike hasn't seen a ball come his way in over three weeks." That was the kind of respect afforded the likes of Herb Adderley and Willie Brown.

Haynes looked at his job in an unambiguous light. "You're always either bad or great. There are no in-betweens. You have to be ready to either make a big play or stop a big play. That's the nature of the game."

"Haynes played man-to-man better than anyone," said Willie Brown, the Hall of Famer who retired from the Raiders a few seasons before Haynes arrived. "He was not afraid. He had confidence, tremendous speed, quickness, and size. There's no question about it, Mike will be in the Hall of Fame."

9. MEL RENFRO—Mel Renfro played both cornerback and safety during his fourteen-year career with the Cowboys (1964–77). He became only the second player after Merlin Olsen to be selected to the Pro Bowl in each of his first ten seasons.

Renfro's coach, Tom Landry, called him "the best coverage back man-to-man. He had great anticipation. He was very quick, with a very good feel for what was going on. . . . When you have Mel Renfro at one cornerback, the other cornerback can expect to see a lot of action."

But football people differ on which position Renfro played better—cornerback or safety.

"As a free safety, he could get to either sideline to help out on deep routes, the fly patterns, as well as any DB ever," said Herb Adderley, who was a teammate of Renfro for a few seasons.

Some football writers, such as *Sports Illustrated*'s Paul Zimmerman, think Renfro should be in the Hall of Fame along with teammate Cliff Harris, a safety.

Renfro is still tops on the Cowboys' all-time lists with 52 interceptions and kickoff returns with a 26.4-yard average.

"There couldn't possibly be a better cornerback than Mel Renfro," Dallas defensive backs coach Gene Stallings said in 1973.

Well, there have been, but not too many.

10. EMMITT THOMAS—Thomas played in five Pro Bowls during his thirteen-year career in Kansas City (1966–78) and intercepted 58 passes, a team record. He is one of only a small group of players to have led the league in interceptions twice in his career (1969 and '74). He is tied with eight other players who had 12 interceptions in a season, two behind Night Train Lane's record.

Thomas started in the AFL just when that league's stars were starting to draw recognition as not being inferior to the older league's players. He was a smart man-to-man defender.

"Emmitt was a student of the game," remembers Hall of Fame linebacker Willie Lanier, Thomas' former teammate. "He played close attention to the nuances of the game. Cornerbacks have to understand they're on an island out there."

"He was a cornerback much like Mike Haynes," says Dick LeBeau. "He could play off or play up on a receiver."

11. JACK BUTLER—Butler played for the Steelers from 1951 to '59 and was once the old-timer nominee for the Hall of Fame. A lot of people say only Night Train Lane was a better cornerback in the fifties, and some football historians call Butler the best defensive player from the 1950s not already in the Hall of Fame.

He was an extremely strong tackler who had a great command of the field. Butler intercepted 52 passes during his career, and he also scored nine touchdowns because he also occasionally played end on offense on third-and-long situations.

Longtime Pittsburgh sportswriter Pat Livingston once wrote that Butler had the "face of a choirboy but the heart of an arsonist. He was a pass defender who made up for his lack of speed by developing the art of intimidation into a defensive weapon."

Butler once cut to the heart of the matter. "The best pass defense is the respect of the receivers. If they figure they're going to get hit as soon as they touch the ball, they're not so relaxed about catching it."

Safeties

The safety is the final tackler. Two decades ago, safeties were cornerback flunkouts, and they were merely designated as right or left safeties. By the seventies, free (or weak) safeties and strong safeties were the norm, and they were real athletes. The free safety, who often calls the signals, is the centerfielder, while the strong safety is more like an extra linebacker in the secondary.

"The eighties was the decade of the great linebacker and how that position changed," says former 49ers coach Bill Walsh. "In the nineties, you're going to see the same thing with safeties."

Today's safeties are a combination of linebacker and cornerback. They are more involved in defending the run than cornerbacks, and they often play near the line of scrimmage. Frequently safeties line up across from the tight end, and in certain blitz packages, they might even line up over the center or tackle. They can get away with getting beat for a touchdown on occasion, but not very often.

LARRY WILSON

1. LARRY WILSON—Every football fan from the sixties remembers the scene: Larry Wilson, with two broken hands, was playing with casts on both of them, but still he made an interception in a game against Pittsburgh.

Bobby Layne, the Hall of Fame quarterback, once called Wilson "pound for pound, the toughest player in the NFL." Layne might well have added, "Of all time." Wilson was only 6-foot and 190 pounds.

In thirteen seasons with the Cardinals (1960–72), Wilson intercepted 52 passes, and he played in eight Pro Bowls in a nine-year period. He didn't invent the safety blitz, but it's his trademark.

"He's probably the toughest strong safety that I ever saw," said Dallas coach Tom Landry. "And he was the most fearless blitzer ever. His body was nothing to him. He just said, 'Heck with it,' and went."

"He's what we call 'the original wildcat,'" said Hall of Famer Ken Houston. "He really started that safety blitz."

Chuck Drulis, the Cardinals' defensive coordinator, knew Wilson was the right man for the safety blitz. "I had to wait for the right player to execute it," Drulis recalled once. "He had to be quick, he had to be a hard tackler and he had to have a lot of guts because he could be belted really hard by those big offensive linemen if anything went wrong. Larry had all those attributes."

The play had the safety, ordinarily the last line of defense, bursting through the offensive line on the snap of the ball, timing his charge perfectly and tackling the quarterback before he had a chance to react. "Wildcat" was the code name for the Cardinals' safety blitz, and Wildcat became Wilson's nickname.

But Wilson's interception total proved that he was equally deadly in pass coverage. A rugged team leader, he led the NFL with 10 interceptions in 1966, including a remarkable string of seven consecutive games in which he had at least one steal (and three in one game).

A running back in college, Wilson shifted to strong safety in the NFL, and that's where he made his name. An outstanding team leader, he was team captain for years and he wound up his career as player-coach.

Wilson didn't brag much. "If you don't come out of a game feeling hurt, you haven't played hard enough," he said.

Pat Summerall, a one-time opponent, best summed up Wilson: "You can run out of superlatives in talking about him. He typified everything great you could possibly expect in a pro football player."

2. KEN HOUSTON—Ken Houston has been called the perfect strong safety, although he was once called pro football's "most underrated superstar." Not much was expected of a player picked in the ninth round of the first combined AFL-NFL draft in 1967, but Houston made the most of a career that ended up in the Hall of Fame.

KEN HOUSTON

When he retired following fourteen stellar seasons with the Oilers (1967–72) and Redskins (1973–80), he had set a record by returning nine interceptions for touchdowns, he had been named All-Pro or All-Conference eight times, and he had been chosen for two AFL All-Star games and a record ten consecutive Pro Bowls. By the time he retired, only Merlin Olsen had played in more Pro Bowls. Houston was inducted into the Hall of Fame in 1986, his first year of eligibility.

Still, he was somewhat unrecognized except by those who watched him play closely. Safety Jake Scott, who was a teammate of Houston with the Redskins, once said, "Ken Houston is the best player I ever lined up with."

Dallas tight end Billy Joe Dupree commented, "The guy I respect more than any one of them is Kenny Houston. Kenny will light you up, he'll light your fire."

And Tom Landry remarked, "He was a good, tough guy who could cover man-to-man. He was real competitive."

Houston had fine speed and he was a bruising hitter.

"I had the speed to cover wideouts and the hitting ability because I was a linebacker in college," he said. "I was a cross between a linebacker and a cornerback."

Houston had the greatest game of his career on December 19, 1971, when he intercepted two passes and returned both of them for touchdowns. That established the all-time record of nine scoring interceptions, as well as tying the season mark of four scoring returns and the single-game mark of two.

Interestingly, he didn't return an interception for a touchdown for the last nine years of his career.

Houston described his abilities to return interceptions for scores this way: "Whenever I get the ball I think right away about getting into the end zone. After I have the football, I like to get back to the center of the field and look over the blocking before cutting back to the sideline. If you are lucky, you go in. One thing that helps is that most offensive players who try to stop me are usually not good tacklers, since that is not something they practice."

He ended his career with 49 interceptions that were returned for 898 yards, an average of 18.3 yards per return. He also scored 12 touchdowns, nine on interceptions and one each on a blocked field goal, a fumble, and a punt return.

RONNIE LOTT

3. RONNIE LOTT—Ronnie Lott has been the hardest hitter in the NFL for the last decade. In ten seasons with the 49ers and the last two with the Raiders, Lott has been named All-Pro six times and has gone to ten Pro Bowls while playing cornerback and both safety positions. He now plays for the Jets.

"Ronnie Lott is like a middle linebacker playing safety," said Tom Landry. "He is devastating. He may dominate the secondary almost better than anyone I've seen. He has a real sense and feel of what's happening on offense, of getting the jump on people."

Lott plays football with abandon. Although he lacks the size of today's big safeties, he sets the standard for aggressiveness. "[That's] the only way to play the game . . . give it your all," says Lott. "That's how the old guys played the game. They played hard."

With 60 interceptions (five that were returned for touchdowns), Lott is the leading active interceptor and seventh all-time. Lott led the NFL in interceptions with 10 in 1986 and nine in '91.

He was voted Rookie the Year in 1981 when San Francisco won its first of four Super Bowls with him in the secondary. He returned three of seven interception for touchdowns that year, tying a record set by Lem Barney.

A sure future Hall of Fame inductee, Lott moved from cornerback to free safety in 1985 and then to strong safety a few years later. He's gotten older, but he hasn't slipped much.

"In his prime, he was one of the best," says Zeven Yaralian, the Giants' secondary coach. "He intimidated receivers and could play that nasty role. He said, 'You come through my area and I'll knock your head off.' He moved to safety because of his hitting ability. He's a better safety than cornerback."

Steve Atwater of the Broncos is another hard hitter in the NFL today, but even he admires Lott's style. "I've seen him hit so many guys running that fade route [in the end zone]. He nails them. He's knocked so many people out," said Atwater.

Which is why it was only fitting that he played part of his career with the Raiders. "Growing up as a kid, I always emulated the Jack Tatums, the George Atkinsons," he says. "I can't believe how many people have told me, 'I can't believe you're in a Niner uniform. You're a Raider player, the way you approach the game, the way you play the game.'"

"I think he has a chance to be the best ever at the position," said pro football historian Jim Campbell. "He plays like a linebacker. He really pops people. 1991 cinched it for me when he went to the Raiders and led the league in interceptions. And he still torpedoes people."

4. EMLEN TUNNELL—Like Night Train Lane, Emlen Tunnell was one of the biggest finds in pro football history. One day he just walked into the Giants' office and asked for a tryout, and he soon became a key to the team's "umbrella defense." He was a pioneer, one of the first defensive stars in pro football. Tunnell played in the fifties, which was a period of defensive evolution, and he developed many of the pass-coverage techniques for the safety position. He was called the Giants' "offense on defense" because of the yards he piled up on punt returns and interceptions. In fact, his interception-yardage record (1,282 yards) still stands.

EMLEN TUNNELL

Tunnell played in nine Pro Bowls and was All-Pro four times in eleven seasons in New York (1948–58) and three in Green Bay.

"He was the hardest-hitting safety who ever played," recalled Herb Adderley, who played with Tunnell for three years in Green Bay. "I think he was the greatest safety man ever. He had recognition of what's happening to get him in the right place at the right time, without relying on quickness or speed."

Tunnell was not only the first black on the Giants, but he was the first black assistant coach in the NFL (with the Giants in 1963) and the first black and the first purely defensive specialist enshrined into the Hall of Fame.

Tunnell retired with the records for most lifetime punt returns (258), most career punt return yards (2,209), most interceptions (79), and, of course, interception yardage. In fact, in 1952, Tunnell accounted for 923 yards on the

52 times he touched the ball—which was more yards than the league rushing leader had that season. Tunnell returned 30 punts for 411 yards, added 364 yards on 15 kickoff returns, and then tacked on 149 yards off seven interceptions.

So why did Tunnell play on defense? Giants coach Steve Owens responded, "He's more valuable to us right where he is. With Em on defense, we have the potential to have the ball on any play for the entire game."

In his first eleven years, Tunnell never intercepted less than six passes in a season. He had an intuitive sense and feel for the ball. He didn't play by the book; he was a free-lancer who let his instincts guide him.

"Tunnell was a genius for setting up the offense for a mistake," said Bobby Layne, who was noted himself for setting up defenses for a killing mistake. "I remember once I thought for sure I had Em sucked up. But as soon as I threw the ball, I knew I'd been suckered. Like a flash, Tunnell was in front of the receiver and touchdown bound for the Giants."

Teammate Frank Gifford still raves about Tunnell's performances. "There was rarely a game in which I wasn't amazed by his reading of plays and his cat-like reactions. At first I thought he was just lucky. Then I realized he was just great."

WILLIE WOOD

5. WILLIE WOOD—The premier free safety of all time, Wood was named All-Pro seven times in an eight-year period from 1964 to '71, and he played in eight Pro Bowls during a twelve-year career with the Packers (1960–71).

Wood was a great leaper who played off the receiver and dared a quarterback to throw in his direction. He learned his job from Hall of Famer Emlen Tunnell, the man he replaced in Green Bay.

"He was my mentor," Wood said. "He understood everything. He made me realize that to play defense you have to understand defense—what the strengths are, what the weaknesses are."

Wood was overlooked by every team in the NFL and AFL in the 1960 draft, and he signed as a free agent with Green Bay. But he compiled the kind of lifetime statistics that are not normally associated with free agents. He intercepted 48 passes, returning them for 699 yards and two touchdowns. He also ran back 187 punts for 1,391 yards and two more scores. He led the NFL in punt returns with a 16.1-yard average in 1961 and in interceptions with nine in '62.

Wood had good but not great speed to go along with superb desire, tenacity, and an impressive leaping ability. He was also very good against the run because he wasn't afraid to tackle players much bigger than him.

He was a quarterback at Southern Cal and being only 5-foot-10 and black could have contributed to not being drafted. So Vince Lombardi signed him as a defensive back. In his first start as a rookie, Raymond Berry burned him for two touchdowns. It wasn't long before Wood was burning Berry and other NFL receivers. And it also wasn't long before Berry would comment, "Wood sets the style for the Packer type of defense. Willie gives them the ability to call one defense and get many interpretations of it. He smells a play and takes off, strictly on his own, to break up a play he should never even been near."

Throughout his career, he had a knack for making big plays at the most crucial times. In Green Bay's 16–7 win over the Giants in the 1962 NFL championship game, Wood made a touchdown-saving tackle on a kickoff return. In 1964, when Green Bay defeated the Bears 17–3, he set up every Packer point on an interception return and punt returns of 64 and 42 yards. But his most famous play came in the first Super Bowl, when his third-quarter interception and fifty-yard return of a Len Dawson pass turned a close 14–10 game into a 35–10 rout of the Chiefs.

6. YALE LARY—Yale Lary was a multi-talented player—as fine a punter as he was a safety, which is why he's in the Hall of Fame. He was All-Pro four times and played in nine Pro Bowls during his eleven-year career with Detroit (1952–53 and '56–64). He was also a dangerous punt returner.

As a safety, Lary was a finesse player who taunted receivers into thinking he was playing off the ball. But his forte was his speed and reaction to the ball.

Lary helped the Lions win NFL titles in 1952 and '53, then spent the next two years in the Army before returning for nine more seasons and another NFL championship in 1957. In eleven years, he intercepted 50 passes (the fifth-highest total when he retired). He also scored three times on punt returns.

Teammate Bobby Layne once said of Lary, "If I had to pick one defensive back who had everything, it would have to be Yale. [He] had everything, especially intelligence and quickness."

But he was also one of the best punters the game has ever seen. He averaged 44.3 yards per punt during his career, and his booming, long-distance kicks kept opponents in consistently poor field position.

"He made our defense look good because he gave us room to work," said Hall of Famer Joe Schmidt.

In 1963, Lary averaged 48.9 yards per punt, the second-highest seasonal average ever. He led the league in punting three times.

7. PAUL KRAUSE—Figure this: Paul Krause has more interceptions than anyone else in NFL history, 81, and he's not in the Hall of Fame.

"He racked up the numbers, and he was the ideal person in Minnesota's defense," says pro football historian Jim Campbell. "He was the product of a zone defense. But his accomplishments are tainted in my book. He was gutless. He didn't like to hit people."

Tom Landry disagrees. "He had all the abilities of the prevent safety. Teams couldn't afford to throw on him. We respected him. He had great range, not speed, which doesn't seem to go together, but he really did."

And Bud Grant, his Vikings coach, obviously throught Krause was a great player, too. "I would have to say that Paul Krause had the game down to a science. His intuition and instincts for playing the receiver and the football were terrific. His ability to make a big play was almost constant. He could turn a game around for us."

Krause was truly a centerfielder. He played in eight Pro Bowls during a long sixteen-year career (1964–79) with the Redskins and Vikings. He returned his 81 interceptions for 1,185 yards (a 14.8-yard average) and three touch-downs.

Krause is upset that he's not yet in the Hall of Fame. "Hey, I wasn't the prettiest tackler in the world, but I made tackles, and I didn't miss many tackles. And I turned the ball over eighty-one times. So I was an offensive free safety. When the ball was in the air, I went for it."

In 1978, one short of Emlen Tunnell's career interception record, Krause failed to pick off a pass. He came back in '79, and had only one interception in the first thirteen games, and his hopes of breaking the record had just about run out. But in Game 14 against the Rams, Krause intercepted two passes. The record was his.

8. JOHNNY ROBINSON—The longest-playing original Chiefs player, Johnny Robinson was the interception king in the AFL with 43 thefts. In his first season in the NFL, after the merger of the two leagues, Robinson intercepted 10 more passes (three in a game twice). When he finally retired in 1971, after a twelve-year career, he was the fifth-leading interceptor of all time with 53. He was a member of the all-time AFL team that was chosen in 1969. A lot of people believe Robinson deserves to be in the Hall of Fame.

"He was a chessmaster," said teammate Willie Lanier. "And it is a chess match out there. You have to get into the mindset of the quarterback. Johnny was intuitive. He had a knack for the game."

A running back early in his career, Robinson was a free safety who forced the run well. He was All-AFL five straight years, but, for all his achievements, he seldom was a headline maker. In fact, the biggest news he might have made was in Super Bowl IV when he played against the Vikings with torn rib cartilage and even made an interception.

KICKERS

Lots of guys can kick in their underwear in practice.
JOHN MADDEN

In the NFL today, nearly every time Nick Lowery, Morten Andersen, Gary Anderson, or Chip Lohmiller kicks a field goal, he's likely to break one of the other's record for accuracy.

In the old days, the best kickers made 50 percent of their field-goal attempts. Today, 70 percent is the average, and the best kickers make 75 percent of their kicks. Those who make just 50 percent last only a few games.

But for punters, the numbers have decreased. Sammy Baugh's single-season average of 51.4 yards per kick will never be broken, because today's best punters—Rohn Stark, Sean Landeta, Reggie Roby, and Rich Camarillo—average nearly ten yards less than that since the emphasis is on hang time and placement rather than distance.

Although it's nearly impossible to compare kickers and punters from different eras because the game and its rules have changed so much, one can certainly compare consistency and accuracy for each kicker in his era.

Placekickers

The debate of straight-on kickers versus soccer-style kickers is no longer, with the straight-ahead kickers having gone the way of dropkicks, the Single Wing, and the Canton Bulldogs.

Today's placekickers are all soccer-style, and the success rate on field goals has risen from about 50 percent in the early sixties to 72.6 percent in 1992, the sixth year in a row they had converted at least seven of every ten attempts. That's a terrific percentage, especially when you consider the weather some players kick in, all the 50-yard-plus attempts, and the pressure that goes with the job.

The biggest difference between today's kickers and those of yesteryear, however, is not that soccer-style kickers are better than straight-on kickers, but rather the rule changes in the last two decades that have made kicking an easier art than the unpredictable task of years past.

In 1974, goalposts were moved from the goal line to the end line and missed field goals were brought back to the line of scrimmage rather than the 20-yard line. Now teams have to get inside the 35-yard line before they even think about kicking a field goal. Years ago, they gambled from near the fifty. The change affected both placekickers and punters.

"Too much is made out of stats," said Jim Turner, the former Jets and Broncos kicker. "What's important is longevity and to be able to kick in big games. And I always put an asterisk next to anybody who kicks indoors because that's like stealing candy."

The best attribute for kickers is not leg strength or accuracy—it's mental toughness. The kicker is all alone. If he misses a kick, he blows it. That might not be quite accurate, because the snap or hold might be bad, but everyone in the stadium blames the kicker.

As ex-Redskin Mark Moseley said, "The best thing you can say about a kicker is that he doesn't choke in the clutch. You need that kind of confidence."

And, on any given Sunday, one or two—or more—kickers is going to miss a kick with the game on the line. And every year, a kicker or three is going to get cut a few weeks into the season because he misses too many kicks—even the easy ones.

These twelve placekickers didn't miss very often.

1. JAN STENERUD—Jan Stenerud is the only full-time placekicker ever to be inducted into the Hall of Fame (1991, his first year of eligibility). He played for nineteen seasons (1967–85), longer than any other full-time placekicker, during which time the straight-on kicker gave way to his soccer-style counterpart.

Stenerud is the second-leading all-time scorer in pro football history, with 1,699 points for the Chiefs, Packers, and Vikings. His 67-percent field-goal accuracy (373-of-558) kept him near the top until a few years ago. He played in six Pro Bowls. In addition to his point total, he holds the career record with 373 field goals. He retired with the record for most seasons over 100 points (seven) and most field goals of 50 yards or more (17), and his 580 extra points placed him third in that category.

"For a sidewinder, he had power, and a lot of them give up power," says historian Joe Horrigan. "He's the prototype pure kicker, the kicker others measure themselves against."

Stenerud was noted for consistency and composure. In Super Bowl IV, Stenerud kicked a 48-yard field goal in the

JAN STENERUD

first quarter; it was a great psychological weapon against the Vikings, for the Chiefs knew that any time they crossed the 50-yard line they had a chance to score.

Stenerud's style was different from conventional soccer-style kickers. "In the old days, soccer-style kickers stood way off to the side and hooked their kicks," said Jim Turner. "Jan came from a little off center and got closer to the ball. That cuts down the hook and increases accuracy. Stenerud was simply unbelievable. He had a thunder leg."

"In 1981 in Green Bay, I made 22-of-24 field goals [then a single-season record for best percentage] in lousy conditions," Stenerud recalled. "In 1984 I was in the same groove for the whole season in Minnesota. I wasn't quite as talented [physically] as I was in '67, but I was at my peak in the eighties. I had learned to practice and groove a swing exactly the same way. I didn't know those things early on. But I was performing out of fear for nineteen years. I always felt, if I had two bad games in a row, I would be cut, even late in my career. It's an extremely insecure position. It's a constant pressure cooker."

His holder in Kansas City, Len Dawson, said, "In those days, we didn't work much on special teams. There's no telling how good Jan could have been had he started his career a decade later."

But it would be hard to be much better than to be the only kicker in the Hall of Fame.

LOU GROZA

2. LOU GROZA—A kicker doesn't get nicknamed "the Toe" unless he's one of the greats. Lou Groza was truly the pioneer, far ahead of the others of his day, which gave Cleveland a tremendous advantage early in his career. He was inducted into the Hall of Fame in 1974.

In twenty-one seasons (1946–59 and 1961–67), he scored 1,608 points for the Browns. He also played tackle for the first fourteen seasons, then just kicked for the last seven.

Altogether, Groza scored 1,608 points, still third on the all-time list (it was the record when he retired). He hit 264 field goals out of 481 attempts (55 percent) and 810 extra points. He was so proficient that the Browns started thinking of making field goals, instead of touchdowns, on fourth downs.

"Back then, the tragedies of playing and kicking weren't thought of," Groza said, "so you did it. I'd play tackle, get a sore back, then have to kick. How was I so successful? I just did what came naturally."

Groza prefers to think of himself as a tackle first (he played in nine Pro Bowls) who just happened to be the Browns' placekicker "because I had the talent." But it was a lot of talent.

"Groza was the best of the olden-day kickers," said Ben Agajanian, who kicked from 1945–64. "He kicked under pressure better than anyone I know."

GEORGE BLANDA

3. GEORGE BLANDA—George Blanda was thirty-one years old in 1958 when the Bears phased him out. In 1967, he was forty when the Oilers let him go. By the time he finally called it quits himself, Blanda was forty-six years old and had scored 2,002 points—all but 54 of them on kicking. In twenty-six seasons and 340 games—both records—he kicked 335 field goals in 638 attempts. He was inducted into the Hall of Fame in 1981.

Blanda is best remembered for the five games in 1970 when, at forty-three, he passed or kicked the Raiders to a final-second tie and four last-minute victories and became a national folk hero.

Longevity is Blanda's biggest asset, but he was a very accurate kicker for his day, as well as a great kicker in the clutch.

"He's my big hero," admits former Redskin placekicker Mark Moseley. "He probably wasn't the greatest kicker in the world, but he had a lot of opportunities to do outstanding things. And he was a great athlete, a real competitor. He had a mind of steel—he never got riled."

4. MARK MOSELEY— The last of the straight-on kickers, Mark Moseley scored 1,382 points over sixteen seasons to rank fifth on the all-time list, mostly with the Redskins. He was very consistent, hitting on 300 of 457 field-goal attempts (66 percent). He played in two Pro Bowls. In 1982, Moseley helped the Redskins get to the Super Bowl by kicking a record 20-of-21 field goals. He was even better a year later when he scored 161 points, a record for kickers. That year he also kicked 23 consecutive field goals without a miss. He is the only pure kicker to be named the league's Most Valuable Player (1982).

MARK MOSELEY

"I had a very easy demeanor," Moseley says. "You don't want to get riled up too often, so, when the team needed me, I'd be at my best. Strict concentration is what it takes. You could run guys over me, run Mack trucks at me, shoot me, but you can't break my concentration."

"The big thing is kicking when it counts [Moseley had 14 last-minute field goals], and he did it," remembered Lou Groza.

5. NICK LOWERY—Nick Lowery is a rags-to-riches story—he was cut eleven times by eight teams before beating out Jan Stenerud in Kansas City in 1980. He is the second-most accurate field-goal kicker in pro football history (behind Miami's Pete Stoyanovich) with an 80.1 percentage (306 of 382), as well as the second-ranked leader on the extra-point accuracy chart. He's a strong kicker who held the league record for most field goals from 50 yards or more for a number of years, and he has done it twice in a game three times. His 306 field goals ranks third all-time.

Lowery had the door slammed in his face by the Jets, Patriots, Buccaneers, Colts, Eagles, Bengals, Redskins, Redskins again, Saints, Chargers, Colts again, and Jets again before finally catching on with the Chiefs in 1980.

NICK LOWERY

"It's impossible to measure what's inside someone," Lowery says, "and that's what keeps sports exciting. If every kicker made every kick at the end of every game, would fourth quarters be exciting anymore? You want to watch robots, go someplace else."

Now the seventh-leading scorer in NFL history with 1,367 points, Lowery owns the record with ten 100-point seasons. He had his best season ever in 1990, when he hit 34 of 37 field goals and scored 139 points.

6. MORTEN ANDERSEN—

Morten Andersen is the third-most accurate kicker ever with a 78.1 percent mark on 246 of 315 field goals. Since he kicks in a domed stadium at least half of the season, he gets downgraded by some, but he was the placekicker on the Team of the 1980s and was selected for the Pro Bowl 1985 through '88 and again in '90 and '92.

Nick Lowery is impressed that Andersen has stayed near the top for so long. "That's an achievement," Lowery says, "because, once they expect it, that's another pressure. It's easier to climb up the ladder than stay on top of it."

In eleven seasons with the Saints, Andersen ranks fifteenth on the all-time scoring list with 1,085 points. His 21 field goals in 42 attempts of 50 yards or more is the all-time record.

7. GARY ANDERSON—The Steelers' Gary Anderson is a pressure kicker with an accurate and powerful leg. He ranks fourth in career accuracy (76.5 percent on 257 of 336 attempts).

He scored 1,123 points from 1982 to '92, ranking thirteenth, including six 100-point seasons. But he has been successful on only seven of 25 kicks of 50 yards or more, one of the lower averages for a top kicker.

Oilers quarterback Warren Moon was once asked who he'd least like to see kick against his team with four seconds left in a game. "Gary Anderson," Moon answered. "I've just seen him make too many big kicks against us. It doesn't matter what kind of weather it is or what kind of kick he needs. Whether it's for the playoffs or it's in overtime, he'd probably be the guy I'd least want to see."

8. PAT LEAHY— Leahy kicked for eighteen seasons with the Jets—a record with one team for a placekicker—and is the third all-time scorer with 1,470 points. He hit 304 of 426 field-goal attempts (71.4 percent). Leahy aged

well—he seemed to get better as he got older, scoring more than 100 points in three of his last four seasons. In 1990, he hit 23 of 26 field goal attempts.

"He impresses me," said Jim Turner. "He withstood Shea [Stadium], which is a bitch to kick in, and the Meadowlands is no picnic, either."

On his ranking on the all-time scoring list, Leahy said, "I'm obviously proud of it. I think it isn't just scooting up on that list. It's actually an indication, I think, of survival, because I'm most proud of not the number of points I score, but that I stayed all these years."

9. JIM TURNER—Pro football's fourth-leading scorer with 1,439 points, Jim Turner hit 62 percent of his field goals (304-of-488) over sixteen seasons while playing in the quagmire of Shea Stadium and the thin air of Denver.

"I liked the pressure," Turner said. "I would like to go in today in the last three seconds of a game."

Turner retired as pro football's No. 2 all-time scorer and field-goal kicker behind George Blanda. He was also the leading scorer for both the Jets and Broncos. And his 34 field goals in 1968 was a league record until 1983. He kicked three field goals in Super Bowl III, providing the margin of victory for the Jets over the Colts.

10. EDDIE MURRAY— In 1988, Eddie Murray hit on 21 of 22 field-goal attempts for the Lions, the best single-season accuracy mark ever. And, the next year, he matched those numbers—a two-year streak unequaled in NFL history. Nicknamed "Money" (as in "on the money"), Murray hit 249 of 334 tries for 75 percent and scored 1,141 points, thirteenth all-time, from 1980 to '92.

"He was very competitive. He wanted to be the best," said Frank Gansz, his kicking coach with the Lions.

11. JIM BAKKEN—Bakken spent seventeen years with the Cardinals (1962–78). In that time he scored 1,380 points, making him the game's sixth-leading all-time scorer. He was successful on 282 of 447 field-goal attempts, a strong 63 percent for his time, and played in four Pro Bowls. He kicked a record seven field goals in nine attempts in a 1967 game, which are both still records.

12. FRED COX—The eighth all-time leading scorer with 1,365 points in fifteen seasons with Minnesota, Fred Cox kicked a field goal in a league-record thirty-one straight games and hit on 282 of 455 during his career (62 percent).

"There's no way in hell his lifetime percentage can compare with a guy who kicks in the Silverdome," said Jan Stenerud. "Cox had to kick in that old [Metropolitan] stadium up there."

Punters

For the NFL's first fifty years, punters just kicked the ball as far as they could. Today hang time, net average, punts inside the twenty, and touchbacks are how to measure the talents of a punter. Instead of kicking the ball past the coverage, the idea is to kick it high and to certain areas and let the cover teams handle the return man.

The same rule changes in 1974 that affected the kicking of field goals had their impact on punting, as well as one that allows only two defenders to go downfield before the kick. That's why the high punting averages of the past are gone forever.

"Several times a game, you have to kick a punt thirty-five yards or less, and it's very difficult to keep a high gross average," says the Giants' Sean Landeta. "It means you have to maximize every chance. When you have seventy yards in front of you, you can't kick it forty-five yards—you need fifty-five."

Hall of Famer Yale Lary admits that all he used to do was just kick the ball as far as he could. "There was no hang time back then," Lary says. "But I'd love to punt it now in the controlled atmospheres of domed stadiums, not in the cold and sleet and snow of outdoors."

So the advantages and disadvantages of the different eras work both ways.

RAY GUY

1. RAY GUY—For fourteen seasons, the headlines usually read: "This Guy is Incredible." And they were right. Ray Guy is the only full-time punter ever to have been selected in the first round of the draft. While his average of 42.4 yards per punt ranks only eighteenth, he was the first to combine hang time with distance and placement. He helped make punting a respectable profession.

Guy was All-Pro six times and played in seven Pro Bowls in eight years from 1973 to '80, leading the NFL in punting three times (1974, '75, and '77). He played his last five seasons without having a punt blocked (619 kicks), and he averaged over 40 yards in thirteen of his fourteen seasons. Someday he might be the first pure punter inducted into the Hall of Fame (he was a finalist for the Hall in 1992).

"He's the first punter you looked at and said he won games," says Joe Horrigan, the historian at the Hall of Fame. "He combined great skills of placement and power, kicking long, high punts, putting the ball where he wanted to. He's the greatest punter we've seen so far."

"He was the first legitimate superstar guy," said ex-Giants and Jets punter Dave Jennings. "He had the perfect style—kicking perfectly straight, with the right leg on his follow-through coming towards his face."

"You know, he was a helluva athlete," said NBC analyst Paul Maguire, the only punter who kicked for the entire ten-year existence of the AFL. "He was an ex-quarterback, and a damn good one at that. He had great extension and power in his leg."

If consistency is the mark of a great punter, Guy was it. "In games, he kicked higher than anybody else consistently," says Sean Landeta. "Others had better numbers, but he had height and very good distance, which is a great combination for an effective punt."

Guy was fearless, inpervious to the menace of eleven charging defensive players or the possibility of a shanked punt. Guy played in 229 consecutive games. He punted 1,049 times—the fourth-highest total ever—and had only three blocked. His 111 punts in postseason games is a record, and few of his kicks were ever returned for a touchdown. He is also remembered for being the first player to ricochet a punt off the overhead scoreboard that hangs ninety feet above the Superdome surface.

When he retired because of a back injury, he said, "I've really accomplished what I set out to do. The only thing that's left would be the Hall of Fame. Hopefully, I'll make that. We'll just have to wait and see. Time will tell."

2. SAMMY BAUGH—Forget that Sammy Baugh played when punters just kicked for distance. Baugh was one of the greatest athletes ever—a star at quarterback, safety, and punter. He's still the all-time punting leader with a 45.1-yard average for his Redskins career. In 1940 he averaged 51.4 yards on 35 kicks. He led the NFL in punting every year from 1940 to '43.

"My two idols growing up were Sammy Baugh and Yale Lary," former Kansas City punter Jerrel Wilson says of the only two punters who are in the Hall of Fame. "They used a different ball back then,

SAMMY BAUGH

and it was a different game. I tried my damnedest to break his record. I hate to say never, but it's going to be awful, awful tough for somebody to have a fifty-yard average for a season. I could stay with it for eight or nine weeks, but then things happen."

"Baugh's average speaks for itself," says Jim Campbell. "Placement is a lost art now. It's just, 'Get the ball off, and we'll make the tackle.' Coffin corner is a term nobody understands anymore. Baugh knew how to coffin-corner."

After watching films of Baugh, Ray Guy was impressed with his ability to control the ball, a talent that sometimes escaped the power-kicking Guy. "He could do things with a football I've never seen," said Guy, who considered Baugh the best punter ever.

HORACE GILLOM

3. HORACE GILLOM—Paul Brown used to tell people that Horace Gillom was the best punter ever. Gillom was certainly the first full-time punter ever, so good that the Browns could afford to make him a specialist. He had a 43.8-yard average during his ten-year career with the Browns (1947–56) and was the first to kick for hang time because he was a tremendously high kicker for his day.

"He was the first guy to move back fifteen yards from center rather than 12 yards," said Paul Maguire. "That allowed them to really spread out the punting team."

"I've asked old-timers about him," says Sean Landeta, "and they tell me he was a tremendous punter back then. He kicked it high and far. The two names that I always heard were Horace Gillom and Glenn Dobbs, who was a great, great punter who fell short of the all-time record because he didn't have 300 punts, but he would have been first by a mile [Dobbs had a 46.4-yard average on 231 punts]."

"Horace was the greatest punter I've ever seen play pro football," said former Browns guard Lin Houston. "They can talk about Ray Guy all the want. He couldn't hold a candle to Horace."

4. ROHN STARK—Rohn Stark of the Colts entered the 1987 season having surpassed Sammy Baugh's record for best lifetime punting average, but he has since slipped back to fourth place with a 44.0-yard career average (although he's higher than anybody who has more than 700 career punts).

"Rohn has a strong leg," says Sean Landeta. "On top of it, he plays indoors, but, even outside, he's very good."

"He plays in all those Eastern cities ouside, and those wind currents are atrocious, but he's done a great job," admits Jerrel Wilson.

Stark has led the NFL in punting three times, more than any other active player and one behind the record held by Sammy Baugh and Wilson. He also has eight of the Colts' ten highest seasonal averages.

ROHN STARK

5. YALE LARY—Yale Lary was a multitalented player, starring at safety, punter, and kickoff returner during his eleven-year career with Detroit. He led the NFL in punting three times and played in nine Pro Bowls. He has the third-best gross punting average of 44.3 yards. He averaged 48.9 yards in 1963 with one of the strongest legs ever.

"I think he's the one who perfected punting," says former Chiefs punter Jerrell Wilson. "He had the great ideas—how to hold the ball, meeting the ball at the right time. I couldn't do what he did."

"Yale invariably put the ball across midfield when punting from the end zone," ex-teammate and Hall of Famer Joe Schmidt said. "He made us [the defense] look good by giving us room to work."

6. SEAN LANDETA—Now the NFL's eighth-leading all-time punter with a 43.4-yard average, the Giants' Sean Landeta has had only one kick blocked during his career, fewer than anyone, until 1992, when he had two blocked. He was the punter on the Team of the 1980s. Landeta is also one of the best directional and "pooch" punters in the game today.

"He's the most consistent punter," said Paul Maguire. "Nobody works harder at it. He doesn't necessarily depend on his ability; it's concentration—total concentration."

"He's a great punter out of the end zone," said Dave Jennings. "That's the true test. That's what separates good punters from not-good punters. You can count on him. Anybody can kick from midfield."

7. JERREL WILSON—The punter on the all-time AFL team, Jerrel Wilson punted 1,072 times (the second-most ever) in sixteen years, mostly with the Chiefs (1962–77), averaging 43.2 yards per punt. He was a power punter, and he's tied with Sammy Baugh for leading the league the most times (four). But he also had twelve punts blocked, the most of the ten best all-time punters.

Players today finesse the ball. As for Wilson? "I attacked the ball," Wilson said. "I tried to bust it every time I kicked it. That was my goal. And two days before I was released by Bum Phillips in Houston [1978], I busted a ball in warmup. I wish it would have happened in a game. I always wanted to see how the referees would react if I busted one and the bladder came out."

8. RICH CAMARILLO—Rich Camarillo is the classic rags-to-riches story for punters—going from free agency to the Pro Bowl. Now with the Cardinals after eight years with the Patriots and Rams, Camarillo is a boomer who gets great hang time and is an excellent directional punter.

"He kicked in a lousy place [New England] and did a great job," said Dave Jennings. "And he's so good aiming away from a returner."

Camarillo, a four-time Pro Bowler, has a career average of 42.8 yards per punt, which ranks twelfth all-time. His 45.3-yard average in 1991 ranks second in Cardinals' history behind Jerry Norton.

9. DAVE JENNINGS—Nobody ever punted more times than Dave Jennings, who did so 1,154 times over fourteen seasons with the Giants and Jets (1974–87). He averaged 40.9 yards and set a record for most consecutive punts without having one blocked, 623, from 1976 to '83. He was a true student of punting, and he was responsible for the NFL keeping record of net average, punts inside the twenty, and touchbacks.

"For a five-year stretch in the middle of his career, you could say he was as good or better than anyone in the game. And that's saying something," says Sean Landeta.

"I liked to aim it out of bounds," Jennings admitted. "I kicked it away from the returner—there's no rules that say you have to kick it to a guy."

Larry Pasquale, his special-teams coach, said, "He had a knack of making the ball land inside the twenty and having it bounce sideways. I still don't know how he did it."

10. REGGIE ROBY—The Dolphins' Reggie Roby can kick the ball like perhaps no other punter ever. But he's also one of the most inconsistent ever, and he outkicks his coverage too often.

"He puts that thing into the ionosphere," says Joe Horrigan. "But the coverage doesn't have the opportunity to get downfield to cover the punt, and the returner has a running start."

Whereas most of the top punters have a season or two in which they average less than 40 yards per punt, Roby's lowest seasonal average is 41.2. He had a career high with a 45.7-yard mark in 1991.

11. TOMMY DAVIS—Tommy Davis' 44.7-yard average is the second-highest ever. He placekicked and punted for the 49ers from 1959 to '69, and he played in two Pro Bowls. He had only two of 511 punts blocked, tied for second-fewest of those on the all-time top ten list. Davis still holds the record with 234 consecutive extra points, and his 99.43 percentage on conversions (348 of 350) is also the record.

12. JERRY NORTON—Jerry Norton's 42.8-yard average is tied for fifth all-time. In eleven seasons with four teams (1954–64) he played in five Pro Bowls. He had only two of 358 kicks blocked. Norton was also a top defensive back who intercepted 35 passes. In 1960, he led the NFL in both punting and interceptions. In one game a year later, he intercepted four Bobby Layne passes, returning two of them for touchdowns. More than any other punter of his day, because of his ball-carrying abilities, Norton was a threat on fake punts.

TEN

KICK RETURNERS

It's like embalming. Nobody likes to,
but someone has to.
TED WATTS

Everybody has seen it at one time or another, either live or on one of those "Greatest Sports Legends" TV shows . . . Gale Sayers backs up to the goal line, cradles a kickoff into his hands, and takes off . . . dodging here, weaving there, all the way to a 100-yard touchdown.

You either saw it twenty-five years ago or you see it now on highlight shows because you don't see it much in the NFL today. Returning a kick for a touchdown is a lost art. Special teams have become so good that about the only time it happens is when everything breaks down and a player scoots through a hole untouched to the end zone.

Gone are the days of Sayers, Travis Williams, and Ollie Matson, stars who danced and zigzagged their way to a score. Very rarely do you see players like Billy "White Shoes" Johnson and Rick Upchurch going all the way on a punt return. Detroit's Mel Gray may be the one exception today, as he is a threat on both kickoff and punt returns.

There are a lot of reasons why. "Every team has a special-teams coach now," says former Eagles coach Dick Vermeil, who was the first special teams coach in the NFL. "And teams are more defensive on their kicks."

Two decades ago, teams didn't place much of an emphasis on kick returns; somebody just did it. "Some did it with speed, some did it with guile, some did it with guts and some did it with no brains," says Jim Campbell.

They did get it done a few decades ago. As Campbell points out, "The only way you score on a kick return now is you get a seam in the wall and—bingo— you're gone. Back then, guys danced around in the open field for half a minute before scoring. Back then, they were truly broken-field runners."

There is a big difference between returning a kickoff and a punt. One of the best ever at both was Abe Woodson, who played from 1958 to 1966. "Kickoffs, they give me time to set myself up and give the blockers time to set themselves up. Punts are almost pure instinct. You have a chance for only one move. You don't have time to readjust. You have to react to the first tackler and try to take it from there. Either you find a hole and get through, or they clobber you."

No matter if it's returning kickoffs or punts, those who do live in a pinball world.

Kickoff Returners

Perhaps the most deflating thing that can happen to a football team is to score and then have the opposing team return the ensuing kickoff for a touchdown. It's enough to change the momentum—and maybe the outcome of the game.

But it doesn't happen much anymore. "You have great coverage guys today," says Frank Gansz, Detroit's special-teams coach. "The parameters of the field haven't changed, and today's players are bigger, stronger, and faster. There's tremendous speed out there, and [the outside] people cover a lot of ground. You won't see people get those big runs anymore."

Former placekicker Jan Stenerud doesn't agree. "I don't buy that about 'better, stronger, faster,'" he says. "Some of the guys I played with twenty years ago were talented, talented athletes. They aren't any better now, in my opinion."

"It's very exciting to try to beat eleven guys at one time," Woodson said. "But it's also very dangerous. You feel like a marked man, like a tackling dummy. Those eleven guys are coming head-on, at full speed, with one thought in mind—to bury you."

The most exciting year ever for kickoff returners was 1967, when Gale Sayers and Travis Williams literally dueled week after week for the NFL lead. When it was over, Williams, a rookie, had returned four of 18 kickoffs for touchdowns and finished with an average of 41.06 yards per return, which is still a record. Sayers averaged 37.69 yards on 16 returns, still second on the single-season list. He returned three for TDs that year.

GALE SAYERS

1. GALE SAYERS—Over an injury-shortened career, Sayers averaged 30.6 yards per kickoff return, a full yard ahead of anyone else ever. He returned six of 91 kickoffs for touchdowns, also a record. No kick returner ever had Sayers' moves. In fact, he would also be the top-ranked punt returner if he had enough attempts.

There's no argument: Sayers was the greatest kickoff returner ever. And—forget that coverages are better—he would score a few touchdowns if he played today.

"Sayers would do equally as well today," Gansz admits. "He was one of the best for setting up—he would hit a tempo and accelerate."

"Oh, yeah . . . he was great," Stenerud said. "If I had to pick one, he had to be the most dangerous."

"Anytime you're in the twenty-five-yard [average] group, you're in that exceptional group," said Vermeil. "And Sayers was over thirty [yards]. That's what I mean. He was as good as the best."

"He was the most versatile guy I've seen in that he could run on his own, setting things up on his own, more or less," said Abe Woodson.

"He did stuff nobody has done before or since—or ever will," asserts historian Campbell. "And kickoffs were where he did it best. He truly was magic."

Joe Horrigan put it another way. "Any way you could put the ball in his hands, he was a potential touchdown. No one else has come that close."

Sayers agrees. "It was one more chance I could get my hands on the football and maybe score," he says. "And that's the way I felt about it—it was an easy way to get back into the football game. I loved doing it. I could see the whole field. I could see everybody coming down on me."

2. OLLIE MATSON—The fastest man in the NFL in the early fifties (he won two medals in the 1952 Olympics), Ollie Matson was truly awesome on kickoffs, where all of his talents—a combination of speed and power—were put on display. He returned six of them for touchdowns and finished with a 26.2-yard average on 143 kicks. In 1958, Matson had a 35.5-yard average, third best of all time.

"Speed and quickness—that's what you need to return kicks," Matson says. "I was big, 210, but I was swift for that size. I could either run around you, over you, or through you. I didn't do a lot of hard cutting like Gale did. But we both had that peripheral vision to know where guys were going to be. And we had the speed to get there."

OLLIE MATSON

Matson was like Sayers in that he was dangerous any time he had the ball, but kickoffs was where he had a chance to do his thing. Over his career he rushed for 5,173 yards, caught 222 passes, and scored 73 touchdowns. But he played on only two teams that ever had a winning record during his fourteen seasons with the Chicago Cardinals, Rams (to whom he was traded for nine players), Lions, and Eagles. He was inducted into the Hall of Fame in 1969.

Hampton Pool, the Rams coach when Matson played, said, "I think he's faster than [Bears Hall of Famer] George McAfee, and he has lots more power. He can run over people."

TRAVIS WILLIAMS

3. TRAVIS WILLIAMS—In five seasons with the Packers and Rams, Travis Williams returned six kickoffs for touchdowns, and his 27.5-yard average still ranks fifth all-time. He led the NFL in 1967 and '71.

"I remember that [1967] season," Sayers said. "You always looked in the papers, you know, what did Travis Williams do this week? But you can't worry about the other fella. Travis had great speed, but not great moves. He was a straight-ahead runner. But once he got in the open, he could fly."

Williams once summed up his talents on kickoffs as, "Go full speed and see what happens." Then he added, "I'm not unusual. I just have unusual speed and those big guys in front of me. They're the ones who do it."

Williams, who called Sayers his idol, was a muscular 215-pounder with 9.3 speed over 100 yards. In 1967, he didn't even return kickoffs until the seventh game. He scored on his third return that game (93 yards), and, two weeks later, he returned two more for touchdowns (87 and 85 yards) in the same quarter.

So, with three TDs on his first six returns, Williams had already tied the single-season record. Then, in the next-to-last game, he broke the record with his fourth TD return, this one 104 yards.

"Travis was another outstanding guy at that time," said Abe Woodson. " He had a lot of power. He was a combination of Sayers and Matson."

4. ABE WOODSON—Abe Woodson was truly a kick-return specialist during his nine seasons with San Francisco and St. Louis (1958–66), and nobody else has ever led the league three different seasons. Woodson also has the most returns among the top twenty kickoff returners, 193. He ranks third all-time with a 28.7-yard average. He returned three for touchdowns in 1963 and five overall.

"I wasn't like those other guys," Woodson admitted. "My style was picking the hole and following the blocking pattern."

"Do I remember Abe Woodson? He was really tremendous," Matson recalls. "Teams didn't want to kick it to him. He could put it on your mind."

Speed was Woodson's forte (he was also a good defensive back). Woodson was once called "King of the Suicide Runners."

"This guy can kill you," said Allie Sherman when he coached the Giants. "We've seen him come out of a corner where he really looked hemmed in. When he gets out of there, his acceleration is really something."

5. LYNN CHANDNOIS—Who, you might ask, is Lynn Chandnois? He's simply the second all-time leading kickoff returner in NFL history with a 29.6-yard average over seven seasons with the Steelers (1950–56). He led the NFL in 1951 and '52 and returned three for touchdowns.

Chandnois was capable of a tremendous upfield burst that was exciting to watch. "He was another great kick returner. He was quick and he was fast," remembers Ollie Matson.

6. BUDDY YOUNG—At 5-foot-5, 170 pounds, Buddy Young was one of the first scatbacks. He played nine seasons (1947–55) with several teams and is fourth all-time with a 27.9-yard average. He was a dodging, all-across-the-field type of runner.

"He was like a little waterbug, tremendously fast and maneuverable," says Bob Carroll.

"There's a difference between being quick and being fast," claims Ollie Matson. "Some guys who are fast are not quick, and some are quick but not fast. When you combine the two together, hey, man, you have something. Buddy Young had that."

7. RON SMITH—Ron Smith's 275 kickoff returns for 6,922 yards are the most ever, and that's how he made his living. He played for ten years (1965–

74) with five teams (Bears, Falcons, Rams, Chargers, and Raiders) He had a 25.2-yard average and three touchdowns.

"I remember when he came up, he said, 'I'm going to beat all your records. You wait and see,'" Woodson remembered. "And he did."

8. TIM BROWN—Tim Brown is one of only three players to return two kickoffs in one game for touchdowns, doing so in 1966. He had a 26.0-yard average and five touchdowns during a ten-year career with the Packers, Eagles, and Colts. Despite a name so similar to Jim Brown's, Tim never got the recognition he deserved in the 1960s, but he was one of the most dangerous runners in the game.

9. BOBBY MITCHELL—Bobby Mitchell was a great open-field runner and breakaway threat for the Browns and Redskins. He averaged 26.4 yards per kickoff return and ran back five for touchdowns. Combined with three TDs on punt returns, his total of eight returns for scores is tied for second all-time to Matson's nine. From 1958–63 he returned either a kickoff or a punt for a score every season. Mitchell still ranks thirteenth all-time on the kickoff list.

10. MERCURY MORRIS—In his day, no one cut the corner like Mercury Morris. And he was as exciting on kickoff returns as his name implied. He didn't return kicks his entire career, but, of the 111 kickoffs he did run back, he took three all the way for touchdowns. His 26.5-yard average ranks tenth.

"He was very dangerous every time he stood back there," remembers Chiefs placekicker Jan Stenerud. "And people don't realize he was strong, too."

Punt Returners

There's nothing in football like watching a punt returner dare to catch a ball with two or three defenders closing in on him, make a few cuts and jukes, and blow by everybody for a long touchdown.

It's something you don't see much of anymore. "Those guys covering punts now have so much speed," says ex-Chiefs punter Jerrel Wilson, "and the game is so conscious of hang time. That's why."

"In football, there's offense and defense," former Denver return specialist Rick Upchurch said. "It's very seldom that an individual really stands out on special teams. It's dangerous, yeah, but I guess that's what makes it so exciting. It's all so helter-skelter out there that the excitement is keeping a cool head and reactions."

But there have been a few over the years, with Upchurch and Billy "White

Shoes" Johnson being the two best. From 1975 to '78, those two players each led the NFL in punt returns twice, usually battling for the lead week by week, often return by return.

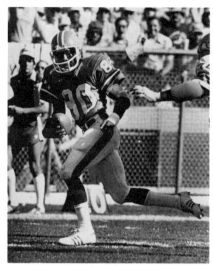

RICK UPCHURCH

1. RICK UPCHURCH—Rick Upchurch combined the lightning speed of a wide receiver, the running ability of a halfback, and a sense of fearlessness into a force that made him one of the best punt returners ever in an era of offensive and defensive stars. Upchurch made special teams one of the most exciting facets of football during his nine years with the Broncos (1975–83).

In that time, he returned 248 punts for 3,008 yards (12.1-yard average, sixth all-time) and eight touchdowns. He set a record for most punt-return yards and tied a record for most returns for touchdowns in a season (four in 1976). Upchurch tied records for most kicks returned for a touchdown in a game (two in 1976 against Cleveland) and most touchdowns on punt returns for a career. He still owns the three longest punt returns in Broncos history (92, 87, and 78 yards). He's one of only two players to lead the NFL three times. And he was named to three Pro Bowl berths on his return abilities alone.

Upchurch's disregard for his body enabled his success. "I never saw the defenders once the ball was snapped," he said. "I knew if I was thinking about them I wasn't concentrating on the rock. I couldn't run without the rock."

Even at 6-foot and 170 pounds, Upchurch was durable. "He's not like the punt returner who, once you really lay it on him, will be hesitant to catch it again," said former Broncos special teams coach Marv Braden. "I've seen 'Uppy' get hit like a ton of bricks, and it didn't faze him. He had no fear of getting hit. Uppy could not be intimidated. He thought the next punt would be the one he breaks for a touchdown."

"Upchurch had more flat-out speed than Billy [Johnson]," says Jerrel Wilson. "If he got behind somebody and started down the sideline, there was no way I could catch him."

2. BILLY "WHITE SHOES" JOHNSON—Say the name "Billy Johnson," and not everybody knows who you are talking about. But say "White Shoes," and every football fan will know you're talking about one of the most exciting kick returners the game has ever seen.

The Oilers were at their low point in 1974 when they decided to use a normally useless 15th-round draft choice on a 5-foot-9, 160-pound running back who ended up being their only draftee to make the team. Head coach Sid Gillman didn't want "midgets" on his team. But Johnson was no midget. And he lasted 12 years with the Oilers and Falcons.

"He changed the game," says Jerrel Wilson. "You couldn't punt to him. Ten guys trying to tackle him wasn't enough. He really thought he could run by everybody on the field. He had a God-given instinct you couldn't teach."

Johnson would cheat up on punters, trying to get them to kick the ball over his

BILLY JOHNSON

head. He returned more punts than anyone (282) for the most yards (3,317), over his fifteen-year career with the Oilers, Falcons, and Redskins. He still ranks seventh all-time with an 11.8-yard average. His six touchdowns (three in 1975, as well as a kickoff returned for a score) is the third-best, and he played in three Pro Bowls.

Punters tried kicking away from Johnson, but, as Dave Green once said, "I'd punt long and I'd punt short. But he still got to the ball quicker than any two safetymen could."

Johnson was a small bundle of energy who could change the outcome of a game in a matter of seconds. "People look for players who take chances," he said. "The return man is a daredevil. Fans love to see him break a run all the way."

And few players ever broke returns all the way more than Billy White Shoes.

3. JACK CHRISTIANSEN—In 1951, his rookie season with the Lions, Jack Christiansen returned four punts for touchdowns, a record that has only been tied (by Upchurch). The next year, he returned 15 punts for 322 yards, a 21.47-yard average that is still the second-highest ever. And his 12.8-yard career average is just fractions below George McAfee's record.

A Hall of Famer, Christiansen returned eight of his 85 punts for touchdowns with an uncanny running style. He wasn't flashy, like Upchurch or Johnson, but he got the ball into the end zone.

"Plus, he had a coach in Buddy Parker who recognized his talents and didn't hesitate using him as a punt returner," says the Hall of Fame's Joe Horrigan.

JACK CHRISTIANSEN

In 1951, Christiansen returned 18 punts for 343 yards and a 19.1-yard average, with the four scores, twice in two different games. The next year, opposing teams started using the spread formation on punts to try to contain him. Still, he returned 15 punts for 322 yards and an even better 21.5-yard average to lead the league and two more touchdowns.

Not bad for somebody who came into the pros at 6-foot-1 and only 162 pounds.

4. GEORGE McAFEE—

George McAfee retired from football over forty years ago, but he still has the highest career punt-return average (12.8 yards). "One-Play" McAfee could change a game quickly during his eight-year career with the Bears.

"Does that record still hold?" McAfee asked recently. "I came from a family of twelve, and you had to be fast to get to the dinner table. I guess I was blessed with pretty good speed."

A star at halfback and defensive back in addition to returning kicks, McAfee was a gamebreaker who was a threat to go all the way every time he touched the ball. Fifteen years after he retired, Gale Sayers was being compared to him and Chicago coach George Halas wouldn't say one was better than the other. Red Grange once called McAfee "the most dangerous man with the football in the game."

McAfee had tremendous speed, but it was deceiving because of his size (6-foot, 177 pounds). He returned two of 112 punts for touchdowns. He was inducted into the Hall of Fame in 1967.

5. MEL GRAY—Mel Gray is the best returner of the last decade. His career average of 12.1 yards on punts is tied with Rick Upchurch for sixth all-time, and he's also the best kickoff returner today (his 5,686 yards on kickoffs is the second-most ever).

CBS broadcaster John Madden says, "He's very dangerous. He's the best kick returner in the league today. When you think of the Lions after Barry Sanders, Mel Gray is their most potent weapon."

The 5-foot-9 162-pounder gets knocked into next week every time he returns a kick. But in 1991 he became the first player to lead the NFL in both kickoff (25.8 yards) and punt returns (15.4) in the same season.

"What an incredible weapon," marvels Lions offensive coordinator Dan Henning. "A great return man adds so much to a team."

Gray says there are two keys to a return man's success: Never think and always move. "When I get out there, everything shuts off," he says. "It has to be that way. And I never stand completely still, even when the ball's coming to me."

6. BILL DUDLEY—The fifth all-time leading punt returner, "Bullet Bill" Dudley returned one 96 yards for a touchdown in 1950, the fifth-longest ever. He played for nine seasons (1946–54) with the Steelers, Redskins, and Lions. In 1946, he led the NFL in rushing, interceptions, and punt returns and was named the league's Most Valuable Player. A year later, he scored 13 touchdowns on one punt return, one kickoff return, seven receptions, and four runs. He also threw two TD passes.

At 5-foot-10, 176 pounds, he was considered too small to play football, but no kick returner ever used his blockers better than Dudley. He wasn't nearly as fast as his nickname would suggest—he had more moves than speed, and he often left would-be tacklers off-balance and grasping at air.

McAfee, who played at the same time as Dudley, said, "He had pretty good speed, not blinding speed. But he was a great runner."

7. EMLEN TUNNELL—A Hall of Fame safety, Emlen Tunnell returned five punts for touchdowns during his fourteen-year career (1948–61) with the Giants and Packers. He was the most prolific returner during his day, holding the career yardage records for both punt and interception returns when he retired.

Tunnell ran back 258 punts for 2,209 yards and an 8.6-yard average. As a rookie, he made too many fair catches, earning the wrath of the impatient fans. "I made up my mind right there," he once said. "Never again would I field a punt without trying to advance it."

8. CHARLEY TRIPPI—Charley Trippi was a great all-around performer, playing halfback, quarterback, and defensive back for nine seasons with the Cardinals (1947–55). But it's in the open field that he made things happen. His 75-yard return on a frozen field in the 1947 NFL championship was the only clutch punt return ever in a big game (he slipped and fell twice on the runback, only to get back up and keep running) and it provided the margin of victory for the Cardinals.

The first of the big-money players, Trippi returned only 63 punts during his career, but he had a 13.7-yard average and two touchdowns.

9. GREG PRUITT—Greg Pruitt was still catching punts late in his career at a time when most running backs have nothing but disdain for a duty given mostly to young players. But, in 1983, when he was thirty-two, Pruitt returned 58 punts for 666 yards, then a record. His 97-yard return that season is the fourth-longest in NFL history.

Pruitt was a versatile runner-receiver and a fine kickoff returner, with speed and quickness. He played twelve seasons for the Browns and Raiders, and is the only player to gain over 2,000 yards rushing, receiving, kick returning, and punt returning.

10. BILLY THOMPSON—Billy Thompson led the AFL in both punt and kickoff returns as a rookie in 1969—the first player ever to do so in any pro league. He was also a fine defensive back who intercepted 40 passes. Thompson played in three Pro Bowls with Denver. His 11.6-yard average on 157 punts ranks ninth all-time.

Who's the Best?

Who's the greatest quarterback ever and who's the best running back of all time are questions that will forever be asked . . . and maybe somewhat answered by this book.

But here's an even bigger question: Who's the greatest pro football *player* of all time? Forget about positions—who's the single best player ever?

In a quick survey, several longtime pro football observers were asked this question. Here's their response.

Name: Rick Korch
Background: Author of this book; managing editor of *Pro Football Weekly*.
The best ever was: Jim Brown

"If Jim Brown hadn't retired after his ninth season, he would have set records that Walter Payton—or any other player—wouldn't even have thought about breaking. He averaged eight-tenths of a yard more per carry than Payton. If he had carried the ball as many times as Payton did, he would have gained 20,031 yards. If he would have played as many games as Payton did, he would have scored 215 touchdowns. They say Brown didn't catch the ball, but he averaged 2.2 receptions per game as compared with Payton's 2.4 (and Payton held the career record for running backs). Brown led the NFL in rushing eight of his nine seasons; only Don Hutson dominated his position like that. It's just too bad Brown didn't play a few more years, because then there wouldn't have been any argument. But he dominated his position like no player ever has."

Name: Jim Campbell
Background: Pro football historian. Former historian for the Pro Football Hall of Fame, research editor for NFL Properties, and director of communications for the NFL Alumni. Currently director of the Bison Club at Bucknell University.
The best ever was: Larry Wilson

"Pound for pound, Larry Wilson was the toughest there ever was. He played safety better than anybody has ever played it, and he revolutionized the position with the safety blitz. Wilson played his ass off for some pretty bad teams when he was with the Cardinals from 1960–72, and I think he got more out of his ability than anybody I can think of. And he did it over an extended period of time. He was a hard-nosed player who never quit. My instant impression of him was a guy with two broken hands who intercepted a ball with what seemed like his elbows."

Name: Joe Horrigan
Background: Research historian at the Pro Football Hall of Fame.
The best ever was: Don Hutson

"Hutson was so far ahead of his contemporaries. He was the prototypical wide receiver, the one by which everyone after him would be measured. His records not only stood the test of time, but no single receiver was ever able to accomplish all that Hutson was able to do during his eleven years as a pro. When he retired, Hutson held nineteen NFL records, including receptions, touchdowns, yards and points. In 1942, when he caught 74 passes—which was the most ever caught in a season until then—the second-leading receiver in the league that year had only 27. For a tall, skinny kid who many thought wouldn't make it as a pro, I'd say that wasn't too bad."

Name: Bob Oates
Background: Pro football writer for the *Los Angeles Times*. He has been covering pro football since 1939.
The best ever was: Dick Butkus.

"Most people will choose an offensive player, but Dick Butkus is the one I think of first. In his prime, he came closer to being a dominating player week in and week out than anybody I've ever seen. He dominated at all times and was always ready to play. He also played an important position, and the way he played it was something else. But here's my most important factor: If you mention anyone else, I'll find a weakness. I can't find any weaknesses in Dick Butkus."

Name: Bob Carroll

Background: Pro football historian and author of 11 pro football books, including *The Hidden Game of Pro Football* and *The 100 Greatest Running Backs.*

The best ever was: Don Hutson.

"From the standpoint of comparison to his peers, it has to be Hutson because he was so far ahead of everybody else at his position. He was the first player to catch pass after pass after pass, and he was also a very good defensive back. He caught 489 passes, and, when he retired in 1947, the next-nearest player was Jim Benton with 288. He was agile and fast, and he could run after the catch, and he set records for yardage and touchdowns that are only just now being broken. From his first game, he was considered the best ever to play the position, and he still is."

Name: Bill Wallace

Background: Sportswriter for *The New York Times* who has covered pro football since 1959.

The best ever was: Lawrence Taylor

"Taylor, more than any player save a quarterback, had the ability to dominate a game by his means, disruption of an offense. His presence was the difference between winning or losing in many games, especially in the Giants' two Super Bowl seasons. He had many roles: pass-rushing end, blitzing inside linebacker or outside coverage on a pass. He had many techniques, like busting through double coverage, or zooming around single coverage, and that overhand clawing tackle at the ball that brought about so many quarterback turnovers. More subtly, he intimidated by his mere presence. Players on offense were handicapped when they come to the line of scrimmage thinking not so much of the play that's been called by a comfortable coach but rather, 'Where is he? What's he going to do next? Will he make a fool of me—again?'"

Name: David Neft

Background: Pro football historian and co-author of *The Football Encyclopedia.*

The best ever was: Ernie Nevers

"If you pick just one player, the one-platoon guys have a tremendous advantage. Ernie Nevers did absolutely everything, and he was superb in everything. He was the fullback in the double-wing, and the whole offense revolved around him. He did the bulk of the ball-carrying, virtually all of the passing, he kicked extra points and field goals and did a lot of punting. And he also played a very good linebacker. Nevers also invented something that was supposed to be a modern innovation—he was the first player to plan strategy based on what the defense gave him. In the double-wing there was little or no huddling—Nevers called plays out of the backfield. He also played major-league baseball and exhibition basketball in what would now be called professional basketball. He was just an incredible athlete. There are not a whole lot like him."

Name: Paul Zimmerman
Background: Senior writer for *Sports Illustrated* and author of *The Thinking Man's Guide to Pro Football.*
The best ever was: Marion Motley

In his book, Zimmerman wrote: "If there is a better football player who ever snapped on a helmet, I would like to know his name. (Jim) Brown was the best pure runner I've ever seen, but Motley was the greatest all-around player, the complete player. He ran, of course, and he caught flare passes and turned them into big gainers, and he backed up the line in an era in which the rest of the world was switching to two platoons, and he pass-blocked like no other back who ever played the game." When asked for this book if he would still choose Motley, Zimmerman replied, "I saw Motley when I was a kid, so that choice is from my heart. Dwight Stephenson, the Dolphins center, is closing fast in my mind—they're all still playing in my mind. But my choice remains Marion Motley."

Name: Beau Riffenburgh
Background: Former senior writer for NFL Properties and author of *The Official NFL Encyclopedia.* Currently researching a Ph.D. in polar history at Cambridge University in England.
The best ever was: Sammy Baugh

"If you want the best football player, it comes down to only one guy— Sammy Baugh. In 1943 he led the NFL in passing, punting and interceptions. He is still the career and season punting leader. He had 28 career interceptions as a defensive back. He led in passing six times, more than anybody, and one year he completed 70 percent of his passes at a time when other quarterbacks were completing 40 percent. He was probably one of the few pre-1950s players who could step into a uniform today and not be bothered by the changes in the passing game. Today he would probably throw 40 touchdowns a season. Was he the best quarterback ever? I doubt it. But, in short, he could do everything, which makes him the best ever."

Name: John Steadman
Background: Sportswriter for the *Baltimore Morning News* who has covered pro football since 1949 and watched it since the early forties.
The best ever was: Marion Motley

"Ohhh, he was an intimidating force. He was an awesome blocker. He ran inside, he ran outside, and he dragged tacklers with him. His overwhelming strength made you feel sorry for the defense. He played linebacker on goal line stands, and he was an excellent pass receiver catching a swing pass from Otto Graham. And Motley ran the trap up the middle better than any other fullback in history. Early in his career he even returned kicks—imagine somebody 240 pounds doing that!"

Name: Cooper Rollow
Background: Sportswriter for the *Chicago Tribune* since 1955.
The best ever was: Walter Payton

"I have to pick Payton because of his ability to produce, his durability. He had an extreme high regard for his body. He was never hurt, and nobody was ever more dependable than he was. Walter had a great football sense, with courage and niftiness. I hate to throw in a negative, but it would be his lack of speed—he wasn't a gazelle, but he could hold his own for 30 yards. Payton was a fine blocker, a fine pass receiver, he could pass, and he was a good kick returner. Basically, he could do everything—he was the total football player. When you talk about Walter Payton you have to say that—he was a total football player."

Name: Jack Clary
Background: President of the Pro Football Researchers Association and author of forty-eight books.
The best ever was: Jim Brown

"Jim Brown was a total dominant force in the game. He was the greatest running back of all time. When he played, defenses were built to stop him. In fact, he was the reason Tom Landry perfected the 4-3 defense (and started the flex concept) for the Giants because he had to stop the Cleveland running game. Brown was a football player who could run like a halfback and catch like a wide receiver. He was incredible, a force, a battering ram, a beauty to watch, Gale Sayers with power."

Name: Chuck Heaton
Background: Sportswriter for the *Cleveland Plain Dealer* since 1946.
The best ever was: Otto Graham

"You just can't take away from the fact that he got his team to the championship game every year. In 10 seasons, he either played in a championship game or he won it every time. Otto was a superb athlete. He could run the ball or throw the ball. As a quarterback, he had a great touch. He could throw it deep or lay it out there. He could throw the long pass so well it seemed to come down in the hands of his deep receivers. He was the best quarterback I ever saw."

Name: Mickey Herskowitz

Background: Sportswriter for the *Houston Post* since the late 1950s and author of thirty-one books, including *The Golden Age of Pro Football.*

The best ever was: Sammy Baugh

"I pick Sammy Baugh, with the criterion being that he changed the game. He is recognized as one of the greatest quarterbacks ever; he was one of the two or three greatest defensive backs ever; and he is in the top four or five as a punter. He played when the game was still evolving, but he used every skill he had. He is the greatest pure passer who ever lived, and he's still the standard by whom other quarterbacks are measured. I've seen film of Baugh and talked to people who played with him, and they all say he was a once-in-a-lifetime player. People talk about him like he was from another planet."

ABOUT THE AUTHOR

Rick Korch is the managing editor of *Pro Football Weekly* and one of the foremost pro football historians in the country.

He has spent sixteen years in and around the National Football League. Korch was previously the public relations director for the NFL Alumni association and a public relations assistant for the Miami Dolphins.

Korch is the author of two other books and is co-author of *The Sports Encyclopedia: Pro Football.* He also is a researcher for HBO's "Inside the NFL." Korch has won five awards from the Pro Football Writers of America, including best feature story in 1990 for a nine-part series called "The Best Ever," which was the forerunner to this book.

Photo Credits

5, Indianapolis Colts; 6, San Francisco 49ers; 8, Cleveland Browns ; 9, photo by George Gojkovich; 10, Transcendental Graphics; 21, Cleveland Browns; 26, Cleveland Browns; 27, Chicago Bears; 38, Transcendental Graphics; 39, San Francisco 49ers; 43, Cleveland Browns; 44, Transcendental Graphics; 53, photo by Laughead Photographers; 61, Indianapolis Colts; 65, Transcendental Graphics; 70, photo by Dick Raphael; 72, Vernon J. Biever Photo; 78, Los Angeles Raiders; 84, Indianapolis Colts; 85, Los Angeles Rams; 93, Dallas Cowboys; 96, Pittsburgh Steelers; 97, photo by Daniel Dmitruk; 103, Houston Oilers; 108, Chicago Bears; 110, photo by Vernon J. Biever Photo; 111, photo by Tom Albert/ Detroit Lions; 112, Chicago Bears; 125, photo by Pete J. Groh; 129, photo by Tom Albert/Detroit Lions; 133, Tom Albert/Detroit Lions; 138, Phoenix Cardinals; 141, New York Giants; 142, photo by Vernon J. Biever; 148 (Lou Garza), Cleveland Browns; 148 (George Blanda), photo by Russ Reed; 149, photo by Don Bok; 150, Kansas City Chiefs; 152, photo by Russ Reed; 153, Transcendental Graphics; 154, Cleveland Browns; 155, photo by Pete J. Groh; 160, Chicago Bears; 161 (Ollie Matson), Phoenix Cardinals; 161 (Travis Williams), Los Angeles Rams; 165, photo by L.D. Fullerton; 166, photo by Tom Albert/Detroit Lions.